ELLERMAN
LINES

ELLERMAN LINES

LINES

REMEMBERING A GREAT BRITISH SHIPPING COMPANY

IAN COLLARD

The
History
Press

First published 2014

The History Press
The Mill, Brimscombe Port
Stroud, Gloucestershire, GL5 2QG
www.thehistorypress.co.uk

© Ian Collard, 2014

The right of Ian Collard to be identified as the Author
of this work has been asserted in accordance with the
Copyright, Designs and Patents Act 1988.

British Library Cataloguing in Publication Data.
A catalogue record for this book is available from the British Library.

ISBN 978 0 7524 8963 6

Typesetting and origination by The History Press
Printed in Great Britain

CONTENTS

Acknowledgements	7
Abbreviations	8
HISTORY	9
The City & Hall Lines	11
The Ellerman Group	16
The First World War	21
Ellerman's Wilson Line	24
From 1920 to 1945	27
Hamburg Süd	46
FLEET LIST	48
Ellerman & Papayanni Line	48
Charters	87
Westcott & Laurence	90
Montgomerie & Workman	91
George Smith & Sons	93
Robert Alexander & Company	136
Ellerman & Bucknall	190
Ellerman's Wilson Vessels	229
Ships Managed for the Ministry of War Transport	230
Ellerman 20 per cent Owned, Ben Line 80 per cent Owned	233
Vessels Chartered for the Ellesmere Port–Mediterranean Services	233
Ellerman City Liners	234
Ellerman Asia Limited (Andrew Weir Shipping Limited), London	234
Other Charters	235

ACKNOWLEDGEMENTS

British Passenger Liners of the Five Oceans (Commander C.R.Vernon Gibbs, RN)
Duncan Haws
Ellermans: A Wealth of Shipping (James Taylor)
Journal of Commerce
Merseyside Maritime Museum
Sea Breezes
Shipping & Transport
The Motorship
The Syren & Shipping
Tyne and Wear Archives and Museums
World Ship Society, *Marine News*

ABBREVIATIONS

B.	built
bhp	brake horsepower
blr	boiler
comp.	compound
cu m	cubic metres
cu ft	cubic feet
cyl.	cylinder
dbl.	double
drg	double reduction geared
dwt	deadweight
E.	engines
exp.	expansion
g	gross
grt.	gross registered tonnage
HP	high pressure
hp	horsepower
ihp	inverted horsepower
inv.	inverted
IP	intermediate pressure
k.	knots
LP	low pressure
MP	medium pressure
nhp	nominal horsepower
P.	passengers
psi	pounds per square inch
quad.	quadruple
rpm	revolutions per minute
sgl.	single
shp	shaft horsepower
srg	single reduction geared
TEU	twenty-foot equivalent units
tpl.	triple
turb.	turbine
2S.DA	two-stroke double acting
2S.SA	two-stroke single acting
4S.SA	four-stroke single acting

HISTORY

I n the second half of the eighteenth and early nineteenth centuries, British merchant shipping was run by the merchant. However, the gradual improvements effected in ships and the experiments in steam navigation introduced the early shipowners to the business. The new vessels required more efficient and experienced mariners to operate them, and the organisation of the trade demanded more expert organisation of the business. It has been claimed, therefore, that the introduction of the steamship resulted in the formation of professional organisations and firms exclusively devoted to the building, management and running of large fleets of merchant ships.

The shipowner of the early nineteenth century was responsible for the operation of a fleet of ships and consequently acquired knowledge to deal with problems experienced with the new steam-operated fleets of vessels. Tonnage laws were revised, as they had been drafted in such a way that they penalised certain vessels (the length and breadth had been taxed for tonnages but not the depth). The introduction of iron, and later steel, in the

Merchants in the Cotton Market, Bombay, *c.* 1870.

construction of ships was a positive step forward and gave the British shipowner the opportunity to purchase vessels far superior to those of any of his foreign rivals. The increase in demand for coal across the world, alongside developments in the use of steam, provided the shipowner with an expanding export trade. The growth of the world's population and the repeal of the Corn Laws also provided him with an expanding import trade.

The Leyland Line was formed by John Bibby, a Liverpool shipowner, and laid the foundations of the Mediterranean services. Bibby & Company had begun its operations by carrying mail between Scotland and Northern Ireland via sailing smacks, which later also carried some passengers. It further developed its fleet into fast schooners, transporting fruit and live cattle from Spain; its first steamer was the *Arno*, which operated on a service to Italy and Sicily. Its fleet of small wooden paddles quickly developed into screw steamers with the help of Harland & Wolff's revolutionary idea of building fast steamers with nine or ten beams to the length.

Frederick Leyland was made a partner in the Bibby Line in 1859 and took control of the company fourteen years later. Bibby's and Frederick Leyland's partnership enabled the firm's business and reputation to increase, and they added new ships to the fleet. They also developed the Lisbon and Oporto route, providing regular services to Portugal, the Mediterranean and the Levant by 1870. Leyland bought out his partner, and the services continued as the Leyland Line, also providing sailings to Boston. On 4 January 1892, Frederick Leyland collapsed and died on the platform at Blackfriars railway station. Following Frederick Leyland's death, the firm became a limited liability company, and John Reeves Ellerman was persuaded to join the board. Christopher Furness became chairman, and Ellerman became managing director. The following year, at the age of 31, Ellerman became chairman of the company.

Port of Calcutta, *c.* 1870.

The City & Hall Lines

The City Line was founded in 1839 by George Smith & Sons when it acquired its first sailing ship. The *Constellation* was sent to Calcutta, inaugurating the line's connection with the Indian trade. The *City of Glasgow* was the first 'City' boat, and this vessel allowed the Smiths to separate themselves from their other commercial activities and devote themselves entirely to shipowning. In 1873, the *City of Madrid* was on a voyage to Australia in company with the *Thermopylae* and covered 349 sea miles in twenty-four hours, whilst her *Thermopylae* covered only 337. That year, the *City of Glasgow* made a day's run at an average speed of fifteen and a half knots per hour, travelling 372 miles in twenty-four hours.

George Smith was the founder of the merchant business, and it was his two sons, Robert and George, who showed great enthusiasm for shipowning. The two brothers did their work standing up at high desks; they would not have chairs in the office because they maintained that sitting down tempted visitors to stay and talk when their business was completed. Nor would they have any liquor on board their ships because there was trouble on the *Constellation*'s first voyage due to her master's intemperance. To avoid alcohol being brought on board for passengers, they carried only missionaries.

In January 1875, George Smith explained the origin of the name *City of Glasgow*, which had introduced the system of nomenclature:

> The first ship which we contracted for and had built to our own specification was the *Majestic*, launched in 1846. Our second, the *City of Glasgow* was built at Kelvinaugh, and launched in 1848. While she was on the stocks, the bounds of the municipality of Glasgow as a city had been extended to the junction of the Kelvin and Clyde westwards, and thus embraced the shipyard in which she was built. Our late Mr R Smith was then a magistrate of the *City of Glasgow*, and this being the first ship built in the extended royalty, we reckoned no name could be more appropriate, and as other ships came into existence, we still kept the *City* and merely added a name in future designations.

When they had established a regular service between the Clyde and Calcutta, they always insisted on their ships sailing on the advertised date from either port. This attracted the attention of Charles Bruce, the Scottish pioneer of tea planting in India, and coupled with the quality of the ships, this caused him to favour the City boats for all his tea shipments to the Clyde. When Lancashire could not get American cotton in 1863, Smith started a regular monthly service to Bombay and Calcutta.

The early ships were built on semi-clipper lines and made some very fast passages; they were driven hard with safety. There were many arguments about which was the fastest ship, and the *City of Perth* appears to have been the most popular choice, although she was run very close by the *City of York* and *City of Hankow*. The latter was built with teak below the waterline and with iron topsides, but she proved to have tremendous strength and was classed A-1 for seventeen years. The *City of Madrid* and *City of Glasgow* both beat the famous *Thermopylae* on the day's run.

In 1869 the Line ordered four steamers and, when the Suez Canal opened that year, the *City of Oxford* was the first to enter service. She left the Clyde on 13 December 1870, calling at Liverpool for Bombay and Calcutta and passing through the canal shortly after it was opened to general traffic. The four steamers had a speed of nine and a half knots, and following their introduction, only two further sailing ships were built: the *City of Benares* and the *City of Madras*.

The company still owned fifty-two sailing ships in 1883, and the increase in the number of steamers ordered meant that there was insufficient trade to keep the whole fleet employed. The sailing ships were therefore engaged in carrying large numbers of immigrants to Australia and New Zealand, and the last sailing ship was not disposed of until 1900. Many of the masters and crew served their apprenticeships on the sailing ships and then moved on to the new steamships.

The City Line became known for providing comfortable accommodation at a reasonable fare on its ships and was popular with junior army officers, Indian government officials and businessmen. Consequently, the company considerably increased the passenger accommodation on its passenger/cargo vessels, and in 1892, it was registered as a limited liability company, controlled by the fourth generation of Smiths and their uncle Mr W.S. Workman. The close connection of the Smith and Workman families, going back to the eighteenth century, proved useful when the firm of Montgomerie & Workman came into the group. It had never been prominent as shipowners, but its brokerage business was considerable and fitted in well with the organisation of the Ellerman Group.

The Sun Shipping Company, later known as the Hall Line, was founded in the early 1860s by Robert Alexander and Liston Young. The firm of Alexander & Young managed the ships under the name of the Sun Shipping Company. The sailing ships owned by the company were operated on the American and Eastern routes, and when the first steamships were purchased, they were placed on the service from Liverpool to Bombay. The company's sailing ships were then employed on secondary routes and trades.

The partnership was dissolved in 1868, when Robert Alexander started his own fleet. He named the ships after historic English halls, beginning with the iron full-rigged *Haddon Hall*, which was followed by *Locksley Hall*. The line sailed on routes that provided profitable business and often competed with the Smiths on the Indian trade. The *Eaton Hall* left Liverpool on 20 April 1874 with first-, second- and third-class passengers and cargo and arrived at Melbourne after a voyage of seventy-two days. She then sailed for San Francisco and loaded a cargo of wheat for Liverpool, arriving there on 10 March 1875. The following month, she sailed for Sydney, where she arrived 90 days later, unloaded her cargo and sailed for Burma in ballast, taking ninety-one days. From there, she loaded a cargo of rice and returned to Liverpool in 115 days – a round voyage of 296 days.

The opening of the Suez Canal in November 1869 and the establishment of coaling stations allowed vessels to avoid the long journey around the Cape of Good Hope. Mail had previously been carried from Bombay to Suez and then overland to Alexandria, where it was shipped onto another vessel. The Suez Canal allowed the steamships to shorten the route to the East by hundreds of miles, and the sailing ship was unable to avail itself of this advantage. Most of the major shipping companies abandoned sail, and orders were placed with British shipbuilders for the new generation of steamships. Alexander built his first steamer, *Rydal Hall*, which was placed on the Indian trade. He formed the Sun Shipping Company and started a regular steamer service to Bombay, which was inaugurated by the transatlantic cargo and passenger vessel *City of Baltimore*, purchased from the Inman Line, pending delivery of his three new steamers.

Eaton Hall, 1870.

Branksome Hall, 1875.

City of Nankin, fitting out by Barclay Curle, October 1859.

City of Hankow, 1869.

City of London, 1868.

City of Benares, 1865.

City of Canterbury passing through the Suez Canal, 1878.

The history and development of the City & Hall Lines were very similar even though they were bitter rivals in the Indian trade. The construction of the North Western Railway of India gave the Hall Line the opportunity for further expansion when, in return for a guaranteed direct service to the port of Karachi, the railway undertook to ship all its material via Hall Line vessels. The direct service was inaugurated in 1860.

In the late 1870s, the firm of Alexander & Radcliffe was formed in Liverpool to manage the Sun Shipping Company and took over some of the ships owned personally by Robert Alexander. In 1881, the firm sold its last sailing ship, the *Locksley Hall*, built in 1869. Two years later, the fleet was divided amongst the Sun Shipping Company, Alexander & Radcliffe and Robert Alexander & Company. The new organisation worked well together. In 1885, the Alexander & Radcliffe partnership was dissolved, and Robert Alexander & Company became the sole manager of the Sun Shipping Company. The passenger side of the business closed in 1898, when it sold its passenger ships to the P&O Company, and it did not enter the Indian passenger trade until 1905, in association with the City Line.

The first passenger vessel built after its incorporation with Ellerman Lines (see below) was *Trafford Hall*, which had accommodation for 100 passengers and was subsequently transferred to the Ellerman & Bucknall South African service. The Hall Line was registered in 1899 and took over the fleet of the Sun Shipping Company, with Robert Alexander as its first chairman. It was acquired by Ellerman Lines two years later. As new ships were introduced into the fleet, the traditional Hall system of nomenclature was allowed to die out, and all new ships were named with the City designation. In the later purchase of the City & Hall Lines, Ellerman interests secured such a position in the Eastern trade that they were able to take a leading part in the development of the British Empire in India. The company was well situated to share in the prosperity of the subcontinent with the help of the British administration. The company's Eastern interests extended to Karachi, the Kathiawar ports and Bombay, Marmagao, the Madras and Malabar Coasts and Rangoon. It also provided regular services to South Africa, Lourenco Marques, Beira and Mauritius, as well as via the Mediterranean to the East African ports.

The Ellerman Group

John Reeves Ellerman was born in Kingston-upon-Hull as the only son of a Lutheran shipbroker and corn merchant, who had immigrated to England from Hamburg in 1850, and an English mother. His father died when he was 9 years of age, and Ellerman spent some of his childhood in France. From the age of 14, he lived independently from his family and was articled to a Birmingham chartered accountant. Upon passing his articles, he moved to London, and after turning down the offer of a partnership in one of the leading firms, he founded his own practice, J. Ellerman & Company. In this practice, he developed the use of modern accounting methods and procedures, and with these he was able to identify companies suitable for takeover. The majority of businesses taken over by him became very successful, so he was able to raise funds from other investors, enabling him to hold large stakes personally. One of these was the Brewery and Commercial Investment Trust, which returned an investment of over 1,000 per cent in nine years.

In 1900, Frederick Leyland (1900) Limited was established following the acquisition of twenty ships owned by the West India & Pacific Steam Ship Company Limited. J. Pierpont

Morgan had formed the International Mercantile Marine and made a determined effort to secure the monopoly of the Atlantic trade for America. He acquired the Leyland, White Star, Red Star and Atlantic Transport Lines, but John Ellerman retained from the purchase the Mediterranean fleet and business of the Leyland Line. He agreed that he would not re-enter the Atlantic trade for a period of fourteen years, except for the Antwerp to Montreal route, which was outside any International Mercantile Marine deal.

The London, Liverpool & Ocean Shipping Company was formed in 1901, and this soon became Ellerman Lines Limited, managing the twenty vessels the company had obtained. These ships were operated on services for which they had been designed, and many of them had names ending in the suffix '-ian', which had been characteristic of the Leyland fleet and the original Bibby Company.

Discussions took place with Basilio Papayanni for the purpose of purchasing the Papayanni Line, which operated a service of steamships between Liverpool, Malta, Egypt, the Levant and the Black Sea, and the Papayanni Line was then taken over in May 1901. The business had been founded in the 1840s by George Michael Papayanni, in partnership with Pierre Mussalini and Basilio Papayanni. George M. Papayanni had come to London to establish a Greek commodity house importing dried fruit and exporting British goods. He moved to Liverpool in 1844, with his brother Basilio acting as his Piraeus agent. The fleet consisted of a number of schooners, and their first steamship, the *Arcadia*, was built in 1855. When the American Civil War stopped grain imports from the United States, Papayanni supplied the deficiency by building a business in grain from south-eastern Europe. The ships were as big as the Danube and Black Sea ports could accommodate and could carry thirty to forty passengers. In addition to carrying the grain, they loaded cotton from Egypt while maintaining regular services. Basilio Papayanni assumed sole control of the company in 1870 until his death in 1897, when he was succeeded by his son, also Basilio. The line became a limited liability company in 1897, but by 1901 it was unable to finance the modernisation of the fleet and was purchased, along with its eight ships, by Ellerman.

In September 1901, Ellerman announced at the Annual General Meeting that negotiations were concluded to purchase the London, Liverpool and Ocean Shipping Company, 50 per cent of George Smith & Sons City Line Limited and 50 per cent of the Hall Line, the other 50 per cent of each being for Ellerman's personal account. In effect, this arrangement allowed Ellerman to take the value in shares, not cash, when London, Liverpool and Ocean Shipping acquired all his personally owned shipping interests from him that year, consolidating them into one group. This was agreed at an Extraordinary General Meeting on 23 December, when the name was also changed to Ellerman Lines Limited. It was effective from 22 January the following year, when Ellerman resigned from Leyland's, becoming chairman of Ellerman Lines Limited.

The directors of the new company were the same as those of the London, Liverpool and Ocean Shipping Company and F.G. Burt. Papayanni & Company operated as a separate business, and the fleet consisted of forty-nine ships as well as eight owned by Papayanni.

The Westcott & Laurence Line owned eight steamers and maintained services to Malta, Alexandria and Odessa, as well as to Piraeus, Syria, Constantinople and the Black Sea and Danube ports. For centuries, the Westcott family had been shipowners, master mariners and, in wartime, privateers in Cornwall. Captain W.G. Westcott, who had founded the company, had obtained a thorough knowledge of the Mediterranean and Black Sea trades as master and marine superintendent in the Greek & Oriental Shipping Company. When that company closed due to a bank crash, he and one of his staff set up as shipbrokers in 1864 and became shipowners three years later. Westcott & Laurence operated nine ships out of London, and it was originally envisaged that William Westcott and his brother John would remain as managers, with John Ellerman as chairman. However, the business was sold to Ellerman's in December 1901, together with Westcott & Flint, their Antwerp subsidiary.

Palgrave, Murphy & Company's Oporto service was purchased by Papayanni for £22,000, together with their two ships, *City of Cork* and *City of Amsterdam*. The ending of the Boer War in 1902 produced overcapacity, and Ellerman Lines and Thos. & Jas. Harrison entered into an agreement with Cayzer Irvine's Clan Line to join the South African Conference. The conference agreed that there would be 108 sailings a year with Clan Line having 78, Hall Line 15 and Harrison Line 15. Hall Line also agreed not to enter the passenger business, and Clan Line received five shillings per ton for three years on freight earning more than twenty-five shillings per ton.

In 1903, a price war developed between Ellerman Lines and Frank Strick, who had decided to extend his Persian Gulf services to Indian ports, loading cargo for this service at Newport. Ellerman decided to enter the Persian Gulf trade briefly, but the situation was resolved two years later with Strick providing a service from Newport and London only. Hall entered the South African business in May 1903 in partnership with the Allan Line, which was a member of the River Plate Conference, but the venture proved unprofitable. The following year, Ellerman adopted new funnel colours that were based on those held by the Alexandra Towing Company of Liverpool. It was also decided that the blue JRE pennant would be worn above the house flag of the constituent fleets, although Ellerman Lines and Papayanni vessels flew only the pennant.

In 1905, John Reeves Ellerman was designated a baronet on the King's Birthday Honours List, and a new Ellerman–Strick joint service was opened to Marmagao. In December 1905, the company came to an agreement with the Glen Line, which was unable, for financial reasons, to contribute sufficient ships to take up its share of the Far East Conference. Four Hall Line ships were sold to the Glen Line and renamed but operated by Hall Line crews. Hall Line received two-fifths of the Glen Line share of the trade for seven years. *Netherby Hall* was renamed *Glenearn* and *Branksome Hall* became *Glenavon*. The other vessels retained their Hall Line names. However, the venture was not successful, and Hall Line withdrew from the arrangement in 1908, although the vessels remained on charter to the Glen Line.

In 1908, the Bucknall Steamship Lines came within the Ellerman Group. The Bucknall family had been involved in the Iberian cork trade from the middle of the eighteenth century and had started owning ships to carry their own cargo in the middle of the nineteenth century. Their first ships were fast schooners weighing between 100 and 200 tons, and by the 1860s they were buying larger ships and operating charter voyages to the River Plate. They ordered their first steamship in 1872, and in 1886 Edward Lloyd took over management of the firm's shipping interests. Bucknall Brothers was formed two years later, and this was followed by Bucknall Nephews in 1890, which took over the ships and the parent company. The British & Colonial Steam Navigation Company was formed in 1891, managed by Bucknall Nephews to take advantage of the campaign against the monopoly of South African Conference Lines. It was backed by G.H. Payne & Company, shipbrokers specialising in South African business, which had been in dispute with the established shipping lines.

The line started with nine small cargo steamers that sailed about every seventeen days to the Cape. They had been successful in obtaining the contract for the carriage of railway material for the Netherlands South African Railways, which was building a line to connect Delagoa Bay with the Transvaal. The contract allowed them to fully load their ships outwards for three years and provided a valuable through-traffic business over the railway.

The first ships were the *Afrikander* and *Kaffir*, which were built with a shallow draught to allow them to cross the bars at Durban and East London. The ships loaded the railway materials at Amsterdam and then completed at the West India Import Dock in London. The railway goods were discharged at Algoa Bay by lighter, but some were kept on board until the vessel reached Cape Town. Over the period of the contract, the railway business increased to the extent that vessels were chartered from Burrell and Andrew Weir Companies. The ships also transported exhibits to the Kimberley Exhibition and gained a reputation for the safe carriage of pedigree stock.

Unfortunately, the volume of homeward cargo was low, and after discharging the outward cargo, the ships would regularly cross to Burma and load cargoes of rice while other charters took them to Australia. The vessels that would return from South Africa in ballast would often call at the Canary Islands to load tomatoes, fruit and potatoes. A service from Marseilles to Madagascar was started, but this was unsuccessful when the French incorporated the route into their imperial reservation, from which all foreign ships were excluded.

During the Klondyke gold rush, the company started a route from Puget Sound to Skagway, but it was only during the gold rush that this prospered. There was a short-lived venture in the North Pacific with Houlder Brothers and another between Vancouver and New Zealand. In 1893, the company signed a contract to carry mules from New York to the Cape Town tramways, and the service was later extended to India to load cargo for the return voyage. Five years later, a full service was advertised between the United States and India, also loading for Canada on the return voyage.

A passenger service to South Africa was started in 1895 with *Johannesburg, Fort Salisbury* and *Bulawayo*, which were sister ships with good cargo capacity and each having accommodation for sixty passengers. The passenger fares were £24, £26 and £28 to Cape Town, according to the position and size of the cabins. The service became popular with passengers because of the comfortable vessels and the very high standard of service. The original route was from London to the Cape, then across to India and back to London through the Suez Canal. The service was so popular that the ships soon took the direct route both outward and back home. The original three passenger ships were sold in 1912, and the South African passenger service was subsequently maintained by ships of the City & Hall Lines.

Bucknall Steamship Lines Limited was formed in 1900 to take over and expand the fleet and services of the British & Colonial Company, with a share and debenture capital of £1,985,000. The new company was forced to pay a high price for the assets it took over and so suffered because of the slump that followed the Transvaal War, when a boom had been expected. It started to recover very slowly following the inauguration of a new service to the Persian Gulf in conjunction with the Strick Line of London. The oil industry was developing rapidly at the time, and the joint service was responsible for shipping large quantities of machinery to the area.

However, by 1908 it had become clear that Bucknall Steamship Lines was under considerable financial pressure, mainly due to an overambitious building programme in the

City of Karachi.

City of Palermo.

early years of the century coupled with the financial slump. The company sought the help of Sir John Reeves Ellerman, as its main problem was shortage of liquidity. Ellerman injected £180,000 to deal with the company's current obligations, and this immediately restored its solvency. The value of the shares in the company was revised, and security for its financial structure was given by Sir John Ellerman. He took control of the company, which held the assets of a fleet of ships valued at £690,000.

At the company's year end in August 1909, it was announced that the loss was significantly less than forecast and the financial position was showing a gradual improvement as freight rates were increasing. On 1 January 1914, the company was renamed Ellerman & Bucknall Steamship Company Limited and became a constituent company of the Ellerman Group.

The acquisition of Bucknall Lines gave Ellerman the opportunity to integrate the various companies into a composite group, without destroying the individual traditions and characteristics of each constituent company. He achieved this by cooperative effort and the tactful treatment of personnel, masters, officers and pursers, who, although remaining with their companies, were temporarily transferred to other ships within the group while the ships were interchanged among the various services. Although the funnel colours of the various parts of the group were changed to the corporate Ellerman colour, the old house flags were retained and flown under the Ellerman pennant.

Routes and services that had formally been in keen competition were combined, but most of the companies ran on their previous routes and some new services were established. A comprehensive and detailed assessment of the company and the fleet was made, and, where required, suitable ships were purchased from other companies and new vessels were ordered and commissioned. The design of ships on the Indian services varied from cargo liners of around 5,000 tons carrying a few passengers to passenger ships from 5,000 to 10,000 tons with comfortable first- and second-class accommodation.

In June 1910, Ellerman, the Clan Line and the Thos. & Jas. Harrison Line started a new service from the west coast of Britain via the Red Sea to East Africa. The first sailing was by Harrison Line's *Traveller*, with Beira becoming the terminal port.

The older City Line passenger ships were transferred to the Mediterranean service and would later be replaced by new vessels under the Ellerman & Papayanni Lines. A two-month round-trip voyage to the Mediterranean, including Greece, Turkey and Black Sea ports, cost £33, and the company offered a six-month season ticket for £50, with any extra time spent on board costing £1 per day. Many of the services could now be combined with routes already existing in the group, therefore allowing the most efficient use of the ships.

The First World War

The task of organising the different units within the Ellerman Group was severely disrupted by the outbreak of the First World War. The government requisitioned many of the ships, and the *City of Oxford* was converted into an imitation of the battleship HMS *St Vincent* to be used in the 'Dummy Squadron' organised by Captain Herbert James Haddock. She later became a kite balloon ship and was used for observing and correcting artillery fire during bombardments. The *City of London* sailed as an auxiliary cruiser.

Twenty-six of the group's vessels carried British, Indian and Dominion troops across the world, and some ships were also placed at the disposal of the Allies. Some of the vessels carried munitions and stores for the army between service as troop-carriers, and several of the Mediterranean ships were employed on the short-distance routes. The Belgravian and Malatian carried munitions to north Russia. Many of the other ships in the fleet were taken over under the Liner Requisition Scheme and were then managed by the Admiralty.

There were no escorted convoys at the beginning of the war, and many ships were lost whilst sailing on long-established steamer routes. When convoys were provided, destroyers and other naval vessels escorted those vessels that were vulnerable to attack by enemy submarines. In the twelve months after they were introduced, only seven outbound and seven inbound ships were lost out of 285 and 329 ships conveyed in the Mediterranean.

Losses from enemy action were heavy, and at the end of hostilities the company looked to replace these ships so as to to return to the business of carrying freight and passengers around the world. It examined a number of standard ships that the shipping controller wished to sell and was able to adapt and modify those that were suitable to the Ellerman business. New tonnage was also ordered, but the shipyards were congested and delivery was liable to long delays. However, the group was soon back in business, and Bucknall's American and India service from New York commenced in 1919 with the *City of Benares* taking the first sailing. The passenger services to Egypt, India, Ceylon, South Africa and the Far East were soon operating, and many of the cargo services were restored, both in the Mediterranean and also on the longer routes. New ships were ordered with an emphasis on fuel economy and operational efficiency.

During the First World War, the Wilson Line of Hull had lost thirty-six ships sunk by German submarines, four through collision, one scuttled and another captured, scuttled and sunk. It was aware of the cost of replacing these vessels and also the increasing competition for business in the North Sea trade. Sir John Ellerman made an initial offer for the line, and this was rejected, but following a revised offer a deal was finalised on 15 November 1916. The name of the company was changed to Ellerman's Wilson Line Limited on 1 February the following year.

City of Canton (2).

City of Canterbury (2).

City of Hong Kong in the Mersey, 1948.

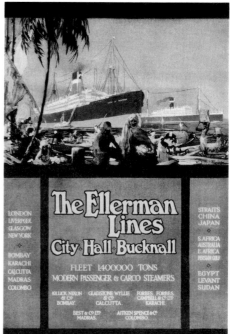

Ellerman & Bucknall advertisement.   Ellerman Lines advertisement.

Ellerman's Wilson Line

This line was founded by Thomas Wilson, who was born in Cottingham, near Hull, in 1792. He became a clerk in the firm of Whitaker, Wilkinson & Company, importers of Swedish iron ore. He progressed to the position of salesman and in 1822 set up his own business as an ore importer with his partner, John Beckinton. Three years later, he recruited two more partners, and the company purchased its first ship. A 100-ton schooner, the *Swift*, was bought in 1830 for the price of £735, and the company traded in iron, bones and oak bark. The company was renamed Wilson, Hudson & Company when John Hudson was recruited as an active partner. By 1841, Hudson had retired, and when Wilson's eldest son joined, the firm was renamed Thomas Wilson Sons & Company.

The fleet totalled nine ships in 1841, and the steamers *Humber* and *Baltic* were added between 1854 and 1856. Sailings were offered between Hull and Stettin, Riga and St Petersburg, and the business continued to be successful and profitable. Thomas Wilson died on 21 June 1869 at the age of 77, and the management of the business was left to his sons, Charles Henry and Arthur. As trade was limited during the Franco–Prussian War of 1870/71, the company started to build up a link with the Adriatic, providing a service with its ships to Trieste. The Stettin trade resumed at the end of the war, and the company was able to extend and develop the Adriatic business, which had proved to be profitable.

The opening of the Suez Canal gave it the opportunity to expand its routes. It started a service to Calcutta and later advertised a service across the North Atlantic, when the route from Hull and Newcastle to New York was opened in 1875. When the Monarch Line went into liquidation, Wilson's purchased three of its vessels and ran them on the service from London to New York. In collaboration with partners, it operated a Newcastle, Hull and Southampton service to New York and a London to New York and Boston route. In 1878, it purchased the Hull firm of Brownlow, Marsdin & Company and its fleet of seven ships. The Wilson fleet then consisted of fifty-two ships, and by 1895, it had increased to ninety-three vessels, including four tugs. Bailey & Leetham Limited and its fleet of twenty-three ships were purchased in 1903. Wilson's vessels now sailed to the Baltic and Scandinavia from Grimsby, Manchester, Liverpool and Hull, and in 1906 it combined with the North Eastern Railway Company to offer services from Hull to Hamburg, Antwerp, Ghent and Dunkirk.

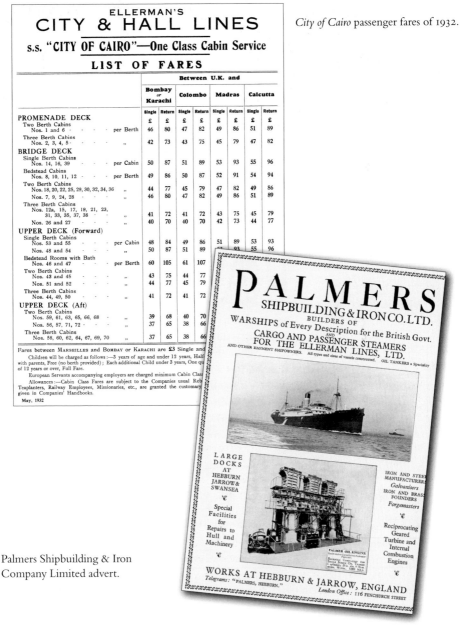

City of Cairo passenger fares of 1932.

ELLERMAN'S
CITY & HALL LINES
s.s. "CITY OF CAIRO"—One Class Cabin Service
LIST OF FARES

	Bombay or Karachi		Colombo		Madras		Calcutta	
	Single	Return	Single	Return	Single	Return	Single	Return
	£	£	£	£	£	£	£	£
PROMENADE DECK								
Two Berth Cabins								
Nos. 1 and 6 · · · per Berth	46	80	47	82	49	86	51	89
Three Berth Cabins								
Nos. 2, 3, 4, 5 · · · ,,	42	73	43	75	45	79	47	82
BRIDGE DECK								
Single Berth Cabins								
Nos. 14, 16, 39 · · · per Cabin	50	87	51	89	53	93	55	96
Bedstead Cabins								
Nos. 8, 10, 11, 12 · · per Berth	49	86	50	87	52	91	54	94
Two Berth Cabins								
Nos. 18, 20, 22, 25, 29, 30, 32, 34, 36 ,,	44	77	45	79	47	82	49	86
Nos. 7, 9, 24, 28 · · ,,	46	80	47	82	49	86	51	89
Three Berth Cabins								
Nos. 12a, 15, 17, 19, 21, 23, 31, 33, 35, 37, 38 · · ,,	41	72	41	72	43	75	45	79
Nos. 26 and 27 · · ,,	40	70	40	70	42	73	44	77
UPPER DECK (Forward)								
Single Berth Cabins								
Nos. 53 and 55 · · per Cabin	48	84	49	86	51	89	53	93
Nos. 48 and 54 · · ,,	50	87	51	89	53	93	55	96
Bedstead Rooms with Bath								
Nos. 46 and 47 · per Berth	60	105	61	107				
Two Berth Cabins								
Nos. 43 and 45 · · ,,	43	75	44	77				
Nos. 51 and 52 · · ,,	44	77	45	79				
Three Berth Cabins								
Nos. 44, 49, 50 · · ,,	41	72	41	72				
UPPER DECK (Aft)								
Two Berth Cabins								
Nos. 59, 61, 63, 65, 66, 68 · ,,	39	68	40	70				
Nos. 56, 57, 71, 72 · · ,,	37	65	38	66				
Three Berth Cabins								
Nos. 58, 60, 62, 64, 67, 69, 70 ,,	37	65	38	66				

Fares between MARSEILLES and BOMBAY or KARACHI are £3 Single and
Children will be charged as follows:—3 years of age and under 12 years, Half
with parents, Free (no berth provided); Each additional Child under 3 years, One qu
of 12 years or over, Full Fare.
European Servants accompanying employers are charged minimum Cabin Class
Allowances:—Cabin Class Fares are subject to the Companies usual Reb
Teaplanters, Railway Employees, Missionaries, etc., are granted the customary
given in Companies' Handbooks.
May, 1932

Palmers Shipbuilding & Iron Company Limited advert.

EGYPT INDIA CEYLON

TRAVEL

in comfort and luxury and book your passage by Ellerman's City & Hall Lines. Steamers specially designed and equipped to meet tropical conditions, having spacious public apartments, extensive promenade and sports decks, with every facility to ensure the comfort of passengers. The rooms are large and airy, each possessing a window or porthole. Above all, passengers receive the personal service of a staff who have been trained to anticipate individual requirements.

Yes, it's LUXURY combined with ECONOMY.

MINIMUM PASSAGE RATES

Bombay - -	} £40
Karachi - -	
Colombo - -	£41
Madras - -	£43
Calcutta - -	£45

Write for particulars of special off-season facilities.

ELLERMAN'S CITY & HALL LINES

Tower Building, Liverpool. Telephone: Central 3840	104-6 Leadenhall Street, LONDON, E.C.3. Telegrams: "Orinoco" London Telephone: Avenue 9340	75 Bothwell Street, Glasgow. Telephone: Central 9222

City & Hall Lines advertisement.

From 1920 to 1945

The main London agents Montgomerie & Workman were amalgamated into the group in 1920, and the shipyard owned by William Gray & Company Limited at West Hartlepool was also purchased that year. During this period, it was also found necessary to purchase a total of forty secondhand vessels to enable the group to maintain its services. Ellerman & Bucknall (Proprietary) Limited was formed in 1927, based at Cape Town with a branch office at Durban. The following year, Lord Kylsant purchased Sir John Ellerman's 46 per cent share in Shaw Savill & Albion but managed to take control of the company, and Ellerman converted this into cash. In 1932, the Papayanni Line came under the group name of Ellerman & Papayanni Lines Limited.

Sir John Reeves Ellerman died on the 16 July 1933 of a heart attack while on holiday at Dieppe. He is reported to have said that he was worth £55 million in 1916, and it was estimated that his shipping interests alone were worth £35 million. Upon his death, his estate was assessed for probate at over £36 million. He lived in London and Eastbourne and never desired to have a country estate or to enter politics. He had little interest in public recognition, although he was made a baronet in 1905 because of his contribution to British shipping during the Boer War By 1918, he had invested in more than seventy breweries and had earlier bought shares in the *Financial Times*, the *Daily Mail*, *The Times*, the *Illustrated London News*, the *Tatler*, the *Sphere* and other publications, which he sold in the 1920s. He also held shares in more than twenty collieries and became a major property owner in London. Following his death, Sir Miles Mattinson took over as chair of the company, and an executive committee was formed to manage the group.

On 1 January 1936, Montgomerie & Workman ceased to be shipowners, and its five ships were absorbed into the Ellerman fleet. A new operation, the Montreal, Australia and New Zealand service, started later that year in collaboration with the New Zealand Shipping Company and Port Line. During the inter-war years, the Ellerman Group offered services covering most of the world except South America and the north-east Pacific. India was the particular interest of the City & Hall Lines, which maintained a regular service from Glasgow and Birkenhead to Calcutta and from Glasgow, Manchester and Birkenhead to the Kathiawar ports and Bombay.

The Hall Line sailed from South Wales, Manchester and Birkenhead for the Middle East, Kathiawar ports, Bombay and Karachi and from South Wales, Glasgow, Birkenhead, Dunkirk, Middlesbrough and Hull for Marmagoa and the Malabar Coast. Homeward, it offered a service from the Burmese ports to the Continent, London, Avonmouth and Liverpool. In conjunction with the Clan and Harrison Lines, it also maintained services from South Wales, Glasgow and Liverpool to South African ports, Lourenco Marques, Beira and Mauritius, as well as via the Suez Canal to East African ports.

The main Ellerman & Bucknall service was from Middlesbrough, Antwerp, Rotterdam, Hamburg and London to South African ports, Lourenco Marques, Beira and Mauritius, but it also ran services from the United Kingdom and the Continent to the Far East. In addition, it offered services from Canada and the United States to the Persian Gulf, South and East Africa, Mauritius, Reunion and Madagascar, to the Far East, to Australia and New Zealand returning to the United States or Britain and also to India and the East Indies. In addition, Ellerman & Bucknall also operated ships to the Persian Gulf in association with the Strick Line.

The Westcott & Laurence Line maintained services from London to Gibraltar, Malta, Alexandria, Cyprus, Greece and Turkey, with calls varying to comply with the seasonal trade, and Ellerman & Papayanni ran from Liverpool to Portugal, Italy, Sicily, the Adriatic, Syria and the Levant and from London to Oporto and the Spanish ports.

In 1939, when the Second World War broke out, the size and equipment of the Ellerman ships made them particularly valuable for carrying troops to the smaller ports, where their cargo gear could deal with the troops' stores and equipment. The Ellerman group, excluding the Wilson Line, which operated as a separate entity, owned 105 ships with a carrying capacity of 919,969 tons. The ships were employed from South Africa or India to the Middle Eastern campaign, with each carrying a brigade or more, within reach of enemy air attack in the Red Sea or Alexandria. Some of the ships returned with prisoners of war. Vessels designed for cargo only were adapted for particular duties when required.

City of Hong Kong leading a convoy out of Gibraltar in 1939. She was under the command of Captain H.L. Walton for most of the Second World War.

City of Durban.

In the early days of the war, several ships carried troops across the Channel to France. When Italy entered the conflict and divided the Mediterranean in two, several of the smaller ships were in the Eastern end, and some of them were retained on the Eastern Mediterranean Feeder service. The Ellerman vessels mostly accomplished the tasks given to them and were complimented by the naval and military officers under whom they were operating.

The *City of Dieppe* was fitted out as a naval issuing ship with stowage for every possible spare part that a warship could require, and finished her work with the Fleet at the surrender of Japan. The *City of Tokyo* carried out similar functions at Freetown. Her aft section was filled with naval stores, amidships was a NAAFI shop, and forward were the victualling stores which were mostly refrigerated items. There were occasions when her generators and refrigerator space acted as a reserve to Freetown.

The *City of Canterbury* and *City of Paris* acted as exchange ships for British and Japanese diplomatic personnel, certain civilians and prisoners of war. The *City of Hong Kong* participated in the invasion of Madagascar and the *City of Edinburgh* was converted to HMS *Lothian*, a base ship in the Pacific campaign. Several vessels were involved in assisting the civilian authorities during air raids at Liverpool and London when the crews used their fire fighting skills on the quays and other vessels which had been damaged. The *Algerian* was converted to a cable layer for the Pluto pipeline under the Channel to keep the forces in France supplied with petrol.

The *City of Canterbury* carried to safety two members of the Greek royal family and the royal jewels at the same time that the *City of London* was evacuating around 3,700 troops from Crete. The troops on board had brought about ninety Bren guns with them and were able to use them on enemy aircraft which attacked the ship on her way to Egypt. When France fell and Italy joined the conflict, three Ellerman vessels brought large numbers of refugees from France and Italy home from Gibraltar.

The company's vessels were present at Dunkirk, Cherbourg and St Nazaire. The *Fabian*, *City of Christchurch*, *City of Mobile* and *City of Windsor* between them brought over 12,000 troops to Britain. The *City of Windsor* also managed to salvage a number of guns which would have been invaluable had the expected invasion occurred. The *City of Mobile* sailing from St Nazaire had over 3,000 troops on board for five or six days in accommodation that was designed for her own crew. Just before the fall of the country to the Japanese, the *City of Canterbury* brought 2,000 refugees from Singapore. Five Ellerman ships took part in the Malta supply convoys, and three were in the 'Mouse Convoy' from Alexandria, designed to tempt the Italian fleet within range of the British ships. Thirteen ships were employed in the Middle Eastern and Tripoline campaign, seven to Greece and Crete, one took troops to Singapore, seven participated in the French North African operations, five in the Sicilian and Italian invasion, four helped in clearing Burma of the Japanese and one was on the Normandy coast.

Many vessels in the fleet continued to carry cargo and passengers to various ports around the world. The *City of Exeter* made a passage from Liverpool to Calcutta via the Panama Canal and New Zealand in 123 days. Under the general requisition, which included the whole of the ocean-going section of the Merchant Navy, all earnings they might have made on their commercial voyages went to the Ministry of Transport. It was very difficult for passengers to travel by sea during the war as all movements were shrouded in secrecy and passengers would not know the time of sailing until the last minute.

City of Edinburgh (5).

City of Exeter.

City of Benares (5).

The *City of Benares* was given instructions by the Ministry of Shipping to sail from Liverpool to Montreal with passengers, including ninety children, who were proceeding to Canada under the Government Evacuation Scheme. Passengers embarked at Princes Landing Stage at Liverpool on 12 September 1940 and she sailed the following day with 406 people on board, including 209 crew, six convoy staff and 191 passengers, including the children. *City of Benares* was the commodore ship of a large convoy and on 17 September she was attacked and hit by a torpedo from the German submarine U-48. She started to settle slowly by the stern, and the master ordered the boats to be lowered and the ship abandoned.

The chief engineer later reported that:

I saw that all the boats had left, but one boat, No. 3 was not far away. I then went down a life-line into the water, swam to the boat and was pulled in by a passenger. I was no sooner in this boat than it got washed under the fore part of the ship and threw everyone at the after end into the water. I was one of those left in the boat. Fortunately it righted itself and shot forward. It was at this period the *City of Benares* sank with her bow high in the air. I managed to pull into the boat two male passengers, fifth engineer, second officer and a naval telegraphist who had managed to swim to the boat, so that in all we were four Indian crew and six Europeans in the boat. We were helpless, as the Fleming gear was damaged, the rudder destroyed, the mast was gone, only one oar was left and the boat was waterlogged. During the next hour or so the second officer was hailing boats to come alongside, eventually one boat did and the second officer, fifth engineer and naval telegraphist transferred to this boat. I remained in the waterlogged boat along with two passengers and four crew, one of whom was the deck serang. In the course of the night, two crew and a passenger died, thus leaving two crew, a passenger and myself in this boat. The following morning at dawn nothing was sighted but oil on the water showed that we were not far from where the ship had gone down. I reckon it was about noon when, on top of a high sea which was running, we sighted two boats and two rafts and in the evening, we sighted the rescue ship. We were so exhausted that the rescuers had to put ropes round us to get us on board.

A few of the survivors, including three children, died on board the destroyer HMS *Hurricane*, which had rescued them, and the remainder were landed at Greenock at noon on 20 September. A further forty-five survivors were also landed at Greenock on 26 September from the destroyer HMS *Anthony*. Their lifeboat had been spotted by a Sunderland flying boat, which dropped a parcel of food and a note stating that assistance was on its way. Only eighty-eight members of crew and fifty-seven passengers survived the sinking, and for the many acts of bravery, several members of the crew and passengers received recognition by the government.

Sixty ships, representing a carrying capacity of 489,851 tons, were confirmed as being sunk by enemy action, and the extent of the line's war activities may be gauged from the fact that 153 awards were granted to the companies' seagoing personnel. Two vessels managed by the company for the Ministry of War Transport (MOWT) were also lost.

Line	Vessels	Deadweight (tons)	War losses	
Hall	49	489,439	26	258,900
City	18	197,686	10	106,292
Ellerman & Bucknall	12	123,976	4	42,764
Ellerman & Papayanni	25	103,345	19	75,744
Westcott & Laurence	1	5,514	1	5,514
	105	**916,969**	**60**	**489,851**

On the conclusion of the war, Ellerman Lines embarked on a building programme to replace the vessels lost and concentrated on re-establishing its worldwide trade routes. It also purchased twelve cargo vessels from the government that it had managed for the Ministry of Transport. There was one class of ship ordered by the Ministry of Transport that promised to suit Ellerman's requirements, especially as several were not completed by the end of the war: the group bought six of the hulls, with a capacity of about 11,000 tons each and a speed varying from 14½ to 15½ knots. They were fitted out according to the group's policy of providing accommodation for twelve passengers in single- and two-berth cabins. Special attention was also given to the crew accommodation, which was air conditioned throughout. The officers' quarters under the bridge were unusually large and ratings were given rooms sleeping four or six people. The placing of these orders demonstrated the enterprise and progressive policy of the line and indicated its determination in playing its part in laying the foundations of national economic recovery, as well as rendering its contribution to the revival of British overseas trade and a profitable future for the company.

City of Khartoum (2).

Florian (2), *Varodd*, *Athenian* (2) and *Palmelian* in Alexandra Dock, Liverpool.

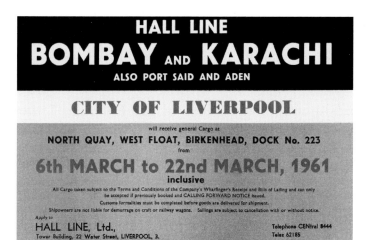

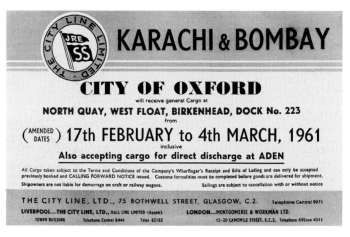

City Line and Hall Line sailing lists.

City of New York and *City of Pretoria* (2) in Alfred Basin, Birkenhead.

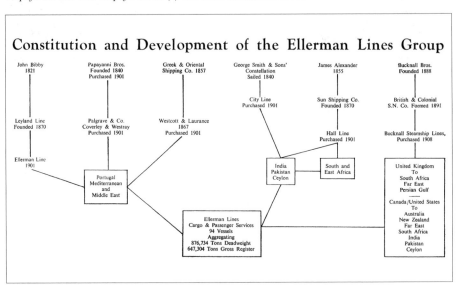

Ellerman Lines constitution, 1953.

On 15 August 1947, India and Pakistan became independent and were soon announcing plans to set up their own merchant fleets, which would be equal members of the particular conferences. The India Steamship Company and Scindia Steam Ship Company were admitted to the conference and competed with the Ellerman ships for business. In 1950, the South African Marine and South Africa Lines joined the South African Conference, and two years later a new class of four passenger vessels was introduced on the South African route by Ellerman & Bucknall. The Burmese services were withdrawn in 1952, and the following year all passenger services to India ceased. In 1954, it was decided to dispose of nineteen of the older ships in the fleet over a three-year period, and by 1955, the fleet consisted of ninety-four ships. The Mossgiel fleet and its two ships on the Glasgow to the Mediterranean service were purchased in 1958. Pakistan Steamship Lines joined the India conference in 1960, and in the following year the United States to India service was withdrawn.

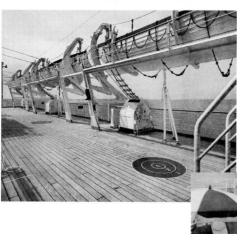

City of Port Elizabeth deck views.

City of Port Elizabeth promenade deck (top), restaurant (middle) and bed-sitting room (bottom).

City of Lancaster (2) and *City of Eastbourne* (2) in the Mersey.

City of Newcastle (2) and *City of London* (4) loading cargo in the West Float, Birkenhead.

City of Lancaster (2) and *City of Liverpool* anchored in the Mersey.

City of Ottawa in Birkenhead Docks.

A busy scene in the West Float at Birkenhead.

City of Liverpool, *City of Lucknow* (6) and *City of Oxford* (4) in Huskisson Dock, Liverpool.

Malatian (2) sailing from Langton Dock, Liverpool.

On 31 December 1965, Ellerman Lines Limited held a nominal capital of £5,450,000, with a book value of fleets, properties and investments amounting to £49,205,000, and a profit on trading for the year of £237,000. This was compared to a profit of £5,706,000 made by the P&O SN Company and £4,650,720 made by the Ocean Steam Ship Company Limited in the same period. Ellerman's profits were about average for British shipping companies operating at the time, with Cairn Line of Steamships recording a loss of £16,654, London & Overseas Freighters Limited a loss of £418,238 and the General Steam Navigation Company a loss of £301,253.

In 1965, the British and Commonwealth Company, Furness Withy, Ocean Steam Company and P&O announced that they were to form a consortium that would be known as Overseas Containers Limited and would provide container services between Europe and Australia. Associated Container Transport was created by the Ben Line, Blue Star Line, Port Line, Ellerman Lines and Harrison Line. The first meeting of the Board of Directors took place on 12 January 1966. In August 1967, Blue Star, Ellerman Lines and Port Line joined together to form Associated Container Transport (Australia) Limited. It was agreed that a new type of ship was required for the carriage of containers, several times the size of the conventional vessels. However, it was expected that they would replace five or six traditional-type cargo vessels. Atlas Line (Australia) Pty Limited was formed by Ellerman, Blue Star and Port Line. The application for membership of the Australia–Far East Conference was rejected, and a fortnightly service was started in August 1967. The competition led to lower freight rates until agreement was reached that resulted in closer relations between the two large groups.

In 1966, an agreement was made with Container Services Incorporated for the supply of a number of containers to be used as an experiment. As *Catanian* and *Malatian* were suitable for the carriage of conventional cargo and around twenty-four containers, they were chosen to be placed on the Lisbon service. It was at this time that the Port of Liverpool was experiencing heavy delays because of labour problems. Ellerman & Papayanni had also been looking at *Cortian*, which was owned by the Bratt Line, as she was making profitable voyages carrying palletised newsprint. *Cortian* was making a profit when other vessels in the same trade were making losses. She was purchased by Ellerman & Papayanni and placed on the Oporto route, handling containers and unitised cargo.

Ellerman's Wilson Line introduced the *Salerno*, which was the first of a new class of five multipurpose vessels and able to carry up to eighty-eight containers. These were followed by *Mediterranian* and *Athenian* for Ellerman & Papayann, and an agreement was reached with Sea Containers Incorporated for the purchase of eight 'Hustler'-class ships. Berths for the new generation of vessels became available at London, but Liverpool was still experiencing heavy delays because of demand for the temporary facilities. *Minho* was introduced in 1969, followed by *Tagus*, *Tamega*, *Tiber*, *Tormes* and *Tua*. Westcott & Laurence started a service between London, Rotterdam and Portugal, and in 1971 Ellerman, Moss Hutchison and the Zim Line established a container service between Liverpool and Israel. Westcott & Laurence, Zim and the Prince Line also operated a joint service from London to Israel, and a container service between Garston and La Spezia was started in 1971 by Ellerman & Papayanni Line.

Ellerman & Papayanni opened a container base at Speke in Liverpool that was adjacent to Garston Docks and the Liverpool Freightliner Terminal. The increased demands on the container berth at Gladstone Dock and the need to provide a regular advertised service meant that Ellerman & Papayanni also loaded cargo at the temporary berth at Hornby Dock. However, this proved unsatisfactory, and an agreement was signed for the line to use the facilities provided by Cawood Containers Limited at Garston on the Mersey.

In May 1972, Cawood Containers Limited opened a container base at Ellesmere Port on the Manchester Ship Canal. When the Seaforth Container Terminal was opened in the same month, *Tagus* was the first vessel to use the new facilities at Liverpool. However, the new terminal continued to experience teething problems, and it was decided to transfer Ellerman's Mediterranean container services to Ellesmere Port.

From 1968, services to the Far East were operated by the joint Ellerman & Ben Line, and in March 1969 a new container vessel, *ACT 1*, entered the Associated Container Transportation Line. The Canadian City Line was formed in 1971, and the three ships transferred from the Australian routes were named after Canadian cities.

The cost of converting to containerisation was proving to be considerable, and at one point Sir John Ellerman offered to back up the company with close to £7,000,000 of his own cash if needed, but this was not required. The container vessel *City of Edinburgh* came into service on 9 November 1973, when she joined her sisters *Benalder* and *Benavon* in the Ben–Ellerman service. She was 58,440 gross tons and designed to accommodate over 2,800 20-foot containers. Ellerman Lines had a share in the vessel although she was owned by the Ben Line.

However, as Ellerman were preparing to welcome its new ship, the historical Finkenwerder Yard where she was built was preparing to close, after its last contract (for an offshore drilling rig) was completed. The yard produced a large number of submarines and torpedo boats for the German Navy during the Second World War and was one of the first shipyards to commence production after the war. It was reported that it was decided to close the yard because its machinery was obsolete and because '*City of Edinburgh* was launched amid the graveyard of surrounding empty shipyards. The shipyard is a barren grave of empty

ELLERMAN & BUCKNALL LINE
Programme of Sailings
TO and FROM

ELLERMAN

1970-71   SOUTH AFRICAN PORTS, LOURENCO MARQUES and BEIRA   1970-71

FROM ENGLAND

VESSEL	LONDON Embark	HAMBURG Arr. Dep.	ROTTERDAM Arr. Dep.	LAS PALMAS Call	CAPE TOWN Arr. Dep.	P. ELIZABETH Arr. Dep.	EAST LONDON Arr. Dep.	DURBAN Arr. Dep.	L. MARQUES Arr. Dep.	BEIRA Arrive
		1971	1971	1971	1971	1971	1971	1971	1971	1971
CITY OF DURBAN	4th Dec.	6.12 7.12	9.12 10.12	15.12	26.12 27.12	29.12 31.12	1.1 1.1	2.1 6.1	7.1 8.1	9.1
CITY OF YORK	1 Jan.	3.1 4.1	6.1 7.1	12.1	23.1 24.1	26.1 28.1	29.1 29.1	30.1 3.2	4.2 5.2	6.2
CITY OF PORT ELIZABETH	29th Jan.	31.1 1.2	3.2 4.2	9.2	20.2 21.2	23.2 25.2	26.2 26.2	27.2 3.3	4.3 5.3	6.3
CITY OF EXETER	12th Feb.	14.2 16.2	17.2 18.2	23.2	6.3 7.3	9.3 11.3	12.3 12.3	13.3 17.3	18.3 19.3	20.3
CITY OF DURBAN	12th March	14.3 16.3	17.3 18.3	23.3	3.4 4.4	6.4 8.4	9.4 9.4	10.4 14.4	15.4 16.4	17.4
CITY OF YORK	7th May	9.5 10.5	12.5 13.5	18.5	29.5 30.5	1.6 3.6	4.6 4.6	5.6 9.6	10.6 11.6	12.6
CITY OF PORT ELIZABETH	4th June	6.6 7.6	9.6 10.6	15.6	26.6 27.6	29.6 1.7	2.7 2.7	3.7 7.7	8.7 9.7	10.7
CITY OF EXETER	18th June	20.6 21.6	23.6 24.6	29.6	10.7 11.7	13.7 15.7	16.7 16.7	17.7 21.7	22.7 23.7	24.7

TO ENGLAND

VESSEL	BEIRA Leave	L. MARQUES Arr. Dep.	DURBAN Arr. Dep.	EAST LONDON Arr. Dep.	P. ELIZABETH Arr. Dep.	CAPE TOWN Arr. Dep.	LAS PALMAS Call	LONDON Disembark
							1971	
CITY OF EXETER	16.12	18.12 20.12	21.12 25.12	26.12 27.12	28.12 28.12	30.12 1.1	12.1	17.1
CITY OF DURBAN	13.1	15.1 17.1	18.1 22.1	23.1 24.1	25.1 25.1	27.1 29.1	9.2	14.2
CITY OF YORK	10.2	12.2 14.2	15.2 19.2	20.2 21.2	24.2 26.2	9.3	14.3	
CITY OF PORT ELIZABETH	10.3	12.3 14.3	15.3 19.3	20.3 21.3	22.3 22.3	24.3 26.3	6.4	11.4
CITY OF EXETER	24.3	26.3 28.3	29.3 2.4	3.4 4.4	5.4 5.4	7.4 9.4	20.4	25.4
CITY OF DURBAN	21.4	23.4 25.4	26.4 30.4	1.5 2.5	3.5 3.5	5.5 7.5	18.5	23.5
CITY OF YORK	16.6	18.6 20.6	21.6 25.6	26.6 27.6	28.6 28.6	30.6 2.7	13.7	18.7

GREEN DENOTES HIGH SEASON SAILINGS

BLACK DENOTES SEASON SAILINGS

BUFF DENOTES OFF SEASON SAILINGS

The dates of arrival and departure at Ports in Southern Africa are subject to alteration according to circumstances prevailing.

ELLERMAN & BUCKNALL LINE
PASSAGE RATES

United Kingdom and Continent to or from	CAPE TOWN SINGLE	CAPE TOWN HALF RETURN	P. ELIZABETH SINGLE	P. ELIZABETH HALF RETURN	EAST LONDON SINGLE	EAST LONDON HALF RETURN	DURBAN SINGLE	DURBAN HALF RETURN	L. MARQUES SINGLE	L. MARQUES HALF RETURN	BEIRA SINGLE	BEIRA HALF RETURN
	£	£	£	£	£	£	£	£	£	£	£	£
With Private Bathroom and Toilet				OFF SEASON FARES per person								
Single Room	240	228	260	247	268	255	283	269	300	285	320	304
Double Bed Sitting Room	230	219	252	240	260	248	275	262	292	278	312	297
Double Room	195	185	215	204	223	212	235	223	255	242	275	261
Three Berth Room	170	162	188	179	195	186	206	196	223	212	240	229
Without Private Bathroom and Toilet												
Single Room	205	195	224	213	231	220	243	231	262	249	280	266
Double Room	150	143	169	161	176	168	188	179	205	195	225	214
Three Berth Room	140	133	158	150	165	157	176	167	193	183	210	200
With Private Bathroom and Toilet				SEASON FARES per person								
Single Room	275	261	295	280	303	288	318	302	335	318	355	337
Double Bed Sitting Room	265	252	287	273	295	281	310	295	327	311	347	330
Double Room	235	223	255	242	261	250	275	261	295	280	315	299
Three Berth Room	205	195	223	212	230	219	241	229	258	245	275	262
Without Private Bathroom and Toilet												
Single Room	235	223	254	241	261	248	273	259	292	277	310	294
Double Room	205	195	224	213	231	220	243	231	260	247	280	266
Three Berth Room	195	185	213	202	220	209	231	219	248	235	265	252
With Private Bathroom and Toilet				HIGH SEASON FARES per person								
Single Room	315	299	335	318	343	326	358	340	375	356	395	375
Double Bed Sitting Room	310	295	332	316	340	324	355	338	372	354	392	373
Double Room	280	266	300	285	308	293	320	304	340	323	360	342
Three Berth Room	240	228	258	245	265	252	276	262	293	278	310	295
Without Private Bathroom and Toilet												
Single Room	270	257	289	275	296	282	308	293	327	311	345	328
Double Room	230	219	249	237	256	244	268	255	285	271	305	290
Three Berth Room	220	209	238	226	245	233	256	243	273	259	290	276

1970–71 sailing list and passage rates to South African ports Lourenco Marques and Beira.

slipways, a graveyard only thinly disguised by the activity around the *City of Edinburgh.*'The 1,600 workers at the yard were, however, offered jobs elsewhere, within the company that owned Finkenwerder.

Ben Line Containers was part of the service provided between Europe and the Far East in a combined conference known as the 'Trio' Lines. The other members of the Far East Conference were Hapag-Lloyd, NYK and Mitsui-OSK Lines. A service for the carriage of refrigerated containers to the east coast of North America

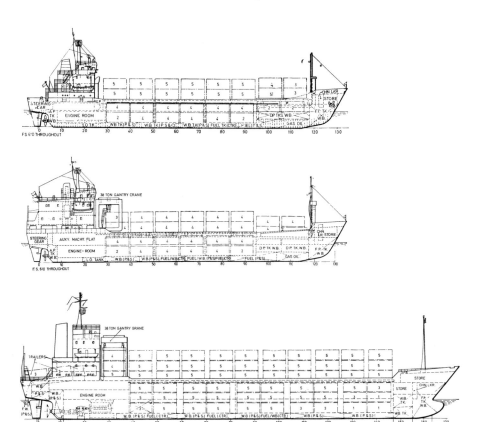

The development of sea containers series of short sea and feeder ships. The initial design was the Hustler class (top), which entered service in 1969. A development of this type was the Tarros class (middle), which employed the same hull form as the Hustler class but with revised superstructure. The Strider-T (bottom) had a higher container capacity and was two knots faster than the earlier versions.

was named the Pacific and America Container Express Line (PACE), operating between St John, New York, Philadelphia, Norfolk, Australia and New Zealand via the Panama Canal. It was operated with cellular container ships and the inaugural sailing was made by *ACT 3* on 15 August 1971 from Australia and *ACT 4* from North America on 25 September. *City of Durban* entered service for the Ellerman–Harrison Container Line in 1978 on the Europe to South Africa route.

Ellerman's became one-third owner of Dilkara for the trade between Australia and the North American ports of Los Angeles, San Francisco, Seattle, Vancouver and Hawaii. The Swedish Transatlantic Line intended to operate two ro-ro ships in cooperation with the Australian National Line, and the *Parella*, *Allunga* and *Dilkara* served this route. In this period, it was still unclear what vessels would be required for the future and how the introduction of containerisation would impact conventional services. However, it was decided to order three conventional ships, so *City of Liverpool*, *City of Hull* and *City of London* were delivered.

A restructuring of the group took place in 1973, when the Papayanni, Westcott & Laurence, Hall and Ellerman & Bucknall Lines were replaced by Ellerman City Liners.

City of Manchester (6).

City of Plymouth.

City of Oxford.

Ellerman's Wilson Lines would become the Transport Division of Ellerman Lines, concerned with heavy intercontinental road vehicles. Ellerman Travel and Leisure took over all travel and leisure interests of the group. Responsibility for investments, property and companies owned overseas, as well as holdings in the United Kingdom, was transferred to the individual lines previously accountable for them and two additional divisions: Investment Services (Camomile Street) and Investment Services (Moorgate). The Moorgate Trust and the Audley Trust held a controlling shareholding in Ellerman Lines limited. As Sir John Ellerman purchased his shipping lines, he decided to let them remain as individual companies with City Line at Glasgow, Hall, Ellerman & Papayanni at Liverpool and Bucknalls and Westcott & Laurence in London. The restructuring created one entity with its headquarters in London. Sir John Ellerman died on 17 July 1973 after suffering a heart attack.

The Ellerman Group was sold for £47 million in 1983 to David and Frederick Barclay. This amount included the brewing and printing interests of the group, and the remaining ships were re-registered in the Isle of Man the following year. Although the fleet consisted of six ships, only one was actually owned by Ellerman City Liners, as the others were chartered from banks. There was a management buy-back in 1985, but the line was purchased two years later for £24.1 million by Trafalgar House, which already owned the Cunard Line. A new freight operation was formed under the name of Cunard-Ellerman, with a fleet of nineteen ships. The organisation controlled stakes in the Atlantic Container Line, Ben Line Containers and Ellerman Harrison Container Line and held a 57½ per cent interest in Associated Container Transportation (Australia) Limited.

Ellerman operated services from northern Europe to Portugal, the Middle East, East and South Africa and the Far East, as well as from Europe to Australia and New Zealand and from the United States to Australia and New Zealand. The agreement included four wholly owned 300 TEU vessels, 65 per cent of the 2,980 TEU container ship *ACT 8*, and the minority shares in ten other container ships of 1,300–3,000 TEU.

On 14 October 1991, the P&O Steam Navigation Company bought the Ellerman shipping and container interests from Trafalgar House for £42.5 million. Sixteen vessels were involved and Trafalgar House retained the Cunard name. The Mediterranean, Middle East, Indian and east African interests in the Cunard–Ellerman Group were sold to Andrew Weir Shipping Limited (The Bank Line).

P&O took over the container ships *ACT 1*, *ACT 2* and *ACT 7*, which were jointly owned by the Blue Star Line, Port Line and Ellerman Lines, *City of Durban* owned by Ellerman Lines and the Charente Steam Ship Company (T&J Harrison), *New Zealand Mariner*, *New Zealand Pacific* and the tanker *Lumiere*. Blue Star Line took over *ACT 3*, *ACT 4*, *ACT 5*, *ACT 6* and *ACT 10*, which were all jointly owned by the Blue Star Line, Port Line and the Ellerman Lines. Andrew Weir Shipping took over four of Ellerman Lines' container ships, *City of Manchester*, *City of Plymouth*, *Liverpool Star* and *Oxford*, but the deal did not affect the Atlantic Container Line's Atlantic Conveyor.

Andrew Weir took over the United Kingdom to Portugal service, the northern Europe to eastern Mediterranean service, the northern Europe to east Africa and the northern Europe to the Red Sea services, as well as the northern Europe to India route. The container vessels *City of Plymouth*, *City of Manchester*, *Liverpool Star* and *Oxford* went to Andrew Weir, and in July 1995 Andrew Weir ordered a 2,000 TEU container vessel from a Polish yard at Gdynia, which was delivered as *City of London* two years later. However, she never sailed on the Weir service but was chartered out to various shipping operators.

Prior to the deal with Hamburg Süd (see next section), Andrew Weir owned the *City of London*, *Baltic Eider* (operated by Finnlines), *Baltic Tern*, *Pacheco* and *City of Manchester*, four cargo vessels deployed on the South Pacific service, and managed the St Helena Line, which operated between the United Kingdom, the Canary Islands, Ascension Island, St Helena and Cape Town.

On 1 January 2003, the Mediterranean, Middle East, African, Indian and Pakistan services were acquired by Hamburg Süd, and they replaced the Ellerman brand exactly two years later. CMA CGM acquired from Andrew Weir the services covering the United Kingdom and Ireland to the Baltic, Spain and Portugal, which included the Ellerman route from Dublin, Liverpool, and Greenock to Leixoes and Lisbon.

Hamburg Süd

Hamburg Südamerikanische was founded as a joint stock company by representatives of eleven Hamburg merchant houses in 1871. By 1906, it had introduced fast steamers on the South American route with *Cap Vilano* and *Cap Arcona*. By 1914, the company operated over fifty ships totalling around 325,000 tons; among them were the large steamers *Cap Finisterre*, *Cap Trafalgar* and *Cap Polonio*.

Following the end of the First World War, the reconstruction of the fleet began with chartered vessels, and by 1922 they were offering cruises on *Cap Polonio*. The *Cap Arcona* entered service in 1927 as the flagship of the fleet. In 1936, Dr August Oetker acquired an interest in the company. At the outbreak of the Second World War, Hamburg Süd had the largest fleet in its history, with fifty-two ships of over 400,000 tons. However, the company lost its entire fleet during the war as ships were lost or were surrendered as part of reparation payments.

By 1951, liner services had resumed between Europe and the east coast of South America. Shipping activities were extended to the tramp market with activity in tanker shipping and the expansion of the refrigerated fleet. Dr August Oetker took over the company in 1955 and they entered the Mediterranean market by the takeover of Deutsche Levante Linie. In 1957 liner services resumed between North America and South America under the name of the Columbus Line, and the services were extended between North America and Australia and New Zealand six years later.

Atlas Levante Linie was taken over in 1967, and a full container service was provided by the Columbus Line with Columbus New Zealand, Columbus Australia and Columbus America operating between the east coast of the United States and Australia and New Zealand in 1971. A container service was opened between Europe and the east coast of South America in 1980, and Deutsche Nah Ost Linie was taken over in 1986. This was followed by the acquisition of a 50 per cent stake in the Spanish line Ybarra y Cia. Sudamérica SA three years later.

The British Furness Withy Group, which owned the Royal Mail Line, and the Pacific Steam Navigation Company, the Swedish Laser Lines, Rotterdam Zuid America Lijn (RZAL) and Havenlijn were acquired in 1990. The Brazilian company Alianca and the South Seas Steamship Company followed in 1998, with South Pacific Container Lines and Transcroll's Europe to South American east coast services in 1999 and the Inter-America Services of Crowley American Transport (CAT) in 2000. The Ellerman services were taken over in 2003, together with the Kien Hung liner services from Asia to South America.

On 1 January 2004, the Columbus Line and Crowley American Transport brands were replaced by Hamburg Süd and the first of six identical 5,552 TEU container ships was christened. She was followed by five sister ships of the 'Monte' class, which were designed with large reefer capacity. The shares of Ybarra y Cia. Sudamérica SA were acquired in December 2005 and cross-trade activities between Australia, New Zealand and Asia, as well as North America were purchased from Fesco in 2006, and later their Australia–New Zealand liner services. The brand Ybarra y Cia. Sudamérica SA was replaced by Hamburg Süd Iberia SA in December 2006.

The company organised a double christening of the *Bahia* and *Bahia Blanca* in Korea in February 2007. The two ships were the first of a total of six identical 3,752 TEU container vessels. Costa Container Lines, which operated to the Mediterranean, South America and the Caribbean, was taken over in December 2007, and the FANZL Fesco Australia, New Zealand Liner Services brand was replaced by Hamburg Süd in January 2008. The company's largest container ship, the *Rio de la Plata*, was christened in March 2008. She was the first built in a series of six identical vessels, each with a capacity of 5,900 TEU. The Costa Container Lines brand was replaced by Hamburg Süd on 1 January 2009, and the 7,100 TEU container ship *Santa Clara* was delivered by the Daewoo Yard in South Korea in October 2010. She is the largest ship ever to have sailed under the Hamburg Süd flag, and a further nine 'Santa'-class vessels were delivered by the end of 2012.

FLEET LIST

Ellerman & Papayanni Line

Arcadia	1855	1,901grt.	92.6×9.66×8.35	Brig	1,221n. 9k.
E.	Sgl. screw, 2 cyl. simple. By builder.				
B.	J. & G. Thompson, Glasgow.				
1855	Completed as a brig for George Michael Papayanni for the Liverpool–Mediterranean service.				
1875	Lengthened by Thompson & Company at Newcastle and a second sgl. exp. engine and new boilers were fitted. Three masts were fitted.				
1898	Broken up at Preston by Thos. W. Ward.				

Thessalia	1855	1,856grt.	92.6×9.66×8.35	Brig	1,206n 9k.
E.	Sgl. screw, 2 cyl. simple. By builder.				
B.	J. & G. Thompson, Glasgow.				
1855	Completed for Basilio Papayanni.				
1875	Lengthened to 92.41 and modified as *Arcadia* (1) by Fawcett & Preston, Liverpool.				
1881	Sold and broken up.				

Laconia	1856	1,982grt.	92.6×9.66×8.35	Brig	1,295n. 9k.
E.	Sgl. screw, 2 cyl. simple. By builder.				
P.	32.				
B.	J. & G. Thompson, Glasgow.				
1856	Completed.				
1870	The first of the three sister ships to be rebuilt by Fawcett & Preston at Liverpool, engines were compounded. Lengthened to 95.8, three masts fitted.				
1874	13 March. On a voyage from Alexandria to Algiers, near Tunis 278 pilgrims from Mecca were washed overboard. Only nine drowned as the rest were rescued.				
1901	17 June. Transferred to J.R. Ellerman.				
1902	March. Broken up at Genoa.				

Agia Sophia	1857	1,437grt.	79.02×10.55×6.71	Barque rig	977n. 9k.
E.	Sgl. screw, 2 cyl. comp. inv. By builder.				
B.	J. & G. Thompson, Glasgow.				
1857	Completed.				
1872	Lengthened to 103.14×10.8 with a new section by Fawcett & Preston, Liverpool. New boilers fitted, twinned engine, four masts fitted. 2,593grt., 1,654n.				

1901	17 June. Transferred to J.R. Ellerman.
1902	Sold to Italian interests and renamed *Tripoli*.
1903	Broken up at Leghorn.

Boetia	1855 951grt. 67.09×8.96×6.92
E.	Sgl. screw, 2 cyl. simple exp.
B.	T.D. Marshall & Company, South Shields.
1855	Completed for J. Dudgeon, London, for the Mediterranean trade.
1858	Purchased by Basilio Papayanni.
1859	Sold to J. Bibby, Sons & Company, Liverpool.
1864	Sold to the West India & Pacific Steam Navigation Company, Liverpool, renamed *Barbadian*.
1865	December. Lost on the Blackwater Bank.

Orontes	1851 701grt. 57.02×8.35×5.18 436n. 8k.
E.	Sgl. screw, 2 cyl. simple inv., 98hp. By Hick & Son, Belfast.
B.	Archibald Denny, Dumbarton.
1851	Completed for Moss Steam Ship Company, Liverpool.
1859	Purchased by Papayanni Brothers.
1861	Sold to Henry W. Withers, Liverpool.
1878	Sold to George P. Forward, Liverpool for the Mersey Steam Ship Companies service to Morocco.
1878	Foundered in the North Sea.

Ionia	1856 1,388grt. 74.49×9.78×7.89 9k.
E.	Sgl. screw, 3 cyl. simple exp.
B.	T.D. Marshall & Company, South Shields.
1856	Completed for Papayanni Brothers. Similar to *Boetia*.
1861	Sold to J. Bibby Sons & Company.
1870	Purchased by the Anglo-Egyptian Navigation Company.
1872	Lengthened to 92.35, compounded and new boilers fitted. 1,758grt.
1875	December. Lost in the River Congo.

Amalia	1860 1,825grt. 84.64×11.28×7.8 1,284n. 9k.
E.	Sgl. screw, 2 cyl. simple exp. By builder.
B.	J. & G. Thompson, Glasgow.
1860	December. Maiden voyage Clyde to Mediterranean, then from Liverpool.
1866	Foundered in the Bay of Biscay.

Macedonia	1867 1,732grt. 87.96×10.76×6.98 10k.
E.	Sgl. screw, 2 cyl. simple inv. By Fawcett, Preston & Company, Liverpool.
B.	Thos. Vernon & Son, Liverpool.
1867	January. Completed.
1875	Engine converted to 2×2 cyl. by G. Forrester & Company, Liverpool.
1881	Lengthened to 106.1, 2,853grt., 1,866n.
1899	Broken up in Italy.

Arafat	1871 2,016grt. 98.57×10.18×7.92 1,305n. 9½k.
E.	Sgl. screw, 2 cyl. comp. inv. By Forrester & Company, Liverpool.
P.	14.
B.	Liverpool Shipbuilding Company, Liverpool.
1871	Delivered to Papayanni Brothers
1901	17 June. Sold to J.R. Ellerman.
1909	Broken up in Italy.

Lord Clive	1871 3,386grt. 116.13×12.22×7.92 2,206n. 10k.
E.	Sgl. screw, 2 cyl. comp. inv. By Forrester & Company, Liverpool.
B.	R. & J. Evans, Liverpool.
1871	28 October. Launched for G.M. Papayanni for the Liverpool to Boston service.
1872	Chartered to the Dominion Line.
1872	15 April. First sailing Liverpool–Quebec–Montreal.
1875	Transferred to the American Line.
1875	15 December. Liverpool–Philadelphia service.
1888	Sold to Lord Clive Steam Ship Company, Liverpool, owned by the American Line and employed on emigrant service Liverpool to Philadelphia. British flag.
1896	Purchased by Gastaldi & Company, Genoa and renamed *Clive* for the New York–Genoa–Naples route. Chartered to Furness Withy & Company.
1897	April. Withdrawn, route sold to Prince Line. Several cargo-only voyages Liverpool–Boston.
1898	April. Broken up.

Lord Gough	1879 3,655grt. 116.68 2,370n.
E.	Sgl. screw, 2 cyl. comp. inv. By builder.
B.	Laird Brothers, Birkenhead.
1878	November. Launched for G.M. Papayanni for charter to American Line.
1879	April. Maiden voyage Liverpool-Philadelphia, American Line.
1888	Sold with *Lord Clive* to Lord Gough Steam Ship Company, Liverpool.
1895	March. Withdrawn.
1896	Sold to the Aberdeen Atlantic Line to carry emigrants to New York.
1898	July. Withdrawn and sold for scrap.
1899	January. Broken up at Genoa.

Roumelia	1877 2,158grt. 97.75×10.79×7.71 1,384n. 10k.
E.	Sgl. screw, 2×2 cyl. comp. inv., 260 nhp. By G. Forrester & Company, Liverpool.
P.	19.
B.	Thos. Royden & Sons, Liverpool.
1877	Delivered to Basilio Papayanni.
1901	17 June. Purchased by J.R. Ellerman.
1905	April. Sold to Parr's Bank Company. Broken up at Garston.

Truthful	1877 956grt. 73.21×9.14×4.91 600n. 9k.
E.	Sgl. screw, 2 cyl. comp. inv., 160 nhp, 70 psi. By builder.
B.	Barrow Shipbuilding Company, Barrow in Furness.
1877	November. Completed for F.H. Powell, Liverpool

1880	Sold to J. Ellis, Liverpool.
1883	Purchased by Papayanni & Company and used for services in the Aegean.
1886	Deleted from register.

Plantain	1879 2,117grt. 96.19×10.73×7.86 1,360n. 9½k.
E.	Sgl. screw, Siamese tandem, 2×2 cyl. comp. inv., 300 nhp, 75 psi. By G. Forrseter & Company, Liverpool.
P.	28.
B.	Thos. Royden & Sons, Liverpool.
1879	September. Delivered to G.H. Horsfall & Company, Liverpool.
1886	Purchased by Papayanni Steam Ship Company Limited.
1901	17 June. Transferred to Ellerman.
1903	Broken up by Robert White & Sons, Glasgow.

Britannia	1885 3,129grt. 107.59×11.98×8.56 2,041n. 10k.
E.	Sgl. screw, 2 cyl. comp., 280 nhp, 75 psi. By G. Forrester & Company.
P.	25.
B.	Thos. Royden & Sons, Liverpool.
1885	Delivered to Papayanni Steam Ship Company.
1901	17 June. Transferred to J.R. Ellerman.
1917	2 April. Torpedoed and sunk by the German submarine U-65 off Pantelaria.

Palm	1869 1,826grt. 91.29×9.69×7.86 1,394n. 9k.
E.	Sgl. screw, 2 cyl. comp., 140 hp. By builder.
B.	McNab & Company, Greenock.
1869	Delivered to G.H. Horsfall & Company, Liverpool.
1885	Purchased by Papayanni Steam Ship Company.
1898	Broken up.

Anatolia	1898 3,848grt. 109.73×14.02×5.36 2,490n. 10k.
E.	Sgl. screw, 3 cyl. tpl. exp., 406 nhp, 180 psi. By G. Clark & Company, Sunderland.
B.	Sir James Laing & Sons, Sunderland.
1898	December. Delivered and employed by Hall Line on the Indian service, managed by Robert Alexander & Company.
1901	17 June. Transferred to Ellerman Lines, Hall Line as managers.
1917	25 June. Sunk by UC-35 off Genoa.

Adalia	1899 3,847grt. 109.73×14.02×5.36 2,482n. 10k.
E.	Sgl. screw, 3 cyl. trl. exp., 406 nhp, 180 psi. By G. Clark & Company, Sunderland.
B.	Sir James Laing & Sons, Sunderland.
1899	August. Delivered to Papayanni Steam Ship Company with Robert Alexander as managers.
1901	17 June. Transferred to J.R. Ellerman with Hall Line as managers.
1917	29 April. Taken over as stores ship to the 16th Squadron, Russian Forces.
1917	29 July. Captured by the German submarine U-94 and sunk by gunfire 53 miles east of Muckle Flugga, Shetland Islands. One crew member died.

Egyptian	1861 1,986grt. 102.1×10.42×7.32 1,356n. 9k.
E.	Sgl. screw, 2 cyl. simple exp. By J. Jack, Rollo & Company, Liverpool.
B.	E.J. Harland, Belfast.
1861	Delivered to J. Bibby, Sons & Company, Liverpool.
1873	Sold with twenty ships to Frederick Leyland & Company.
1879	G. Forrester, Liverpool compounded the engines and she was fitted with two masts.
1889	Re-boilered.
1901	25 April. Frederick Leyland was taken over by J. Pierpoint Morgan and became part of the International Mercantile Marine Company.
1901	26 May. Sold to John Ellerman with twenty other vessels of the fleet of Frederick Leyland. The ships were transferred to the London, Liverpool & Ocean Shipping Company Limited, which changed its name to Ellerman Lines Limited on 31 December.
1902	22 January. The ships were transferred to Ellerman Lines Limited, with the eight Papayanni ships remaining separate as they were personally owned by J.R. Ellerman.
1903	Broken up.

Arabian	1862 1,995grt. 102.1×10.42×7.32 1,356n. 9k.
E.	Sgl. screw, 2 cyl. simple exp. By J. Jack, Rollo & Company, Liverpool.
B.	Harland & Wolff, Belfast.
1862	April. Completed for J. Bibby, Sons & Company.
1871	Engines compounded by G. Forrester, Liverpool. Two masts fitted.
1872	Transferred to Frederick Leyland & Company.
1901	Purchased by J.R. Ellerman, owned by Ellerman Lines Limited.
1902	Broken up.

Persian	1863 2,075grt. 110.28×10.36×7.41 1,396n. 10k.
E.	Sgl. screw, 2 cyl. comp. inv. By J. Jack, Rollo & Company, Liverpool.
B.	Harland & Wolff, Belfast.
1863	Delivered to J. Bibby, Sons & Company, Liverpool.
1873	Purchased by Frederick Leyland & Company.
1901	26 May. Owned by J.R. Ellerman.
1902	22 January. Ellerman Lines as managers.
1902	July. Broken up.

Lesbian	1874 1,559grt. 92.14×9.51×7.07 1,019n. 9k.
E.	Sgl. screw, 2 cyl. comp. inv. By J. Jack, Rollo & Company, Liverpool.
B.	Thos. Royden & Sons, Liverpool.
1874	Delivered to Frederick Leyland & Company.
1901	26 May. Purchased by J.R. Ellerman.
1902	22 January. Ellerman Lines as managers.
1903	Broken up in Italy.

Athenian	1875 1,619grt. 92.14×9.51×7.07 1,019n. 9k.
E.	Sgl. screw, 2 cyl. comp. inv. By J. Jack, Rollo & Company, Liverpool.
B.	Thos. Royden & Sons, Liverpool.
1875	Delivered to Frederick Leyland & Company.

1901	26 May. Purchased by J.R. Ellerman.
1902	22 January. Ellerman Lines as managers.
1905	Broken up.

Algerian	1876 1,757grt. 95.1×9.51×7.28 1,152n. 9k.
E.	Sgl. screw, 2 cyl. comp. inv. 220 hp. By J.Jones & Sons, Liverpool.
B.	Bowdler, Chaffer & Company, Seacombe.
1876	Completed for Frederick Leyland & Company.
1901	26 May. Purchased by J.R. Ellerman.
1902	22 January. Ellerman Lines as managers.
1903	Funnel heightened.
1904	Lost her funnel in a gale in the Bay of Biscay. A canvas replacement was fitted but as she could only make 5k she arrived at Liverpool two days late.
1912	Broken up in Italy.

Alsatian	1877 1,765grt. 95.1×9.51×7.28 1,158n. 9k.
E.	Sgl. screw, 2 cyl. comp. inv., 220 hp. By J.Jones & Sons, Liverpool.
B.	Bowdler, Chaffer & Company, Seacombe.
1876	Laid down.
1877	Because of a strike at the shipyard the ship was completed in Birkenhead docks by Frederick Leyland.
1901	26 May. Purchased by J.R. Ellerman.
1902	22 January. Ellerman Lines as managers.
1907	Broken up.

Andalusian	1877 1,763grt. 95.1×9.51×7.28 1,158n. 9k.
E.	Sgl. screw, 2 cyl. comp. inv. 220 hp. By J.Jones & Sons, Liverpool.
B.	Bowdler, Chaffer & Company, Seacombe.
1877	Because of a strike at the shipyard the ship was completed in Birkenhead docks by Frederick Leyland.
1901	26 May. Purchased by J.R. Ellerman.
1902	22 January. Ellerman Lines as managers.
1909	Broken up.

Falernian	1880 2,252grt. 104.67×10.52×7.16 1,479n. 9½k.
E.	Sgl. screw, 2×2 cyl. comp., 288 nhp. By Fawcett, Preston & Company.
B.	Oswald Mordaunt & Company, Woolston, Southampton.
1880	Delivered to Frederick Leyland & Company.
1894	Re-boilered.
1901	26 May. Purchased by J.R. Ellerman.
1902	22 January. Ellerman Lines as managers.
1911	November. Broken up at Garston by J.J. King & Sons.

Fabian	1881 2,248grt. 104.67×10.52×7.16 1,476n. 9½k.
E.	Sgl. screw, 2x2 cyl. comp., 288 nhp. By Fawcett, Preston & Company.
B.	Oswald Mordaunt & Company, Woolston, Southampton.
1881	Delivered to Frederick Leyland & Company.

1901	26 May. Purchased by J.R. Ellerman.
1902	22 January. Ellerman Lines as managers.
1916	26 October. Attacked by German submarine in St George's Channel. Later escaped but several direct hits and one member of crew lost his life.
1917	20 September. Torpedoed and sunk by UB-50 off Cape Spartel, near Tangier.

Flaminian	1880 2,131grt. 101.5×10.15×7.19 1,381n. 9½k.
E.	Sgl. screw, 2 cyl. comp. inv., 208 nhp. By builder.
B.	Palmers & Company, Newcastle.
1880	Delivered to S.S. Flaminian Company Limited, Leyland's as managers.
1895	Re-boilered.
1901	26 May. Purchased by J.R. Ellerman.
1902	22 January. Ellerman Lines as managers.
1912	Sold with Flavian to G. Longueville and broken up in France.

Flavian	1880 2,139grt. 101.5×10.15×7.19 1,387n. 9½k.
E.	Sgl. screw, 2 cyl. comp., inv., 208 nhp. By builder.
B.	Palmers & Company, Newcastle.
1880	Delivered to S.S. Flanian Company Limited, Leyland's as managers.
1896	Re-boilered.
1901	26 May. Purchased by J.R. Ellerman.
1902	22 January. Ellerman Lines as managers.
1913	Sold to G. Longueville and broken up.

Oporto	1888 739grt. 64.61×8.26×5.12 460n. 10k.
E.	Sgl. screw, 2 cyl. comp. 80 hp. By D. Rollo & Sons, Liverpool.
B.	Charles J. Bigger, Londonderry.
1888	June. Delivered to Frederick Leyland for the Iberian service.
1901	26 May. Purchased by J.R. Ellerman.
1902	22 January. Ellerman Lines as managers.
1918	Sold to Bombay Steam Navigation Company.
1925	Broken up at Bombay.

Minho	1890 825grt. 64.34×8.23×5.12 510n. 9k.
E.	Sgl. screw, 2 cyl. comp. By builder.
B.	J.Jones & Sons, Liverpool.
1890	May. Delivered to Frederick Leyland & Company.
1901	26 May. Purchased by J.R. Ellerman.
1902	22 January. Ellerman Lines as managers.
1913	Sold to J.B. Pla, Valencia and renamed *Manuela Pla*.
1916	Purchased by Dutrus & Carsi, Velancia.
1924	Managed by Fabregas y Garcias.
1931	Broken up.

Mexican	1891 3,488grt. 109.73×13.17×8.11 2,270n. 10k.
E.	Sgl. screw, tpl. exp. 399 nhp. By builder.
B.	Naval Construction & Armament Company, Barrow in Furness.

1891	October. Delivered to the West India & Pacific Steam Ship Company, Liverpool.
1900	1 January. Company and fleet were taken over by Frederick Leyland & Company.
1901	26 May. Purchased by J.R. Ellerman.
1902	22 January. Ellerman Lines as managers.
1903	Sold back to Frederick Leyland & Company.
1913	Sold to De Gregori & Gennaro, Genoa and renamed *Messicano*.
1918	Lost in Mediterranean.

Almerian	1897 2,984grt. 107.14×12.86×7.1 1,910n. 10k.
E.	Sgl. screw, tpl. exp., 284 nhp, 200 psi. By G. Clark, Sunderland.
B.	Robert Thompson & Company, Sunderland.
1897	Delivered to Frederick Leyland & Company.
1901	26 May. Purchased by J.R. Ellerman.
1902	22 January. Ellerman Lines as managers.
1903	Sold to Frederick Leyland & Company.
1918	19 October. Sunk by a mine 13 miles west by south of Licata, Sicily. Mine laid by UC-52.

Albanian	1898 2,930grt. 107.14×12.86×7.1 1,876n. 10k.
E.	Sgl. screw, tpl. exp., 284 nhp, 200 psi. By G. Clark, Sunderland.
1898	Delivered.
1901	26 May. Purchased by J.R. Ellerman.
1902	22 January. Ellerman Lines as managers.
1903	Sold to Frederick Leyland & Company.
1921	Purchased by Oughtred & Harrison, Hull managers of the Hull Beacon Shipping Company.
1928	Sold to V. Saglimbene, Catania, Sicily, and renamed *Burgandrea*.
1933	Broken up in Italy.

Tagus	1898 937grt. 67.08×8.75×4.97 509n. 9½k.
E.	Sgl. screw, 2 cyl. comp., 88 hp, 160 psi. By builder.
B.	Caledon Shipbuilding & Engineering Company, Dundee.
1898	October. Delivered to Frederick Leyland & Company.
1901	26 May. Purchased by J.R. Ellerman.
1902	22 January. Ellerman Lines as managers.
1916	6 September. Attacked and sunk by UB-39, 35 miles north-east of Ushant.

Douro	1900 1,028grt 71.63×9.36×4.97 638n. 9½k.
E.	Sgl. screw, 2 cyl. comp., 88 hp, 160 psi. By builder.
B.	Caledon Shipbuilding & Engineering Company, Dundee.
1900	Delivered.
1909	Wrecked at Oporto.

Belgian	1900 3,657grt. 116.53×13.82×7.87 2,364n. 11k.
E.	Sgl. screw, tpl. exp., 366 nhp, 200 psi. By T. Richardson & Sons, Hartlepool.
B.	Sir James Laing & Sons, Sunderland.

1900	October. Delivered to Frederick Leyland & Company for the Antwerp–Montreal service.
1901	26 May. Purchased by J.R. Ellerman.
1902	22 January. Ellerman Lines as managers.
1909	Sold to Frederick Leyland & Company.
1917	24 May. Attacked and torpedoed by U-57, 50 miles from Fastnet, and two members of her crew lost their lives. She managed to sail back to port but was declared a constructive total loss and scrapped.

Orchis	1870 1,765grt. 85.5×10.3 1,138n. 9k.
E.	Sgl. screw, 2 cyl. comp. inv., 187 nhp, 2 dbl. blrs. By J. Howden & Company, Glasgow.
B.	J.G. Lawrie & Company, Glasgow.
1870	November. Delivered to William Johnson, Liverpool.
1884	Purchased by Hornstedt & Carthorne, Liverpool. Re-boilered.
1889	Sold to Westcott & Laurence for the London–Mediterranean route.
1901	August. The fleet and ships of Westcott and Laurence joined the Ellerman Group, operating as a separate company, with J.R. Ellerman as chairman.
1913	Bought by A/S Brunkeberg with Moller & Perrson as managers. Name changed to *Birka*.
1916	January. Wrecked.

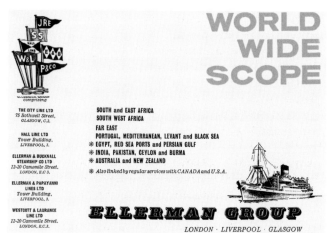

Ellerman Group advertisement.

Tenedos	1873 1,280grt. 73.67×9.84×6.92 953n. 9k.
E.	Sgl. screw, 2 cyl. comp., 162 nhp, 60 psi, 2 sgl. blrs. By builder.
B.	London & Glasgow Engineering & Iron Shipbuilding Company, Glasgow.
1873	November. Delivered to the Globe Steamship Company, London for the Glasgow–India service and later London–India route.
1889	Purchased by Westcott & Laurence Line.
1901	August. The fleet and ships of Westcott & Laurence joined the Ellerman Group, operating as a separate company with J.R. Ellerman as Chairman.
1904	Sold to Scounaki, Ibrahim & Company, Salonika and renamed *Salonique*.
1917	Broken up.

Perim	1877 1,348grt. 73.55×9.94×6.92 1,016n. 9k.
E.	Sgl. screw, 2 cyl. comp., 118 nhp, 65 psi, 2 sgl. blrs. By builder.
B.	London & Glasgow Engineering & Iron Shipbuilding Company, Glasgow.
1877	April. Delivered to R.W. Cousins & Company, London.
1891	February. Purchased by the Westcott & Laurence Line.
1901	August. The fleet and ships of Westcott & Laurence joined the Ellerman Group, operating as a separate company with J.R. Ellerman as chairman.
1917	21 October. Sank following a collision off Tarragona.

Gulf of Suez	1880 1,608grt. 79.25×10.36×6.61 1,014n. 9k.
E.	Sgl. screw, 2 cyl. comp., 170 nhp, 80 psi, 2 blrs. By Blair & Company, Stockton.
P.	6.
B.	William Gray & Company, West Hartlepool.
1880	May. Delivered to the Greenock Steam Ship Company, Greenock (Gulf Line).
1887	Engine conversion by Blair & Company, Stockton-on-Tees. Purchased by Westcott & Laurence Line.
1901	August. The fleet and ships of Westcott & Laurence joined the Ellerman Group, operating as a separate company with J.R. Ellerman as Chairman.
1924	February. Sold to A. Coker & Company, Liverpool, and scrapped.

Joshua Nicholson	1880 1,853grt. 82.29×10.67×7.47 1,196n. 9½k.
E.	Sgl. screw, 2 cyl. comp., 160 nhp, 90 psi, 2 blrs. By R. & W. Hawthorn, Newcastle.
B.	Tyne Iron Shipbuilding Company, Wilmington-on-Tees.
1880	October. Delivered to Charles Tully & Company, North Shields.
1886	The business collapsed and fleet laid up. Owned by Joshua Nicholson Steam Ship Company.
1889	Purchased by Stephens & Mawson Limited.
1894	Engines tripled by Palmers at Jarrow.
1898	Purchased by Westcott & Laurence Line.
1901	The fleet and ships of Westcott & Laurence joined the Ellerman Group, operating as a separate company with J.R. Ellerman as Chairman.
1917	18 March. Torpedoed and sunk by U-70 off Wolf Rock Light on a voyage from London to Alexandria. All twenty-six crew were lost.

Cedardene	1881 2,197grt. 87.02×11.34×7.44 1,437n. 10k.
E.	Sgl. screw, 2 cyl. comp., 300 nhp, 90 psi, 2 blrs. By R. & W. Hawthorn, Newcastle.
B.	Bartram, Haswell & Company, Sunderland.
1881	8 November. Launched as *Clan Monroe* for the Clan Line.
1882	Converted to quad. exp. by Westray, Copeland, Barrow in Furness.
1897	Sold to Dene Steam Shipping Company Limited, Newcastle. J.T. Lunn as managers.
1899	Purchased by Westcott & Laurence for the Black Sea route.
1901	August. The fleet and ships of Westcott & Laurence joined the Ellerman Group, operating as a separate company with J.R. Ellerman as chairman.
1903	24 February. She was wrecked north of Azile, Morocco on a voyage from Glasgow to Alexandria.

Avoca	1883 1,539grt. 76.2×10.73×5.49 995n. 9k.
E.	Sgl. screw, 2 cyl. comp. inv. By North East Marine Engineering Company, Sunderland.
B.	Strand Slipway Company, Sunderland.
1883	March. Delivered to Westcott & Laurence Line. London–Antwerp–Mediterranean service.
1901	August. The fleet and ships of Westcott & Laurence joined the Ellerman Group, operating as a separate company with J.R. Ellerman as Chairman.
1906	Sold to Captain J.R. Laurence, owned by the London Avoca Steam Ship Company and managed by Westcott & Laurence Line.
1908	Sold to Brodrene Biornstad's Acties Avoca and renamed *Christiania*.
1912	Purchased by A.H. Arvesen.
1913	Wrecked.

Plymothian	1883 1,626grt. 79.4×10.97×5.64 1,053n. 9k.
E.	Sgl. screw, 2 cyl. comp., 198 nhp, 85 psi, 2 sgl. blrs. By Wallsend Slipway Company, Newcastle.
B.	Swan Hunter & Company Limited, Wallsend.
1883	Delivered to Port of Plymouth Steam Ship Company. Managed by Bellamy.
1894	Sold to Westcott & Laurence Line.
1901	August. The fleet and ships of Westcott & Laurence joined the Ellerman Group, operating as a separate company with J.R. Ellerman as chairman.
1906	Purchased by G. Andrada, Piraeus, and renamed *Marika*.
1908	Sold to Domestinis Oeconomou, Piraeus.
1909	Property of the Bank of Athens. Managers A. Sachtouri and G. Andreon.
1913	Purchased by George Coulouras, Andros.
1917	Deleted from register.

Orestes	1888 1,779grt. 79.25×11.06×5.88 1,434n. 9k.
E.	Sgl. screw, 2 cyl. comp., 207 nhp, 2 sgl. blrs. By Black, Hawthorn & Company, Gateshead.
B.	Schlesinger, Davies & Company, Newcastle.
1888	Delivered to H. Collings & Company, London.
1894	Purchased by Westcott & Laurence Line.
1901	August. The fleet and ships of Westcott & Laurence joined the Ellerman Group, operating as a separate company with J.R. Ellerman as chairman.
1907	Sold to Kingsdyke Steam Ship Company, managed by Ross, Allan & Johnston, Glasgow. Renamed *Kingsdyke*.
1917	Purchased by the Lowland Steam Shipping Company, J. Crass & Company, Glasgow as managers.
1918	17 January. Torpedoed and sank by UB-80, 20 miles north-east of Cape Barfleur. Sixteen crew lost their lives.

Barcelona	1882 2,307grt. 90.13×11.55×6.1 1,506n. 9k.
E.	Sgl. screw, 2 cyl. comp. inv., 261 nhp, 115 psi, 2 sgl. blrs. By North East Marine Engineering Company, Sunderland.
B.	James Laing & Company, Sunderland.

1882	January. Delivered to Jones Brothers & Company, Newport as *Friary*.
1899	Owned by the Friary Steam Ship Company, H.W. Hartmann & I. Howard Jones.
1900	February. Renamed *King Edward VII*.
1903	Sold to Rabassa, Montevideo. Renamed *Barcelona*.
1904	May. Purchased by Westcott & Laurence Line.
1912	30 November. Foundered.

Egyptian (2) 1891 2,923grt. 94.95×12.51×6.16 1,934n. 10k.

E.	Sgl. screw, tpl. exp., 246 nhp, 160 psi, 2 sgl. blrs. By Blackwood & Gordon, Port Glasgow.
B.	Russell & Company, Port Glasgow.
1891	Delivered to Cynthiana Steam Ship Company as *Cynthiana*. McLean & Sutherland as managers.
1892	Sold to the British Maritime Trust, London.
1899	Purchased by T. Ronaldson & Company. Renamed *Saxon King*.
1904	Sold to Ellerman Lines Limited with Westcott & Laurence as managers. Renamed *Egyptian*.
1912	Wrecked off Great Yarmouth.

City of Cork 1870 1,001grt. 69.95×9.14×5.24 622n. 9k.

E.	Sgl. screw, 2 cyl. simple, 129 nhp, 60 psi, 2 blrs. By T. Richardson & Son, Hartlepool.
B.	T.R. Oswald & Company, Sunderland.
1870	Delivered to Palgrave, Murphy & Company, Dublin as *Marquess of Lorne* for the Dublin–Liverpool service.
1877	New high-pressure boilers fitted and compounded by T. Richardson & Son, Hartlepool. Renamed *City of Cork* for the Dublin–Oporto service.
1902	Purchased by Ellerman Lines Limited with *City of Amsterdam* and the Dublin–Oporto service. Managed by Fred Smith.
1906	September. Broken up.

City of Amsterdam 1877 823grt. 67.21×9.2×4.75 503n. 9k.

E.	Sgl. screw, 2 cyl. comp.,129 nhp, 60 psi, 2 blrs. By T. Richardson & Son, Hartlepool.
B.	Richardson Duck & Company, Stockton-on-Tees.
1877	May. Delivered to Palgrave Murphy & Company, Dublin.
1902	Purchased by Ellerman Lines Limited with *City of Cork* and the Dublin–Oporto service. Managed by Fred Smith.
1908	Sold to Bravo Steam Ship Company. G. Smith manager for the City Line services.
1913	Purchased by Asia Minor Steam Ship Company. G. Smith manager for the Papayanni services.
1913	March. Wrecked.

Assiout 1889 3,146grt. 105.34×12.47×8.14 1,994n. 11½k.

E.	Sgl. screw, tpl. exp., 305 nhp, 180 psi, 2 dbl. blrs. By builder.
B.	Harland & Wolff and Company, Belfast.
1889	April. Delivered to British Ship-owners Company Limited, Liverpool as *British Empire*.
1901	Sold to Ellerman Lines Limited. Fred Swift as manager, renamed *Assiout*.
1914	Managed by Graham Smith.

1914	November. Seized by the Turks.
1915	April. Sunk by Turkish Navy.

Austrian	1894 3,127grt. 96.56×12.25×5.88 2,028n. 11k.
E.	Sgl. screw, tpl. exp., 278 nhp, 160 psi. By builder.
B.	William Denny Brothers, Dumbarton.
1894	6 August. Launched.
1894	11 September. Delivered to the British & Burmese Steam Navigation Company as *Bhamo*. Paddy Henderson & Company, Glasgow.
1901	Purchased by Ellerman Lines Limited. Fred Swift as managers. Renamed *Austrian*.
1921	Sold to the Ognam Shipping Company, London.
1926	Seized in Italy as the company owed money. Sold by Italian Admiralty Court.
1926	August. Broken up at Preston by Thos. W. Ward.

Belgravian	1891 2,521grt. 95.1×11.89×7.16 1,592n. 11k.
E.	Sgl. screw, tpl. exp., 305 nhp. By builder.
B.	William Doxford & Sons, Sunderland.
1891	14 February. Launched.
1891	March. Delivered to the Clan Line as *Clan McNeil*.
1902	Purchased by Ellerman Lines Limited. Fred Swift as manager, renamed *Belgravian*.
1922	Sold to Kenneth Saunders, Glasgow.
1929	Broken up in Italy.

Bosnian	1891 2,507grt. 95.1×11.89×7.16 1,576n. 11k.
E.	Sgl. screw, tpl. exp., 305 nhp. By builder.
B.	William Doxford & Sons, Sunderland.
1891	25 March. Launched.
1891	May. Delivered to the Clan Line as *Clan Macleod*.
1902	Purchased by Ellerman Lines Limited. Fred Swift as manager, renamed Bosnian.
1922	Sold to M. Basiliades, Chios and renamed *Psara*.
1929	Broken up.

Bulgarian	1891 2,515grt. 95.1×11.89×7.16 1,613n. 11k.
E.	Sgl. screw, tpl. exp., 305 nhp. By builder.
B.	William Doxford & Sons, Sunderland.
1891	28 April. Launched.
1891	June. Delivered to the Clan Line as *Clan MacIntyre*.
1902	Purchased by Ellerman Lines Limited. Fred Swift as manager, renamed *Bulgarian*.
1917	20 January. On a voyage from Cartagena to Liverpool she was torpedoed and sunk by U-84 in the Atlantic. Fourteen crew lost their lives.

Sardinia	1888 2,474grt. 94.49×12.28×6.89 1,500n. 10k.
E.	Sgl. screw, tpl. exp., 361 nhp, 170 psi, 3 sgl. blrs. By Blair & Company, Stockton.
P.	20.
B.	Hawthorn Leslie & Company, Hebburn.
1888	August. Delivered to the Greenock Steam Ship Company (Gulf Line) as *Gulf of Corcovado*.

1900	Sold to P. Viale di G.B., Genoa and renamed *Paolo V.*
1902	Renamed *Sardinia.*
1908	25 November. On a voyage from Malta to Alexandria with 152 deck passengers bound for Mecca a fire broke out in the nitrate in number 2 hold. The engine room was abandoned and the vessel steamed in circles. As all the lifeboats were on fire the crew and passengers were forced to jump into the water. The ship finally went aground on the Ricasoli Rocks and burned out; 120 people lost their lives.

Sardinia at Malta.

Alexandria	1890 3,501grt. 111.35×12.86×5.79 2,194n. 10k.
E.	Sgl. screw, tpl. exp., 387 nhp, 180 psi. By G. Clark & Company, Sunderland.
B.	James Laing & Sons Limited, Sunderland.
1880	Delivered to Cie. Havraise Peninsulaire de Navigation a Vapeur, Le Havre as *Ville de Paris.*
1902	Purchased by Ellerman Lines Limited and renamed *Alexandria.*
1914	Broken up by J. J. King & Company.

Gascon	1890 1,106grt. 70.6×9.48×5.03 683n. 9½k.
E.	Sgl. screw, tpl. exp., 181 nhp, 160 psi, 1 dbl. blr. By D. Rowan & Company, Glasgow.
B.	S. Mc Knight & Company, Ayr.
1890	April. Delivered to the Moss Steam Ship Company, Liverpool as *Gascony.*
1904	Purchased by J. McCormick & Company, Leith, and renamed *Gascon.*
1906	Sold to Ellerman Lines Limited.
1909	23 December. She went aground at Douro on a voyage to Liverpool. Total loss.

Avon	1880 2,199grt. 86.35×10.73×8.93 1,395n. 9k.
E.	Sgl. screw, 2 cyl. comp. inv., 200 nhp, 75 psi, 1 dbl. blr. By North Easy Marine Engineering Company Sunderland.
B.	James Laing & Sons Limited, Sunderland.
1880	Delivered to the Royal Mail Steam Packet Company.
1903	Sold to Ellerman Lines Limited.
1916	April. Sunk in fog in the Mersey.

Bavarian	1895 3,012grt. 104.55×12.53×7.92 1,950n. 10k.
E.	Sgl. screw, tpl. exp., 326 nhp, 160 psi, 2 sgl. blrs. By North Easy Marine Engineering Company, Sunderland.
B.	Sunderland Shipbuilding Company, Sunderland.

1895	January. Delivered to the Shire Line as Merionethshire.
1907	Purchased by Ellerman Lines Limited. Fred Swift as manager, renamed *Bavarian*.
1928	August. Broken up.

Algerian	1896 3,837grt. 110.95×13.78×7.92 2,404n. 10k.
E.	Sgl. screw, tpl. exp., 326 nhp, 160 psi, 2 sgl. blrs. By North Easy Marine Engineering Company, Sunderland.
B.	Sunderland Shipbuilding Company, Sunderland.
1896	June. Delivered to Jenkin's Shire Line as *Flintshire*.
1907	Taken over by the Royal Mail Steam Packet.
1913	Sold to Ellerman Lines Limited. Fred Swift as manager, renamed *Algerian*.
1916	12 January. Sunk by mine laid by UC-52, 2½ miles from the Needles, Isle of Wight.

Wharfedale / Arcadian	1891 2,855grt. 97.54×12.8×5.42 1,833n. 9k.
E.	Sgl. screw, tpl. exp., 254 nhp, 160 psi, 3 sgl. blrs. By W. Allan & Company, Sunderland.
B.	Short Brothers, Sunderland.
1891	May. Delivered as *Nerano* to the Columbia Steam Navigation Company Limited. W. & T. W. Pinkney as managers.
1903	Owned by Cia. Algortena de Nav. Bilbao, renamed *Alangueta*.
1904	Purchased by Sir James Laing & Sons, renamed *Wharfedale*.
1908	Purchased by Ellerman Lines Limited. Fred Swift as manager, renamed *Arcadian*.
1910	2 January. On a voyage from London to Glasgow she sank following a collision with Turnbull Martin's *Ayrshire* in thick fog off Tuskar Rock. There were fifty-one people on board and twelve lost their lives.

Volta / Venetian	1891 2,734grt. 99.85×12.01×6.71 1,723n. 10½k.
E.	Sgl. screw, tpl. exp., 253 nhp, 160 psi, 2 sgl. blrs. By builder.
P.	44 (first), 14 (second).
B.	Naval Construction & Armament Company, Barrow in Furness.
1891	8 August. Launched.
1891	September. Delivered to the British & African Steam Navigation Company with Elder Dempster & Company, Liverpool, as managers.
1908	Purchased by Ellerman Lines Limited. Fred Swift as managers, renamed *Venetian*.
1916	Transferred to Papayanni Line.
1924	June. Broken up in Holland.

Castilian	1890 1,923grt. 82.42×11.43×4.94 1,232n. 10½k.
E.	Sgl. screw, tpl. exp., 232 nhp, 150 psi, 2 sgl. blrs. By Central Marine Engineering Works, West Hartlepool.
B.	William Gray & Company, West Hartlepool.
1890	March. Delivered to Bullard King & Company, London, as *Umbilo*.
1903	Re-boilered.
1909	Purchased by Ellerman Lines Limited. Fred Swift as manager, renamed *Castilian* for Papayanni services.
1917	18 April. Torpedoed and sunk by U-61, 110 miles from Tory Head, Ireland.

Italian	1887 2,581grt. 100.58×11.67×5.7 1,645n. 10½k.
E.	Sgl. screw, tpl. exp., 346 nhp, 160 psi, 3 dbl. blrs. By builder.
B.	Wigham Richardson & Company, Newcastle.
1887	December. Delivered as *Port Fairy* to William Milburn & Company's Anglo-Australian Steam Navigation Company, London.
1888	2 January. Maiden voyage, London–Melbourne–Sydney.
1892	When the line withdrew from passenger services they disposed of the relevant vessels. She was sold to J.H. Andressen Successores, Oporto, renamed *Dona Maria*.
1907	Sold to the Booth Steamship Company (1901) Limited, renamed *Port Fairy*.
1907	17 August. Maiden sailing Liverpool–Manaus.
1909	Sold to be broken up but purchased by Ellerman Lines Limited, renamed *Italian*. Fred Swift as managers.
1913	Broken up at Preston by Thos. W. Ward & Company.

Asturian	1889 3,193grt. 106.68×12.19×6.16 2,070n. 10k.
E.	Sgl. screw, tpl. exp., 315 nhp, 160 psi, 2 dbl. blrs. By J. & J. Thompson, Glasgow.
B.	Chas. Connell & Company, Glasgow.
1889	January. Ordered for Rathbone Brothers Star Line as *Capella* but taken over on the stocks by T. & J. Harrison.
1890	Delivered to T. & J. Harrison for the Liverpool–West Indies service.
1899	Re-boilered.
1910	March. Purchased by Ellerman Lines Limited, renamed *Asturian*. Fred Swift as managers.
1917	18 February. Attacked by German submarine in the Mediterranean. British warship came to her rescue.
1921	Sold to the Franco-British Steam Navigation Company.
1922	September. Evacuated Greek nationals from Smyrna to Piraeus.
1922	10 November. In a gale, 260 miles west of Ushant, she ran out of coal and was towed into Corcubion by the Admiral Cochrane of the Byron Steam Ship Company.
1923	Laid up in Queens Dock, Cardiff, then sold and broken up in Germany.

Douro (2)	1881 1,603grt. 77.77×10.55×6.98 1,022n. 9½k.
E.	Sgl. screw, tpl. exp., 192 nhp, 150 psi, 2 sgl. blrs. By G. Clark & Company, Sunderland.
B.	William Doxford & Sons, Sunderland.
1881	December. Delivered as *Congella* to Bullard King & Company, London.
1910	Purchased by Ellerman Lines Limited, renamed Douro. Fred Swift as managers.
1915	5 September. Attacked and sunk by U-20, 75 miles south-west of Bishop Rock. She was Papayanni's first war loss.

Estrellano	1910 1,161grt. 70.13×10.61×5.03 703n. 10½k.
E.	Sgl. screw, tpl. exp., 132 nhp, 150 psi. By builder.
B.	Ramage & Ferguson Limited, Leith.
1910	The first new ship built for Papayanni services since Ellerman Lines took over.
1917	31 October. Torpedoed and sunk by UC-71 off Pillier Island, Greece. Three of her crew lost their lives.

Lisbon (2)   1910   1,203grt.   70.56×10.88×5.03   724n.   10½k.
E.   Sgl. screw, tpl. exp., 132 nhp, 150 psi. By Ramage & Ferguson, Leith.
B.   W. Harkess & Company, Middlesbrough.
1910   Delivered.
1917   30 May. Mined and sunk off the Royal Sovereign Lightship by mines laid by UC-62.

Favorian   1894   3,039grt.   97.6×12.68×7.89   1,957n.   12k.
E.   Sgl. screw, tpl. exp., 287 nhp, 160 psi, 2 sgl. blrs. By J. Dickinson, Sunderland.
B.   Tyne Iron Shipbuilding Company, Newcastle.
1894   6 February. Launched.
1894   March. Delivered as *Alnwick* for Norwick Steam Ship Company, Hunting &
                Sons as managers.
1910   Purchased by Ellerman Lines Limited , renamed *Favorian*. Westcott & Laurence
                as managers for their London services.
1916   4 August. Torpedoed and sunk by U-35, 24 miles south-west of Planier Island.

Andalusian (2) 1911   2,349grt.   90.98×12.34×6.92   1,452n.   10½k.
E.   Sgl. screw, tpl. exp., 304 nhp, 215 psi, 2 sgl. blrs. By Richardsons, Westgarth &
                Company, Middlesbrough.
B.   W. Harkess & Company, Middlesbrough.
1911   June. Delivered to Ellerman Lines Limited.
1915   12 March. Attacked by U-29, 25 miles off Bishop Rock and scuttled.

Palmella   1913   1,352grt.   70.96×11.31×5.06   759n.   10k.
E.   Sgl. screw, tpl. exp., 192 nhp, 220 psi, 2 sgl. blrs. By builder.
B.   Ramage & Ferguson Limited, Leith.
1913   February. Delivered to Ellerman Lines Limited. Fred Swift as managers.
1915   Graham Smith as managers.
1918   22 August. Torpedoed and sunk by UB-92 , 25 miles northwest of South Stack.
                All 25 crew on board were lost.

Mardinian   1913   3,322grt.   95.4×12.92×6.58   2,125n.   10½k.
E.   Sgl. screw, tpl. exp., 344 nhp, 215 psi, 2 sgl. blrs. By Richardsons, Westgarth &
                Company, Middlesbrough.
B.   W. Harkess & Company, Middlesbrough.
1913   August. Delivered to Ellerman Lines Limited. Fred Swift as manager.
1914   Graham Smith as managers.
1917   19 May. Torpedoed and sunk by U-34, 4 miles west of Tabraca Island.

Falerian (2) / *Volturno*   1914   3,419grt.   96.93×12.19×6.58   2,917n.   10½k.
E.   Sgl. screw, tpl. exp., 344 nhp, 215 psi, 2 sgl. blrs. By Richardsons, Westgarth &
                Company, Middlesbrough.
B.   W. Harkess & Company, Middlesbrough.
1914   July. Delivered.
1914   4 August. She was detained in dock in Turkey at the outbreak of the First World War.
1914   September. Seized for money owed.
1914   29 October. Seized when Turkey entered the war.

1919	Reverted back to Ellerman Lines Limited.
1928	In a damaged state, she was sold to E. Cesano and renamed *Bosforo*. She was repaired and re-purchased by Ellerman & Papayanni. Later managed by Montgomerie & Workman, renamed *Volturno*.
1943	24 June. Bombed by German aircraft off Cape St Vincent, Portugal. Sank next day.

Maronian	1913 3,385grt. 97.2×12.92×6.64 2,182n. 10½k.
E.	Sgl. screw, tpl. exp., 343 nhp, 215 psi, 3 sgl. blrs. By builder.
B.	Earle's Shipbuilding Company, Hull.
1913	Delivered.
1938	Sold to E. Szabados, Venice and renamed *Luciano*.
1941	15 April. Sunk by allied aircraft off Valona.

Malatian	1914 3,427grt. 98.45×22.55×6.64 2,224n. 10½k.
E.	Sgl. screw, tpl. exp., 343 nhp, 215 psi, 3 sgl. blrs. By builder.
B.	Earle's Shipbuilding Company, Hull.
1914	January. Delivered.
1925	In Bucknall livery on the Australia–Dutch East Indies service.
1936	November. Sold to Cia. Ligure di Navegazione, Genoa, and renamed *Santa Maria*.
1943	September. Under German control and managed by Mittelmeer Reederei GmbH.
1944	October. Sunk at Venice by Allied aircraft.

Flaminian (2)	1914 3,439grt. 98.45×12.86×6.64 2,224n. 10½k.
E.	Sgl. screw, tpl. exp., 343 nhp, 215 psi, 3 sgl. blrs. By builder.
B.	Earle's Shipbuilding Company, Hull.
1914	Delivered.
1915	29 March. Attacked and sunk by U-28, 50 miles south-west of the Scilly Isles.

Roumelian	1914 2,687grt. 95.09×13.11×7.25 1,710n. 11k.
E.	Sgl. screw, tpl. exp., 331 nhp, 220 psi, 2 sgl. blrs. By Richardsons, Westgarth & Company, Newcastle.
B.	Palmers, Newcastle.
1914	Delivered.
1936	December. Sold to Soc. Anon di Nav. Transmediterranea, Sicily, renamed *Drepanum*.
1942	Under German control, managed by Neptun Dampschiffahrts Ges., Bremen.
1943	20 November. Lost following a collision off Gothenburg.

Flaminian (3)	1917 3,227grt. 96.01×12.92×7.25 2,068n. 11k.
E.	Sgl. screw, tpl. exp., 331 nhp, 220 psi, 2 sgl. blrs. By Richardsons, Westgarth & Company, Newcastle.
B.	W. Harkess & Son, Middlesbrough.
1917	Delivered for the Mediterranean service. Graham Smith as manager.
1939	September. Transferred to Admiralty control, renamed *Empire Flaminian*. Managed by Ellerman & Papayanni.
1946	Royal Engineers depot ship at Southampton. Returned to Papayanni Line as Flaminian.
1950	21 July. Arrived at Dover to be broken up by Dover Industries.

Italian (2)   1899   3,648grt.   105.15×13.41×4.33   2,302n.   12½k.

E.   Sgl. screw, tpl. exp., 370 nhp, 180 psi, 4 sgl. blrs. By builder.

B.   Barclay, Curle & Company, Glasgow.

1899   April. Delivered as *Fantee* to the African Steam Ship Company. Elder Dempster as managers.

1901   Collided with a submerged rock at Cape Palmas, Liberia, and was looted by local people until the arrival of HMS *Dwarf*.

1904   3 May. Went aground at Douala, Cameroon and was towed off by Elder Dempster's *Egga*.

1913   Purchased by Ellerman Lines Limited. Graham Smith as manager, renamed *Italian*. Also operated on Ellerman & Bucknall services during the First World War.

1921   Transferred to the Ellerman's Wilson Line, renamed *Rollo*.

1932   September. Broken up at Copenhagen.

Lesbian (2)   1915   2,555grt.   93.06×12.86×7.07   1,625n.   11k.

E.   Sgl. screw, tpl. exp., 226 nhp, 180 psi, 2 sgl. blrs. By Richardsons, Westgarth & Company, Middlesbrough.

B.   W. Harkess & Son, Middlesbrough.

1915   Delivered to Ellerman Lines Limited. Graham Smith as managers.

1917   5 January. Attacked and sunk by U-35, 125 miles east of Malta.

Border Knight 1899   3,774grt.   109.72×14.02×7.83   2,394n.   10k

E.   Sgl. screw, tpl. exp., 325 nhp, 160 psi, 3 sgl. blrs. By builder.

B.   D. & W. Henderson & Company, Glasgow.

1899   July. Delivered to Border Union Steam Ship Company. J. Little & Company, Liverpool as managers.

1917   14 November. Torpedoed and sunk by UC-17, near the Lizard, Cornwall. One crew member lost his life.

Darino   1917   1,349grt.   72.02×11.12×5.21   830n.   11k.

E.   Sgl. screw, tpl. exp., 203 nhp, 210 psi, 2 sgl. blrs. By builder.

B.   Ramage & Ferguson Limited, Leith.

1917   October. Delivered to Ellerman Lines Limited. Graham Smith as managers.

1939   19 November. Torpedoed and sunk by U-41 off Spain. Sixteen of her crew lost their lives.

Andalusian (3) 1918   3,074grt.   98.00×13.78×7.38   1,907n.   11k.

E.   Sgl. screw, tpl. exp., 241 nhp. By builder.

B.   Earle's Shipbuilding Company, Hull.

1918   Delivered. Graham Smith as managers.

1940   20 June. Attacked by U-51 but the submarine's torpedoes malfunctioned.

1941   17 March. Torpedoed and sunk by U-106 in the Atlantic.

Serbino   1919   4,080grt.   104.36×14.02×7.56   2,636n.   11k.

E.   Sgl. screw, tpl. exp., 388 nhp, 220 psi, 2 sgl. blrs. By builder.

B.   Ramage & Ferguson Limited, Leith.

1919   May. Delivered to Ellerman & Papayanni Line.

1922	Transferred to the Hall Line, managers, with Ellerman Lines Limited as owners.
1933	Ellerman & Papayanni as managers.
1941	21 October. Torpedoed and sunk by U-82 in convoy SL 89.

Fabian (2)	1919 3,059grt. 100.95×14.26×7.07 1,861n. 11k.
E.	Sgl. screw, tpl. exp., 407 nhp, 180 psi, 3 sgl. blrs. By Central Marine Engineering Works, West Hartlepool.
B.	William Gray & Company, West Hartlepool.
1919	September. Delivered.
1940	17 June. Transported 1,000 troops and civilians from St Nazaire to Britain.
1940	16 November. Torpedoed and sunk by U-65 in the Atlantic.

Bulgarian (2)	1904 2,064grt. 89.15×12.56×5.73 1,268n. 10k.
E.	Sgl. screw, tpl. exp., 200 nhp, 170 psi, 2 sgl. blrs. By builder.
B.	Flensburger SG, Flensburg.
1904	Delivered as *Marie Menzell* to Menzall & Company Hanseatische Dampfer, Ges, Hamburg.
1915	Sold to Vulkan Reederei 'Otto Kalthoff' GmbH, Hamburg, renamed *Otto Kalthoff*.
1918	November. Managed by N.V. Handel & Maats, Vulcaan, Rotterdam.
1919	Became responsibility and ownership of Westcott & Laurence Line, renamed *Bulgarian*.
1936	24 April. Stranded and declared a total loss. Broken up at Dalmuir by W. Arnott Young.

Gerano	1914 2,080grt. 78.73×12.34×4.94 1,289n. 10k.
E.	Sgl. screw, tpl. exp., 156 psi, 1 sgl. blr. By builder.
B.	Stettiner Oderwerk, Stettin.
1914	Delivered as *Stern* to Rudolf Christian Gribel.
1919	Became the responsibility and ownership of Ellerman Lines Limited. Westcott & Laurence as managers.
1920	Renamed *Gerano*; also serving on the Ellerman's Wilson Line services.
1934	Sold, renamed *Leonidis M. Valmas*.
1940	Torpedoed; towed to the Clyde where she was broken up.

Cressado	1913 1,227grt. 73.58×11.03×4.85 717n. 9½k.
E.	Sgl. screw, tpl. exp., 154 nhp, 200 psi, 2 sgl. blrs. By Ottsener Maschinen Fabrik, Altona, Hamburg.
B.	Henry Koch AG, Lubeck.
1913	Delivered as *Cressida* to Adolf Kirsten, Hamburg.
1919	Became the responsibility and ownership of Ellerman Lines Limited. Westcott & Laurence as managers.
1920	Owned by Gulf of Suez Steam Ship Company, London, renamed *Cressado*.
1938	Transferred to Ellerman & Papayanni Line as managers.
1942	8 May. Collided with HMS *Pozarica* off the Sherries and sank.

| *Mardinian* (2) | 1919   2,434grt.   92.41×13.11×6.34   1,426n.   10k. |
| E. | Sgl. screw, tpl. exp., 266 nhp, 180 psi, 2 sgl. blrs. By Richardsons, Westgarth & Company, Sunderland. |

B.	S.P. Austin & Son Limited, Sunderland.
1919	August. Delivered to Ellerman Lines Limited.
1940	9 September. Torpedoed and sunk by U-28 in the Atlantic. Thirty-one survivors were transferred to HM Trawler *Apollo*.

Castilian (2)   1919   3,067grt.   100.98×14.26×7.07   1,849n.   10k.

E.	Sgl. screw, tpl. exp., 310 nhp, 2,580 ihp, 180 psi, 2 sgl. blrs. By Richardsons, Westgarth & Company, Middlesbrough.
B.	Sir Raylton Dixon & Company, Middlesbrough.
1919	Delivered to Ellerman Lines Limited, Westcott & Laurence as managers.
1937	Owned by Westcott & Laurence Line.
1943	12 February. On a voyage from Manchester to Lisbon she was wrecked near the Skerries in fog.

Destro / Destrian   1920   3,553grt.   95.7×13.78×8.75   2,177n.   10½k.

E.	Sgl. screw, tpl. exp., 240 nhp, 180 psi, 2 blrs. By builder.
B.	Dunlop, Bremner & Company, Port Glasgow.
1920	18 July. Delivered as *Destro* to Ellerman's Wilson Line but operated on Ellerman & Papayanni's Mediterranean services.
1926	Transferred to Ellerman Lines Limited.
1940	12 June. Attacked by Italian war planes off Milos, little damage.
1941	Employed as a supply ship in the Mediterranean.
1941	April. Participated in the Greek campaign, including the evacuation of Crete, surviving many bomb attacks.
1942	27 March. Survived sixty-eight air attacks in two weeks and was damaged by bombs at Tobruk.
1946	19 March. Transferred to Ellerman & Papayanni service, renamed *Destrian*.
1948	January. Sent a distress signal during a gale but survived the storm without assistance.
1950	Sold to Bock, Goddefroy's Deutsche Levant Line, renamed *Pergamon*.
1956	Purchased by Rudolf A. Oetker's Hamburg Süd Amerika Group.
1964	Broken up at Bremerhaven.

Dido   1920   3,554grt.   95.7×13.78×8.75   2,175n.   10½k.

E.	Sgl. screw, tpl. exp., 240 nhp, 180 psi, 2 blrs. By builder.
B.	Dunlop, Bremner & Company, Port Glasgow.
1920	Delivered to Ellerman's Wilson Line.
1922	Transferred to Ellerman & Papayanni routes.
1932	Laid up at London.
1941	January. Taken over in dry dock at Brest by the Germans, renamed *Dorpat*. Operated by Leth & Company of Hamburg.
1943	11 April. Mined and sank at Aarhus, later raised.
1945	3 May. Bombed by Allies off Langeland. Sold to Finnish interests and renamed *Leila*. Owned by W. Rostedt, Abo. Varnstamo Rederi.
1963	September. Broken up.

Palmella (2)   1920   1,568grt.   74.95×11.64×5.15   978n.   10k.
E.   Sgl. screw, tpl. exp., 210 nhp, 220 psi, 2 sgl. blrs. By builder.
B.   Ramage & Ferguson Limited, Leith.
1920   May. Delivered to Ellerman Lines Limited for Papayanni services.
1940   11 December. Torpedoed and sunk by U-37 off Portugal.

Palmella (2).

Estrellano (2) 1920   1,963grt.   74.95×11.64×5.15   1,226n.   10k.
E.   Sgl. screw, tpl. exp., 230 nhp, 220 psi, 2 sgl. blrs. By builder.
B.   Hall, Russell & Company, Aberdeen.
1920   November. Delivered to Ellerman Lines Limited.
1941   9 February. Torpedoed and sunk by U-37 off Portugal in convoy HG 53. *Estrellano*, Currie Line's *Courland* and the *Brandenburg* were all sunk within two hours.

Lesbian (3)   1923   2,532grt.   82.94×12.71×6.06   1,460n.   10k.
E.   Sgl. screw, tpl. exp., 274 nhp, 220 psi, 2 sgl. blrs. By Wallsend Slipway Company.
B.   Swan Hunter & Wigham Richardson, Newcastle.
1923   September. Delivered to Ellerman Lines Limited.
1940   23 June. Detained at Beirut by French authorities.
1941   June. Destroyed.

Egyptian (3) 1920   2,866grt.   96.41×13.44×7.10   1,806n.   11k.
E.   Sgl. screw, tpl. exp., 233 nhp, 220 psi, 2 sgl. blrs. By Richardsons, Westgarth & Company, Middlesbrough.
B.   W. Harkess & Son, Middlesbrough.
1920   Completed.
1943   7 March. Torpedoed and sunk by U-230 in convoy in the Atlantic.

Lisbon (3)   1920   1,964grt.   76.44×11.64×5.21   1,242n.   11k.
E.   Sgl. screw, tpl. exp., 230 nhp, 220 psi, 2 sgl. blrs. By builder.
B.   Hall, Russell & Company, Aberdeen.
1920   September. Delivered.
1940   29 October. Wrecked on Rattray Head, Scotland.

Manchurian 1905   2,819grt.   89.03×12.59×7.83   1,760n.   9½k.
E.   Sgl. screw, tpl. exp., 229 nhp, 185 psi, 2 sgl. blrs. By builder.
B.   A.G. Neptun, Rostock.
1905   Delivered as *Tilly Russ* to Ernst Russ, Hamburg.
1919   Transferred to the Shipping Controller.
1920   Purchased by Ellerman Lines Limited, renamed *Manchurian*.
1934   November. Broken up at Milford Haven by Thos. W. Ward.

Assyrian   1914   2,962grt.   101.19×13.65×7.04   1,761n.   10k.
E.   Twin screw, oil 2×2 stroke dbl. acting diesels, 1,660 ihp. By builder.
P.   9.
B.   Blohm & Voss, Hamburg.
1914   24 February. Launched as *Fritz* for Woermann Line.
1914   August. Entered service on the west African routes.
1919   13 November. Transferred to Britain under the responsibility of the Shipping Controller.
1920   March. Ellerman Lines Limited, renamed *Assyrian*. Graham Smith as managers. Company's first motor ship.
1923   Problems with German engine. Converted to steam by Cooper & Greig Limited, Dundee.
1932   Laid up at London.
1940   19 October. Torpedoed and sunk by U-101 in the SC7 convoy. She was the commodore lead ship in the fifth column, followed the periscope of a German submarine and the submarine was forced to outrun her. The convoy was attacked for two days by eight submarines which fired thirty-two torpedoes and sank twenty-three ships. The survivors from *Assyrian* were picked by the sloop *Leith*.

Hero   1895   775grt.   65.99×9.14×4.14   331n.   9k.
E.   Sgl. screw, tpl. exp., 239 nhp, 2 sgl. blrs. By builder.
B.   Earle's Shipbuilding Company, Hull.
1895   June. Delivered to Thomas Wilson Sons & Company.
1905   Transferred to Wilson's North East Railway Shipping Company, Hull.
1916   Purchased by the General Steam Navigation Company.
1923   Transferred to the North East Railway Shipping Company, then to Ellerman Lines Limited.
1926   Owned by the General Steam Navigation Company as *Hero*.
1933   Broken up.

Torcello   1911   1,479grt.   70.62×11.09×4.48   875n.   9½k.
E.   Sgl. screw, tpl. exp., 105 nhp, 185 psi, 2 sgl. blrs. By builder.
B.   Stettiner Oderwerke, Stettin.
1911   Delivered as *Stahlhof* for Neue Dampfer Cie. AG, Stettin.
1919   November. Transferred to the Shipping Controller.
1920   Purchased by Ellerman's Wilson Line, renamed *Torcello*.
1923   Transferred to Ellerman Lines Limited.
1938   Sold to the African & Continental Steam Ship Company, renamed *Lutine*.
1938   September. Sold to Piero & Mario Martini, operated by CICOMA, renamed *Zenobia Martini*.

1943	23 March. Torpedoed and sunk by HM Submarine *Unseen* in the Gulf of Gabes, Tunisia.

Algerian (3) 1924   2,305grt.   89.91×13.32×6.4   1,441n.   11k.
E.   Sgl. screw, tpl. exp., 300 nhp, 225 psi, 2 sgl. blrs. By builder.
B.   Barclay, Curle & Company, Glasgow.
1924   23 April. Launched.
1924   May. Delivered.
1943   Requisitioned by the Admiralty. Converted by Green & R.H. Silley Weir for the laying of a pipeline to carry petrol under the Channel to Normandy.
1944   June. The pipeline was laid between Sandown and Cherbourg and later from Dungeness to Boulogne.
1946   Returned to Ellerman Lines.
1957   12 December. Sold to be broken up.

Malvernian / City of Kobe   1924   4,373grt.   111.89×15.15×8.35   2,743n.   12k.
E.   Sgl. screw, tpl. exp., 301 nhp, 180 psi, 4 blrs. By builder.
B.   Ramage & Ferguson Limited, Leith.
1924   Delivered to Ellerman Lines, managed by Ellerman & Papayanni.
1925   Transferred to Hall Line.
1927   Renamed *City of Kobe*.
1939   19 December. Mined and sunk off Great Yarmouth.

City of Lancaster / Lancastrian   1924   3,040grt.   100.64×13.72×6.89   1,923n.   12k.
E.   Sgl. screw, tpl. exp., 362 nhp, 225 psi, 3 sgl. blrs. By builder.
B.   Palmers Shipbuilding Company, Jarrow.
1924   February. Delivered to Ellerman Lines Limited for the Papayanni Mediterranean services.
1929   Lengthened to 102.17 with an extension on the bow.
1940   16 June. At St Nazaire, the Cunard liner *Lancastria* was hit by bombs at 16.30, which opened up her hull causing her to sink within twenty minutes. *City of Lancaster* was nearby for the evacuation of troops and brought back 2,500 people to Plymouth, but around 3,000 troops lost their lives that day.

Lancastrian.

1943	January. She carried the British spy Edward Chapman back to Europe.
1947	Renamed *Lancastrian*.
1953	December. Broken up at Troon.

City of Leicester	1926 3,351grt. 105.16×14.48×7.19 1,994n. 11½k.
E.	Sgl. screw, tpl. exp., 389 nhp, 220 psi, 2 sgl. blrs. By Central Marine Engineering Works, West Hartlepool.
B.	William Gray & Company, West Hartlepool.
1926	January. Delivered to Ellerman Lines Limited.
1937	20 April. Transferred to Hall Line.
1942	6 January. Transferred to Westcott & Laurence Line.
1952	9 August. Arrived at Troon to be broken up.

City of Oxford (3)	1926 2,759grt. 99.58×14.14×6.37 1,633n. 11k.
E.	Sgl. screw, tpl. exp., 306 nhp, 185 psi, 3 sgl. blrs. By Wallsend Slipway Company, Wallsend.
B.	Swan, Hunter & Wigham Richardson Limited, Wallsend.
1926	December. Delivered to Ellerman Lines Limited.
1942	16 June. On a voyage from Huelva to Garston in convoy HG 84 she was torpedoed by U-552. She continued to steam ahead and turned over and sank. U-552 sank five ships in the convoy including Ellerman's Wilson's *Thurso*. U-552 was accompanied by U-575 which fired four torpedoes into the convoy. Three missed and when the other torpedo struck a vessel it failed to explode.

Como	1910 1,246grt. 76.2×10.73×4.78 706n. 10k.
E.	Sgl. screw, tpl. exp., 116 nhp, 2 sgl. blrs. By Amos & Smith Limited, Hull.
B.	Earle's Shipbuilding & Engineering Company, Hull.
1910	Delivered to Thomas Wilson & Company, Hull.
1914–18	In commercial service on the Kirkwall–Norway routes.
1916	15 November. Purchased by Ellerman, managed by Ellerman's Wilson Line
1921	Operated by Westcott & Laurence.
1926	Transferred to Ellerman Lines Limited.
1930	Transferred to Ellerman's Wilson Line.
1945	Sold to Lenaghans Limited, Belfast, then to John Carlblom & Company, Hull, and renamed *Nelkon*.
1948	Renamed *Kerempe* when sold to Vapurcul Kollektif Sirketi, Istanbul.
1954	Broken up.

Oporto	1928 2,352grt. 82.48×12.25×5.61 1,437n. 10½k.
E.	Sgl. screw, tpl. exp., 269 nhp, 220 psi, 2 sgl. blrs. By builder.
B.	Ramage & Ferguson Limited, Leith.
1928	July. Completed.
1943	12 March. On a voyage from the United Kingdom to Freetown she was torpedoed and sunk by U-107.

Anatolian	1932 1,944grt. 81.65×12.19×5.94 1,138n. 12k.
E.	Sgl. screw, tpl. exp., 1,600 ihp, 200 psi, 2 sgl. blrs. By builder.
B.	Swan, Hunter & Wigham Richardson Limited, Wallsend.
1932	March. Completed as a refrigerated vessel.
1933	January. Sold to Cie. Generale d'Armaments Maritimes and renamed *Grande Terre* to carry bananas from the Antilles to France.
1939	Purchased by Skibs A/S Pasat, Oslo, T.B. Torgersen as managers.
1940	Sold to Kyukyo Hogei KK, Tokyo, and renamed *Koa Maru*.

Malvernian (2)	1937 3,133grt. 104.34×15.27×6.31 1,397n. 13k.
E.	Sgl. screw, tpl. exp., LP turb. drg and hydraulic coupling, 606 nhp, 225 psi, 3 sgl. blrs. By Central Marine Engineering Works, West Hartlepool.
B.	William Gray & Company, West Hartlepool.
1937	3 June. Trials.
1937	June. Delivered to Ellerman Lines Limited.
1940	Requisitioned by the Admiralty as an ocean boarding vessel HMS *Malvernian*.
1941	19 July. Bombed by German aircraft off Spain. Following a fire she sank.
1941	21 July. Thirty-two crew reached Corunna and twenty-five landed at Vigo the following day. The remaining 107 crew were captured by German minesweepers as they neared land.

Belgravian (2)	1937 3,133grt. 104.34×15.27×6.31 1,397n. 13k.
E.	Sgl. screw, tpl. exp., LP turb. drg and hydraulic coupling, 606 nhp, 225 psi, 3 sgl. blrs. By Central Marine Engineering Works, West Hartlepool.
B.	William Gray & Company, West Hartlepool.
1937	Delivered to Ellerman & Papayanni Limited.
1941	5 August. Torpedoed and sunk by U-372 in convoy SL 81.

Corinthian	1938 3,198grt. 109.33×15.27×9.14 1,342n. 13k.
E.	Sgl. screw, tpl. exp., LP turb. drg and hydraulic coupling, 606 nhp, 225 psi, 3 sgl. blrs. By Central Marine Engineering Works, West Hartlepool.
B.	William Gray & Company, West Hartlepool.
1938	August. Delivered to Ellerman & Papayanni Limited.
1963	4 April. Arrived at Dalmuir to be broken up by W. Arnott Young.

Ionian	1938 3,144grt. 104.34×15.27×6.31 1,397n. 13k.
E.	Sgl. screw, tpl. exp., LP turb. drg and hydraulic coupling, 606 nhp, 225 psi, 3 sgl. blrs. By Central Marine Engineering Works, West Hartlepool.
B.	William Gray & Company, West Hartlepool.
1938	November. Delivered to Ellerman & Papayanni Limited.
1939	29 November. On a voyage from London to Hull she struck a mine 3½ miles from Newark light vessel. The master attempted to sail her to a port but she had to be abandoned and sank.

Florian	1939 3,174grt. 104.34×15.27×6.31 1,397n. 13k.
E.	Sgl. screw, tpl. exp., LP turb. drg and hydraulic coupling, 606 nhp, 225 psi, 3 sgl. blrs. By Central Marine Engineering Works, West Hartlepool.

B.	William Gray & Company, West Hartlepool.
1939	Delivered to Ellerman & Papayanni Limited.
1941	18 January. Left Oban on a voyage from Hull to New York in ballast.
1941	20 January. Torpedoed and sunk by U-94 in the North Atlantic. She sank within forty-two seconds and all forty-four crew lost their lives.

Pandorian	1940 3,146grt. 109.57×15.27×7.31 1,306n. 13k.
E.	Sgl. screw, tpl. exp., LP turb. drg and hydraulic coupling, 606 nhp, 225 psi, 3 sgl. blrs. By builder.
B.	Swan, Hunter & Wigham Richardson Limited.
1940	March. Delivered to Ellerman & Papayanni Limited.
1963	10 January. Sold to N. Epiphaniades, Greece, and renamed *Kyrakali*.
1964	Purchased by Bluesky Corporation, Monrovia, and renamed *Bluesky*.
1969	Sold to Nereus Maritime Company Limited, Cyprus, and renamed *Varosi*.
1970	28 March. Arrived at Shanghai from Kuwait to be broken up.

Pandorian.

Samarina / City of Ely	1943 7,258grt. 134.63×17.37×10.61 4,473n. 11k.
E.	Sgl. screw, tpl. exp., 2,500 bhp at 76 rpm, 240 psi, 2 blrs. By Central Machinery Corporation, Hamilton, Ohio.
B.	Bethlehem Fairfield Corporation, Baltimore.
1943	Launched as *James Blair*.
1943	September. Completed as *Samarina* for the United States War Shipping Administration on charter to the Ministry of War, Westcott & Laurence as managers.
1947	Sold to Ellerman & Bucknall Lines Limited, renamed *City of Ely*.
1961	12 May. Sold to Trader Line Limited, London and renamed *Paget Trader*.
1965	2 November. Fire on board and vessel docked at Singapore.
1966	January. Laid up at Hong Kong.
1966	August. Broken up at Kaohsiung.

Samois / City of Lichfield   1943   7,263grt.   134.63×17.37×10.61   4,448n.   11k.

E.	Sgl. screw, tpl. exp., 2,500 bhp at 76 rpm, 240 psi, 2 blrs. By Worthington Pump and Machinery Corporation, Harrison, New Jersey.
B.	Worthington Pump and Machinery Corporation, Harrison, New Jersey.
1943	Launched as *Samuel H. Ralston*.
1943	November. Completed as *Samois Samarina* for the United States War Shipping Administration on charter to the Ministry of War, Westcott & Laurence as managers.
1847	August. Renamed *City of Lichfield* by Ellerman & Bucknall Limited.
1959	12 June. Sold to Panamanian Oriental Steamship Company, Wheelock, Marden & Company and renamed *Camerona*.
1961	Sold to Eddie Steamship Company, Keelung, renamed *Chee Lee*.
1963	Sold to the Far Eastern Navigation Corporation, Taiwan.
1967	April. Broken up at Kaohsiung.

Samboston / City of Rochester   1943   7,265grt.   134.63×17.37×10.61   4,448n.   11k.

E.	Sgl. screw, tpl. exp., 2,500 bhp at 76 rpm, 240 psi, 2 blrs. By Central Machinery Corporation, Hamilton, Ohio.
B.	Bethlehem Fairfield Corporation, Baltimore.
1943	Launched as *Willis J. Abbot*.
1943	December. Completed as *Samboston* for the United States War Shipping Administration on charter to the Ministry of War, Ellerman & Papayanni as managers.
1947	Managed by Ellerman & Bucknall Line, renamed *City of Rochester*.
1962	10 April. Sold to Sivikari Cia Nav. SA, Piraeus, and renamed *Fotini Xilas*.
1964	Purchased by Cardinal Shipping Corporation, Monrovia, and renamed *Resolute II*.
1967	4 December. Arrived at Kaohsiung to be broken up.

Ben H. Miller / City of Shrewsbury   1944   7,262grt.   134.63×17.37×10.61   4,468n.   11k.

E.	Sgl. screw, tpl. exp., 2,500 bhp at 76 rpm, 240 psi, 2 blrs. By Worthington Pump and Machinery Corporation, Harrison, New Jersey.
B.	Worthington Pump and Machinery Corporation, Harrison, New Jersey.
1943	December. Launched as *Ben H. Miller*.
1944	Completed for the United States War Shipping Administration on charter to the Ministry of War, Ellerman & Papayanni as managers.
1947	Purchased by Ellerman & Bucknall and renamed *City of Shrewsbury*.
1959	30 April. Sold to Cia. de Nav. Arcoul, Beirut, and renamed *Marucla*.
1969	Broken up in Japan.

Samtorch / City of Stafford   1944   7,208grt.   134.63×17.37×10.61   4,715n.   11k.

E.	Sgl. screw, tpl. exp., 2,500 bhp at 76 rpm, 240 psi, 2 blrs. By Ellicott Machinery Corporation, Baltimore.
B.	Bethlehem Fairfield Corporation, Baltimore.
1944	Completed as *Samtorch* for the United States War Shipping Administration on charter to the Ministry of War, Ellerman & Papayanni as managers.
1947	Purchased by Ellerman Lines Limited and renamed *City of Stafford*, Ellerman & Bucknall as managers.
1961	6 October. Sold for £117,500 to Stuart Navigation (Bahamas) Limited, Nassau, renamed *Kuniang*.

1962	Purchased by Sygiamore Steam Ship Company, Hong Kong.
1963	Company became part of the World Wide Shipping Group.
1965	Sold to Jupiter Shipping Company, Hong Kong.
1966	Owned by Trefoil Navigation Incorporated, Monrovia, renamed *Prospect*.
1967	13 April. Arrived at Kaohsiung to be broken up.

Anglian	1947 2,219grt. 93.48×14.08×5.45 867n. 12k.
E.	Sgl. screw, tpl. exp., LP turb., 225 psi, 2 sgl. blrs. By Central Marine Engineering Works, West Hartlepool.
B.	William Gray & Company, West Hartlepool.
1947	June. Delivered to Ellerman & Papayanni Line. After one voyage she was chartered to Ellerman's Wilson Line for the Hul–Sweden service.
1963	Sold to African Coasters (Proprietary) Limited, Durban, renamed *Bulwark*.
1968	Owned by Amenkroog Marine Corporation, Panama, renamed *Aroma*.
1970	Renamed *Froma* when purchased by Formosa Navigation Incorporation.
1973	Broken up.

Crosbian	1947 1,518grt. 82.9×12.86×4.54 647n. 12k.
E.	Twin screw, oil, 2×6 cyl. By British Polar Diesels, Glasgow.
B.	William Gray & Company, West Hartlepool.
1947	August. Delivered to Ellerman & Papayanni for the Liverpool–Oporto–Lisbon service.
1963	Transferred to Mossgiel Steam Shipping Company Limited, John Bruce (Shipping) Company as managers.
1967	29 August. Sold to Davao Reawood Corporation, Davao, Philippines, and renamed *Mabuhay*.
1978	Owned by Solid Shipping Corporation, Philippines.
1980	11 November. Arrived at Manila to be broken up.

Darinian.

Darinian	1947 1,533grt. 83.3×12.86×4.54 644n. 12k.
E.	Twin screw, oil, 2×6 cyl. By British Polar Diesels, Glasgow.
B.	Henry Robb Limited, Leith.
1947	November. Delivered to Ellerman & Papayanni but also operated on Westcott & Laurence services out of London.

1970	24 June. Sold to Cia. Naviera Evdelia SA, Panama, renamed *Kostandis Fotinos*.
1971	Purchased by Rosade Lines SAL, Lebanon, renamed *Tania Maria*.
1973	Owned by Koutourada Shipping Company Limited, Cyprus, renamed *Nektarios*.
1978	16 April. Wrecked on Perim Island, Aden and abandoned. Twelve of her crew were rescued by the *Jag Deesh*.

Lucian	1948 1,516grt. 83.3×12.86×4.54 644n. 12k.
E.	Twin screw, oil, 2×6 cyl. By British Polar Diesels, Glasgow.
B.	William Gray & Company, West Hartlepool.
1948	February. Delivered.
1964	14 May. Sold to Seaways Incorporated, Panama, for £50,000, renamed *Amorgos* for the Liverpool/Ellesmere Port–Piraeus service.
1970	Sold to Amorgos Shipping Company SA, Panama.
1974	Owned by Ligeas Shipping Company, Greece.
1975	Owned by Viadora Cia. Naviera SA, Greece and sold to Antilles Marine Cargo Limited, Liberia.
1976	Owned by Kadi Cia. Naviera SA, Greece and renamed *Yashoo*.
1979	Sold to Crystal Star Cia. Naviera SA, Greece.
1986	Broken up.

Mercian	1948 1,517grt. 83.3×12.86×4.54 657n. 12k.
E.	Twin screw, oil, 2×6 cyl. By British Polar Diesels, Glasgow.
B.	Swan, Hunter & Wigham Richardson Limited, Newcastle.
1948	March. Delivered to Westcott & Laurence Line, later to Ellerman & Papayanni.
1970.	18 August. Sold to Canopus Shipping SA, Famagusta, renamed *Rinoula*.
1971	Purchased by Rigel Shipping Company Limited, Famagusta.
1974	Owned by Kamara Cia. Nav. SA, Panama.
1975	Renamed *Gabriella* by Adnamar SA, Panama.
1977	Owned by Caobamar SA, Panama, and renamed *Donatella 1*.
1978	Sold to Rotary Traffic SpA. di Nav., Italy, and renamed *Stabia 1*.
1979	4 January. On a voyage from Brazil she was driven onto rocks at Salerno during a storm and became a total loss. All of her crew were saved.

Mercian.

Pamelian / Palmelian   1948   1,535grt.   83.21×12.86×4.54   644n.   12k.

E.   Twin screw, oil, 2×6 cyl. By British Polar Diesels, Glasgow.

B.   Henry Robb & Company, Leith.

1948   March. Launched as *Pamelian* but completed as *Palmelian*.

1970   11 July. Arrived at Bilbao to be broken up by Algonso & Fernadez.

Palmelian.

Egyptian (4) / *City of Leicester* (3)   1947   3,607grt.   113.69×15.51×6.61   1,452n.   12½k.

E.   Sgl. screw, 3 steam turb. LP and MP sgl., HP drg, 3,775 shp. By Wallsend Slipway
               Company, Wallsend.

B.   J. & L. Thompson & Sons Limited, Sunderland.

1947   January. Delivered to Ellerman & Papayanni Line.

1964   Renamed *City of Leicester*.

1965   Sold to Gardenia Shipping Company SA, Piraeus, renamed *Gardenia*.

1966   Sold to the Great Pacific Navigation Company, Panama, renamed *Chung Hsin* and
               re-sold to Chung Lien Navigation Company SA, Panama.

1967   Broken up at Taiwan.

Ionian (2) / *City of Durham* (2)   1947   3,596grt.   83.21×12.86×4.54   1,442n.   12k.

E.   Sgl. screw, 3 steam turb. LP and MP sgl., HP drg, 3,775 shp. By Wallsend Slipway
               Company, Wallsend.

B.   J. & L. Thompson Limited, Sunderland.

1947   March. Delivered to Ellerman & Papayanni Line.

1964   Replaced *Anatolian*, renamed *City of Durham* for the services to India.

1964   20 October. Sold for £48,000 to Eurata Shipping Company, SA, Greece, and
               renamed *Angelica N.*

1968   Sold to Theresia Limited, SA, Panama, and renamed *Eliza*.

| 1971 | 17 February. She went aground at Abijan and suffered bottom damage. She proceeded to Amsterdam and was assessed to be beyond economical repair. Sold to Eisen and Metall AG, Hamburg. |
| 1971 | 29 March. Arrived at Hamburg to be broken up. |

Patrician	1947 3,604grt. 83.21×12.86×4.54 1,457n. 12k.
E.	Sgl. screw, 3 steam turb. LP and MP sgl., HP drg, 3,775 shp. By Wallsend Slipway Company, Wallsend.
B.	J. & L. Thompson Limited, Sunderland.
1947	June. Delivered to Ellerman & Papayanni Line.
1963	8 July. Sank in the Strait of Gibraltar following a collision with the American ship *Santa Emilia*.

Venetian (2) / *City of Leeds* (2) 1947 3,578grt. 83.21×12.86×4.54 1,433n. 12k.	
E.	Sgl screw, 3 steam turb. LP and MP sgl, HP drg, 3,775 shp. By Wallsend Slipway Company, Wallsend.
B.	J. & L. Thompson Limited, Sunderland.
1947	August. Delivered to Westcott & Laurence Line, managed by Ellerman & Papayanni Line.
1964	Renamed *City of Leeds*, transferred to Ellerman & Bucknall.
1965	7 May. Sold to Orizon Shipping Company Limited, Monrovia, and renamed *Carina P* (Owners Papank Shipping Company SA).
1966	Renamed *Transrodopi III*, operated by Transrodopi SA, Piraeus, and owned by Kyriacos Shipping Corporation.
1968	The fleet of four ships were sold to Navigation Maritime Bulgare, Varna; renamed *Acrux*.
1970	Renamed *Silistra*.
1975	Sold to Brodespas.
1975	28 December. Arrived at Split to be broken up.
1976	30 June. Breaking up commenced.

Sicilian	1948 3,351grt. 110.03×15.27×6.34 1,426n. 12k.
E.	Sgl. screw, 3 steam turb. LP, HP drg through a hydraulic coupling, 3,775 shp. By builder.
B.	Ailsa Shipbuilding Company, Troon.
1948	October. Delivered to Ellerman & Papayanni Line.
1964	6 November. Sold to Bluesea Corporation, Monrovia, and renamed *Bluesea*.
1970	Sold to Nereus Maritime Company Limited.
1971	15 July. Left anchorage at Singapore Roads for Shanghai, to be broken up.

Grecian	1949 3,347grt. 110.03×15.27×6.34 1,517n. 12k.
E.	Sgl. screw, 3 steam turb. LP, HP drg through a hydraulic coupling, 3,775 shp. By builder.
B.	Ailsa Shipbuilding Company, Troon.
1949	28 January. Launched.
1949	June. Delivered to Ellerman & Papayanni Line.
1966	9 February. Sold to Astropropicio Cia. Nav. SA, renamed *Alexandra*.
1969	26 May. Arrived at Split to be broken up.

Andalusian (4)/ City of Ely   1950   3,913grt.   114.24×16.18×6.43   1,964n.   13k.

E.   Sgl. screw, tpl. exp. with LP turb. drg by hydraulic coupling,
                     225 psi, 2 sgl. blrs. By Central Marine Engineering Works, West Hartlepool.

B.   William Gray & Company, West Hartlepool.

1950   June. Delivered to Ellerman & Papayanni.

1962   Renamed *City of Ely*.

1964   Reverted to *Andalusian*.

1966   28 August. Sold to Aghia Barbara Cia. Nav. SA, Panama, renamed *Capetan Andreas P*,
                     later sold to Ezkos Maritime Technical Company, Panama.

1973   January. Boiler room fire at Constanza, declared uneconomic to be repaired and
                     broken up.

Maltasian / City of Norwich (2) / Maltasian
                     1950   3,910grt.   114.24×16.18×6.43   1,964n.   13k.

E.   Sgl. screw, tpl. exp., LP turb. drg by hydraulic coupling,
                     225 psi, 2 sgl. blrs. By Central Marine Engineering Works, West Hartlepool.

B.   William Gray & Company, West Hartlepool.

1950   September. Delivered to Westcott & Laurence Line.

1962   Transferred to Hall / City Line routes, renamed *City of Norwich*.

1964   Reverted to *Maltasian*.

1967   25 January. Sold to Kallisto Cia. Maritima SA, Panama, renamed *Capetan Christos P*.

1975   Purchased by Conga Marine Nav. SA, Greece, renamed *Aias* for voyage to the ship
                     breakers.

William Gray &
Company Limited
advertisement.

Anatolian (2) / City of Durham (3)   1955   3,799grt.   114.88×16.25×6.71   1,637n.

E.   Sgl. screw, tpl. exp., LP turb. drg with hydraulic coupling, 225 psi, 2 sgl. blrs. By
             Central Marine Engineering Works.

B.   William Gray & Company, West Hartlepool.

1955   November. Delivered to Ellerman & Papayanni.

1963   Transferred to Hall Lines Indian services, renamed *City of Durham*.

1964   Reverted to *Anatolian*.

1966   April. Chartered to the Cunard Line for the Liverpool–Chicago service, renamed
                     Ascania. Ellerman & Papayanni as managers.

1966	September. Reverted to *Anatolian*.
1968	Chartered again to the Cunard Line, renamed *Ascania*, then reverted to *Anatolian* on completion of charter.
1968	11 December. Sold to M. J. Lemos & Company, London, renamed *Agia Sophia*. Owned by the Gulf Shipping Corporation, Cyprus.
1970	Owned by Wavecrest Shipping Company, Famagusta.
1971	Sold to Millwala & Sons (England) Limited, London, renamed *Fulka*.
1974	Owned by the Arabian Gulf Trading Company, Sharjah, United Arab Emirates, renamed *Khalid*.
1975	Sold to Sharjah Shipping Company Limited, Sharjah, renamed *Gulf Unity*.
1977	Owned by the Gulf Shipping Lines, Sharjah.
1978	19 February. Arrived at Gadani Beach to be broken up.

Castilian (3) / *City of Peterborough*   1955   3,803grt.   114.97×16.25×6.71   1,619n.

E.	Sgl. screw, tpl. exp., LP turb. drg with hydraulic coupling, 225 psi, 2 sgl. blrs. By Central Marine Engineering Works.
B.	Alexander Stephen & Sons Limited, Glasgow.
1955	24 May. Launched.
1955	July. Delivered to Westcott & Laurence Line. Ellerman & Papayanni as managers.
1963	Renamed *City of Peterborough*.
1964	Reverted to *Castilian*.
1966	Chartered to the Cunard Line for the Great Lakes service, renamed *Arabia*.
1967	On completion of charter she reverted back to *Castilian*.
1971	15 February. Sold to Maldivian Nationals Trading Corporation (Ceylon) Limited, Colombo, renamed *Maldive Freedom*. Maldives Shipping Limited as managers.
1977	31 January. On a voyage from Aqaba to the Straits of Tiran she ran aground.
1977	6 February. Refloated.
1977	17 March. Arrived at Karachi to be broken up.

Lancastrian (2) / *City of Leicester* (2)   1956   3,799grt.   114.88×16.25×6.71   1,641n.

E.	Sgl. screw, tpl. exp., LP turb. drg with hydraulic coupling, 225 psi, 2 sgl. blrs. By Central Marine Engineering Works.
B.	William Gray & Company, West Hartlepool.
1956	February. Delivered to Ellerman & Papayanni Line.
1962	Renamed *City of Leicester* for Hall Line services, although the company press release gave the name as *City of Lancaster*.
1964	Reverted to *Lancastrian*.
1966	April. Chartered to the Cunard Line, renamed *Alsatia*.
1966	October. Reverted back to *Lancastrian* on completion of charter.
1969	9 April. Sold to M. J. Lemos & Company, London, renamed *Theokrates*, owned by the Ionian Shipping Company Limited, Famagusta, Cyprus.
1974	Owned by Sharjah Sea Transport Company, Sharjah, United Arab Emirates, renamed *Khorfaken*.
1975	2 February. Driven ashore in gale at Sharjah, declared a total loss.

Almerian (2) / *City of Leeds*   1956   3,649grt.   114.88×16.25×6.71   1,519n.

E.   Sgl. screw, tpl. exp., LP turb. drg with hydraulic coupling, 225 psi, 2 sgl. blrs. By
            Central Marine Engineering Works.

B.   Caledon Shipbuilding & Engineering Company, Dundee.

1956   October. Delivered to Ellerman & Bucknall Line. Ellerman & Papayanni Line as
            managers. Final steamship for Ellerman Lines Limited.

1962   Renamed *City of Leeds.*

1964   Renamed *Almerian.*

1966   Chartered to the Cunard Line, renamed *Assyria.*

1966   October. Reverted to *Almerian.*

1967   Chartered to the Cunard Line, renamed *Asia.*

1967   October. Reverted to *Almerian.*

1969   18 December. Sold to Galaction Shipping Company Limited, Famagusta, renamed
            Theokletus.

1974   Purchased by Marcoroma Cia Naviera, Panama.

1974   5 May. Left Singapore Roads anchorage for China to be broken up.

Almerian (2).

Florian loading in
Alexandra Dock,
Liverpool.

Florian	1955 3,134grt. 107.08×15.94×6.19 1,126n. 13½k.
E.	Sgl. screw, oil, 8 cyl. 2S SA, Clark–Sulzer, 3,850 bhp. By Sulzer.
B.	William Gray & Company, West Hartlepool.
1955	May. Delivered to Ellerman & Papayanni.
1956	May. Fire broke out in cargo of cotton dock in Liverpool and she suffered buckled deck plates.
1956	December. Following another fire she had to have the deck plating renewed.
1971	20 December. Sold to Maldive Shipping Limited, renamed *Maldive Loyalty*.
1982	5 October. Arrived at Gadani Beach to be broken up.

Flaminian (4) / *City of Izmir* 1956 3,100grt. 107.08×15.94×6.19 1,115n. 13½k.	
E.	Sgl. screw, oil, 8 cyl. 2S SA, Clark–Sulzer, 3,850 bhp. By G. Clark and North East Marine (Sunderland) Limited.
B.	Henry Robb & Company, Leith.
1956	February. Delivered to Westcott & Laurence Line.
1965	September. In collision with the tanker Floreal off Gibraltar. A small fire developed on her but this was extinguished.
1969	Transferred to Ellerman & Papayanni management.
1973	1 January. Moved to Ellerman City Liners Limited.
1974	Renamed *City of Izmir*.
1975	April. Sold to Climax Shipping Corporation, Maldives, renamed *Climax Pearl*.
1981	Renamed *Maldive Pearl*, owned by Maldive Shipping Limited.
1984	3 April. Arrived at Gadani Beach to be broken up.

City of Izmir.

Malatian (2) 1958 1,407grt. 82.26×13.06×4.51 597n. 12½k.	
E.	Sgl. screw, oil, 7 cyl. 2S SA, Sulzer, 2,100 bhp. By G.Clark and North East Marine (Sunderland) Limited.
B.	Henry Robb & Company, Leith.
1958	May. Delivered to Westcott & Laurence Line, Ellerman & Papayanni as managers
1969	Transferred to Ellerman & Papayanni ownership.
1971	18 November. Sold to Maldive Shipping Limited, renamed *Maldive Victory*.
1981	13 February. On a voyage from Singapore she struck a reef while entering Male harbour and sank.

Malatian (2).

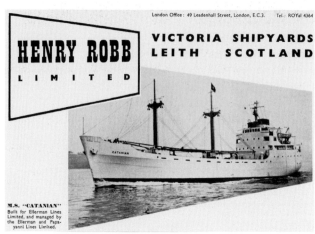

Henry Robb Limited
advertisement.

Catanian	1958 1,408grt. 82.26×13.06×4.51 597n. 12½k.
E.	Sgl. screw, oil, 7 cyl. 2S.SA, Sulzer, 2,100 bhp. By G. Clark and North East Marine (Sunderland) Limited.
B.	Henry Robb & Company, Leith.
1958	August. Delivered to Ellerman & Papayanni Line.
1972	14 February. Sold to Pacific Ocean Lines Limited, Male, Madive Islands, renamed *Ocean Glory*.
1977	Purchased by Gala Shipping Limited, Male, renamed *Ocean Glory No 6*.
1986	Reverted to *Ocean Glory*, owned by the Century Shipping Corporation, Panama.
1987	1 January. Arrived at Gadani Beach to be broken up.

Arcadian (2) / *City of Famagusta*	1960 3,402grt. 111.83×16.58×6.4 1,419n. 14k.
E.	Sgl. screw, oil, 7 cyl. 2S.SA, Sulzer, 3,500 bhp. By Fairfield Shipbuilding Company, Glasgow.
B.	Henry Robb & Company, Leith.
1960	July. Delivered to Ellerman & Papayanni Line.
1973	1 January. Transferred to Ellerman City Liners.
1974	Renamed *City of Famagusta*.
1977	May. Sold to Associate Levant Lines SAL, Beirut, with *City of Limassol*. Renamed *Batroun*.
1986	18 December. Arrived at Gadani Beach to be broken up.

Arcadian (2).

Cortian	1962 537grt. 71.41×10.42×3.82 279n. 11k.
E.	Sgl. screw, oil, 8 cyl. 4S.SA, 1,200 bhp. By Motoren Werke, Mannheim.
B.	A/B Lodose Varv, Lodose, Sweden.
1962	April. Delivered to Erik Kekonius, Skarhamn, Sweden as *Cortia*.
1966	Managed by Lars Johansson, Skarhamn, Sweden and purchased by Ellerman & Papayanni Line, renamed *Cortian*.
1968	Transferred to Mossgiel Steam Ship Company, John Bruce as managers. Remained on Ellerman & Papayanni service.
1971	Sold to Captain Folke Patriksson, Sweden and reverted to *Cortia*. Owned by Anders F. Partriksson Partrederi.
1974	Sold to Cala d'Olivio S. p. A., Italy, renamed Austerity and converted into livestock carrier.
1978	Owned by Neptune SpA., Palermo, renamed *Bruno Alphina*.
1986	Sold to SIBA S p A., Brescia, owned by Balzarini, Corvi & Cia., renamed *Siba Foggia*.
1994	4 December. Abandoned after she started taking in water off Port Said on a voyage from Port Jeddah to Trieste, three crew were lost. She remained afloat and was taken in tow the following day to Limassol.
1994	7 December. Arrived at Limassol and placed under arrest by the local court.
1995	10 March. Released from arrest and towed to Vassilikis for repairs and returned.
1996	Sold to Peril Investments SA, Belize, renamed Nehmet Allah.
1998	Became *Fighter II*.
2000	Renamed *Madar I*.
2004	22 December. Arrived at Sachana to be broken up.

Athenian (2) / *City of Valetta*	1966 2,702grt. 93.84×13.93×6.71 1,432n. 14k.
E.	Sgl. screw, oil, 6 cyl. 4S.SA, 2,580 bhp. By Mirrlees National Limited, Stockport. Controllable pitch propeller.
B.	Henry Robb & Company, Leith.
1966	July. Delivered to Westcott & Laurence Line, Ellerman & Papayanni as managers. One of six similar ships of advanced design ordered at the Leith shipyard for companies in the Ellerman Group. All were designed to carry general and pallatised cargo and were readily adaptable to become carry containers. Athenian differed from the sister ships as she was adaptable as either an open or closed shelter deck-type.

She was built with clear holds with large hatches. The hatch covers on the upper deck were the latest MacGregor single-pull type, and those on the second deck were flush steel-hingeing, hydraulically operated, and strengthened to take 4-ton forklift trucks. The cranes were Strother & Pitt's electro-hydraulic 'Stevedore' level-luffing type, with a maximum jib ratio of 48 feet. Special techniques were used for the treatment of hatch covers and runways to combat the excessive corrosion found in these areas. All holds and 'tween decks had independent mechanical supply and exhaust ventilation at over thirty air changes per hour with empty holds, for the carriage of fruit.

1973	1 January. Transferred to Ellerman City Liners.
1974	Renamed *City of Valetta*.
1980	Sold to Pacific International Lines (Pte), Singapore, renamed *Kota Jade*.
1986	Broken up at Taiwan.

Storry Smithson Group (marine division) advertisement.

Mediterranian / City of Istanbul   1968   1,460grt.   94.00×14.6×5.09   730n.   13k.

E.	Sgl. screw, oil, 6 cyl. 4S.SA, 2,580 bhp. By Mirrlees National Limited, Stockport. Controllable pitch propeller.
B.	Henry Robb & Company, Leith.
1968	October. Delivered to Ellerman & Papayanni Line.
1973	1 January. Transferred to Ellerman City Liners.
1974	Renamed *City of Istanbul*, Ellerman & Papayanni as managers.
1978	Owned by Gracechurch Shipping Limited, Newcastle, renamed *Fenchurch*.

1983	Sold to Angelopoulos & Sarlis, Greece, renamed *Pelor*.
1993	Renamed *A.m. Spiridon*.
2003	Sold and renamed *Sara*.
2011	2 January. Arrived at Aliaga to be broken up.

Charters

Estremadurian 1958 1,921grt.
Ex *Varodd*, Nils Naesheim A/S.

1968	Chartered by Ellerman & Papayanni for the Liverpool–Oporto service. Carried fifty-six containers. First vessel to load at Gladstone Dock Container Terminal.
1970	Charter completed, reverted to *Varodd*.
1975	Renamed *Petrola XL*.

Iberian 1964 455grt.
Built as *Yuki Hansen* for Knud Hansen A/S, Copenhagen.

1966	Renamed *Iberian* for the Hull–Oporto service.

Evorian 1963 455grt.
Built as *Karin Smits* for M. Smits, Netherlands.

1969	Renamed *Evorian* for the Hull–Oporto service.

Italian 1963 454grt.
Built as *Dita Smits* for M. Smits, Netherlands.

1968	Renamed *Italian*.
1971	Completed charter, renamed *Duel*, owned by H. Rasmussen, Denmark.

Grecian 1966 1,450grt.
Built as *Andromeda* for M. Moermaus, Netherlands.

1969	Renamed *Grecian* on five-year charter.
1974	Completed charter, renamed *Sela*, owned by Hafskip, Iceland.

Marmorian 1966 1,174grt.
Built as *Marmorhav* for Hvide & Schjott, Norway.

1967	Renamed *Marmorian*.
1968	Completed charter, reverted to *Marmorhav*.

Anglian 1966 499grt.
Built as *Wilhelm S.* for Tim Schepers & Sohne, Germany.

1968	Renamed *Anglian* for the Hull-Oporto service.
1970	Completed charter and reverted to *Wilhelm S.*

Silvian 1956 1,877grt.
Built as *Transsylvania* and renamed *Stahleck* in 1971.

1971	Renamed *Silvian*.
1972	Completed charter, renamed *Kathy*, owned by Katrien NV, Netherlands.

Minho / City of Milan (2)   1969   1,578grt.   85.31×13.75×4.17   892n.   13k.

E.	Sgl. screw, oil, 6 cyl. 4S.SA, 3,200 bhp at 512 rpm to 275 rpm. By N.V. Werkspoor, Amsterdam. Controllable pitch propeller.
B.	A. Vuijk & Zonen, Capelle, Rotterdam.
1969	10 October. Launched.
1969	December. Delivered to Sea Containers as one of a 'Hustler' class of seventeen ships.
1970	On charter to Ellerman & Papayanni Line for the Liverpool–Oporto service. Crewed by Ellerman Lines.
1974	Renamed *City of Milan*.
1978	Charter completed with the delivery of five larger and faster ships of the *City of Plymouth* class.
1979	Sold to Ope Investment & Marine Company SA, Panama, renamed *Eco Mondego*.
1994	Became *Ana Raquel*.
2001	8 November. Arrived at Lisbon to be broken up.

Tagus / City of Lisbon   1970   1,578grt.   85.31×13.75×4.17   892n.   13k.

E.	Sgl. screw, oil, 6 cyl. 4S.SA, 3,200 bhp at 512 rpm drg to 275 rpm. By N.V. Werkspoor, Amsterdam. Controllable pitch propeller.
B.	Astilleros del Cadagua, Bilbao.
1970	7 January. Launched.
1970	March. Chartered to Ellerman & Papayanni.
1972	First vessel to berth at the Royal Seaforth Container Terminal.
1974	Renamed *City of Lisbon*. Ellerman obtained the contract to carry mail on the Mersey–Lisbon route and she was the first ship of the line to carry the Royal Mail pennant.
1979	Renamed *Cape Hustler*, Sea Containers Incorporated.
1983	9 April. On a voyage from Durban to Cape Town, she sustained engine damage and diverted to Port Elizabeth, where she was later placed on the market.
1985	Purchased by Bona Mercantile Company Limited, Hondoras, renamed *Cape*.
1989	Sold to Mirror Navigation Inc., St Vincent, renamed *Despo*.
1989	20 November. Abandoned with engine problems.
1989	Sank off Zante.

Tamega / City of Genoa (2)   1970   1,578grt.   85.31×13.75×4.17   892n.   13k.

E.	Sgl. screw, oil, 6 cyl. 4S.SA, 3,200 bhp at 512 rpm drg to 275 rpm. By N.V. Werkspoor, Amsterdam. Controllable pitch propeller.
B.	A. Vuijk & Zonen, Capelle, Rotterdam.
1970	19 June. Launched as *Tamega*.
1970	September. Completed, on charter to Ellerman & Papayanni.
1974	Renamed *City of Genoa*.
1982	Renamed *Hustler Ebro*, Sea Containers Incorporated.
1983	Renamed *Bermudiana*.
1987	Sold to Honduras interests, renamed *Minart*.
1987	Renamed *Anita*, same owners.
1988	Renamed *Prince Hamlet*, same owners.
1989	Renamed *Lloyd Bermuda*, same owners.
1989	Sold to Excelsior Navigation Company Limited, renamed *Zim Levant*.

1992	Renamed *Jason*.
1992	Sold to Atlantic Gulf Shipping Company Limited, Cyprus, renamed *Idmon*.
1993	Purchased by Filippos Shipping Company, SA, renamed *Filippos*.
1996	Sold to Avante SRL, Paraguay.

Tormes / City of Oporto   1970   1,578grt.   85.31×13.75×4.17   892n.   13k.

E.	Sgl. screw, oil, 6 cyl. 4S.SA, 3,200 bhp at 512 rpm drg to 275 rpm. By N.V. Werkspoor, Amsterdam. Controllable pitch propeller.
B.	Zaarndamsche Schips. Maats., Amsterdam.
1970	April. Launched.
1970	June. Completed.
1974	Renamed *City of Oporto*.
1980	Purchased by Econave Comp. Costeira e Oceania de Nav., Portugal, renamed *Eco Guadiana*.
1989	Sold to Whirry First Marine Incorporated, Panama, renamed *Dina*.
1995	Sold to Mar-Whirry Marine Corporation, Panama.

Tua / City of Florence (4)   1970   1,599grt.   85.31×13.75×4.17   892n.   13k.

E.	Sgl. screw, oil, 6 cyl. 4S.SA, 3,200 bhp at 512 rpm drg to 275 rpm. By N.V. Werkspoor, Amsterdam. Controllable pitch propeller.
B.	A.Vuijk & Zonen, Capelle, Rotterdam.
1970	18 August. Launched.
1970	November. Completed.
1974	Renamed *City of Florence*.
1983	October. Renamed *Hustler Fal* by Sea Containers Incorporated. Laid up at Manchester.
1984	Purchased by Seaco Holdings, Cyprus, renamed *Confrigo 1*.
1989	Renamed *Lorelei*, Maltese flagged.
1990	30 September. Suffered main engine damage on a voyage from El Guamache to Cristobal.
1990	5 October. Arrived at St Anna Bay in tow.
1990	21 December. Engine dismantled and vessel placed on sale by auction.
1991	Sold to Cabotage Venezolano, Venezuela, renamed *Halcon Del Mar*.
1992	Sold to Argosy Shipping Corporation, Panama.
1995	Purchased by Aguilla Shipping Corporation Inc., Panama.

Tiber / City of Naples (2)   1970   1,599grt.   85.31×13.75×4.17   892n.   13k.

E.	Sgl. screw, oil, 6 cyl. 4S.SA, 3,200 bhp at 512 rpm drg to 275 rpm. By N.V. Werkspoor, Amsterdam. Controllable pitch propeller.
B.	Zaarndamsche Schips., Maats., Amsterdam.
1970	2 October. Launched.
1970	December. Completed.
1974	Renamed *City of Naples*.
1979	Reverted to *Tiber* and sold to Atlantic Clipper Limited, Cayman Islands, renamed *Atlantic Clipper*.
1983	Sold to Hyde Shipping Corporation, Cayman Islands, renamed *Hybur Clipper*.
1983	Owned by Bay Island Shipping Limited, Georgetown, Grand Caymen.
1995	Sold to Verset Holdings Inc., St Vincent & Grenadines, renamed *Island Clipper*.

Tronto / City of La Spezia   1971   1,559grt.   85.31×13.75×4.17   909n.   13k.
E.   Sgl. screw, oil, 6 cyl. 4S.SA, 3,200 bhp at 512 rpm drg to 275 rpm. By N.V.
                Werkspoor, Amsterdam. Controllable pitch propeller.
B.   A.Vuijk & Zonen, Capelle, Rotterdam.
1971   Laid down as *Tigris*.
1971   16 October. Launched as *Tronto*.
1972   January. Completed.
1974   Renamed *City of La Spezia*.
1979   Reverted to *Tronto*. Sold to Atlantic Intrepid Limited, renamed *Atlantic Intrepid*.
1983   Sold to Bahia Shipping Limited, Cayman Islands, renamed *Hybur Intrepid*.
1997   Purchased by Island Intrepid Limited, Antigua & Barbuda, renamed *Island Intrepid*.

Mondego / City of Venice (4)   1972   1,559grt.   85.31×13.75×4.17   909n.   13k.
E.   Sgl. screw, oil, 6 cyl. 4S.SA, 3,200 bhp at 512 rpm drg to 275 rpm. By N.V.
                Werkspoor, Amsterdam. Controllable pitch propeller.
B.   Astilleros de Atlantico, Santander.
1972   10 June. Launched.
1972   December. Delivered.
1974   Renamed *City of Venice*.
1980   Reverted to Sea Container Chartering Limited, renamed *Atlantic Resolute*.
1982   Renamed *Hustler Indus*. Later on the Jacksonville–Bermuda service.
1989   Renamed *Marlago III*.
1989   Renamed *Medeleine*.
1991   Renamed *Hustler Bell*.
1994   Renamed *Terrapin Flyer*.
1995   Renamed *Panama Flyer*.
1995   Renamed *Terrapin Flyer*.
2001   Renamed *Panama Flyer*.
2001   Renamed *Miami-F.*

Westcott & Laurence

Harriet Agnes   1865   624grt.   59.44×7.92×4.63   473n.   9½k.
B.   Sweden.
1867   Purchased by Westcott & Houseden.
1878   Owned by W.G. Westcott.
1879   Sold to R. Fell, junior, London.
1886   Deleted from Lloyd's Register.

Rhone   1868   1,343grt   76.07×9.17×5.36   868n.
E.   Sgl. screw, 2 cyl. simple exp.
B.   W. Pile & Company, Sunderland.
1868   February. Launched as *Rhone* for the Ryde Line, London for the London–
                Antwerp–Falmouth–Rio de Janeiro–Montevideo–Buenos Aires service.
1871   Lengthened and engines compounded by Millwall Dock Engineering Company.
                New speed 11k.

1879	Purchased by Westcott & Laurence for the Mediterranean service.
1898	Sold to Soc. Anon. Belge de Nav. a Vap. Schaldis, Antwerp with De Clerck & Van Hemelryk as managers.
1904	Purchased by G. Lauro, Naples.
1906	Sold to L. & G. Agarinis, Venice, and broken up.

Science	1868 1,348grt. 76.07×9.17×5.36 868n.
1868	March. Launched as *Richard Cobden* for the Ryde Line.
1871	Lengthened and compounded. 11k.
1874	Valparaiso via the Straits of Magellan was added to her ports of call.
1876	Sold to Sala y Vidal, Barcelona, renamed *Vidal Sala*.
1876	Owned by Cie. Gantoise de Nav., Ghent, renamed *Lys*.
1899	Purchased by Westcott & Laurence Line, renamed *Science*.
1899	26 March. Sunk in a collision off Cape St Vincent.

Juan	1864 1,585grt. 82.48×10.09×7.04 1,020n. 10k.
E.	Sgl. screw, 2 cyl. comp. inv., 200 nhp, 30 psi. By Maudsley Son & Field, London.
B.	A. Leslie & Company, Hebburn.
1864	Built as *Galileo* for the Lamport & Holt Line, Liverpool, for the Liverpool–Brazil and River Plate service.
1869	Purchased by T. H. Jackson & Company, Liverpool, renamed *Juan*.
1874	Sold to J. Jack & Company, Liverpool. New engines fitted.
1878	Sold to J.B. Palmer, London.
1882	Purchased by William Banks, London for the South American services.
1884	Sold to T.A. Hinton, London.
1888	Purchased by Westcott & Laurence Line.
1898	Sold to H. Diedrichsen, Kiel, for a service to China from Hong Kong.
1898	26 August. Left Hong Kong for Kiaochow and was declared missing.

Montgomerie & Workman

City of Quebec	1855 729grt. 56.2×9.33×6.13 708n.
B.	Robert Steele, Greenock.
1855	June. Delivered to Montgomerie & Greenhorne for service with George Smith's City Line.
1877	Owned by Montgomerie & Workman.
1895	Purchased by Berneaud & Cia., Para, Brazil. Hulked.

City of Hamilton	1850 524grt. 38.92×8.02×5.79 517n.
B.	Aberdeen.
1850	Delivered.
1856	Owned by Montgomerie & Greenhorne.
1865	Owned by Edmonstone, Allen & Company for the London to the United States service.
1872	Sold to Gillespey & Company.
1874	Lost at sea.

Duke of Rothesay   1864   999grt.   60.87×10.18×6.37
B.	Denny & Rankin, Dumbarton.
1864	November. Delivered to Montgomerie & Greenhorne.
1866	Lost at sea.

Duke of Athole   1865   963grt.   60.72×10.12
B.	Denny & Rankin, Dumbarton.
1865	February. Delivered to Montgomerie & Greenhorne.
1877	Owned by Montgomerie & Workman.
1878	First sailing ship to transit the Suez Canal under tow.
1880	Sold to Devitt & Moore, London.
1889	Owned by German interests.
1897	Abandoned at sea.

Duke of Argyll   1865   960grt.   60.72×10.12
B.	Denny & Rankin, Dumbarton.
1865	Delivered to Montgomerie & Greenhorne.
1877	Owned by Montgomerie & Workman.
1896	Sold to Georg T. Monsen, Stavanger. Renamed *Signe*.
1904	Owned by A. Bech, Tvedestrand.

Duke of Abercorn   1869   1,096grt.   64.62×10.7×6.25
B.	Chas. Connell & Company, Glasgow.
1869	October. Delivered to Montgomerie & Greenhorne for the Australia and China routes.
1877	Owned by Montgomerie & Workman.
1892	She was lost on a voyage from Cardiff to Callao with a cargo of coal.

Duke of Hamilton   1850   524grt.
1850	Delivered to Edmonstone, Allan & Company, London.
1868	Purchased by Montgomerie & Greenhorne.
1871	Sold.
1876	She was lost on a voyage from Philadelphia to Hamburg with a cargo of petrol.

Xantippi   1893   972grt.   64.4×10.76×5.27
B.	Workman, Clark & Company.
1893	June. Delivered to Montgomerie & Workman. Four-masted barque.
1895	Lost at sea.

George Smith & Sons

The City Line

Constellation	1839 334grt. 32.49×7.28×5.15
B.	Quaco, New Brunswick.
1839	August. Launched. Completed one trans-Atlantic voyage with timber and was then advertised for sale.
1840	Purchased by George Smith & Sons, Glasgow, and carried out one voyage from the Clyde to Calcutta.
1841	Placed on the United States and South African trade.
1848	Purchased by Captain P. McPhee.
1854	Sold to J. Loveday, West Hartlepool.
1864	5 November. Lost at sea.

Oriental	1843 346grt. 33.31×7.25×5.42
1843	Delivered for the Calcutta service.
1846	Sold to Captain J. Neill, who joined Thomas Dunlop as a partner for service on the Glasgow–West Indies route.
1865	Sold to Morris & Company, Rhyl, North Wales, to operate out of Liverpool.
1868	Wrecked.

Majestic	1846 565grt. 38.19×7.62×5.79 458n.
1846	Delivered to George Smith & Sons for the Calcutta service.
1860	Sold to R. & J. Craig, Glasgow for the Glasgow–Java service.
1868	Broken up.

Asia	1846 450grt.
B.	A. McMillan & Son, Dumbarton.
1846	Delivered to George Smith & Sons, Glasgow.
1862	25 January. Foundered off the Cape of Good Hope.

City of Glasgow	1848 509grt. 38.92×8.11×6.1
B.	Barclay, Curle & Company, Glasgow.
1848	Delivered to George Smith & Son, Glasgow, becoming the first 'City' boat.
1866	Sold to Connell & Company, Glasgow.
1872	November. Owned by John Wright & Sons, Glasgow.
1873	She was abandoned on a voyage from Greenock to Pensacola.

City of Calcutta	1850 541grt. 38.92×8.11×6.1
B.	Barclay, Curle & Company, Glasgow.
1850	Delivered to George Smith & Son, Glasgow, for the Calcutta service.
1859	August. After her cargo was loaded at Calcutta she rolled over onto her side. All of the crew were saved but a passenger lost his life.

City of London	1851 541grt. 40.69×8.9×6.1
B.	Barclay, Curle & Company, Glasgow.
1851	Delivered.
1867	Sold to Hendry & Company, Greenock.
1870	Wrecked in the Solway Firth.

City of Edinburgh	1852 599grt. 42.37x7.95x6.1
B.	Barclay, Curle & Company, Glasgow.
1852	Delivered.
1867	Sold to J. McAlister.
1869	Wrecked in the Bay of Bengal.

City of Benares	1853 692grt. 49.93×8.35×6.37
B.	Barclay, Curle & Company, Glasgow.
1853	Delivered for the East Indies services.
1865	31 January. Destroyed by fire at Calcutta, where she was burnt down to the water level.

City of Manchester	1854 766grt. 50.44×8.26×6.43 iron hull
B.	Robert Steele & Company, Greenock.
1854	Delivered as one of six similar sister ships.
1871	Sold to J. McAlister.
1874	Purchased by W. Kenneth & Company, Glasgow.
1876	She was reported to have been lost in a cyclone off the Arracan coast but arrived at Rangoon.
1883	Broken up.

City of Madras	1855 800grt. 61.05×9.2×6.31 iron hull
B.	Robert Steele & Company, Greenock.
1855	Delivered as one of six similar sister ships.
1856	1 March. Wrecked off Corsewell Point, near Stranraer in a gale.

City of Dublin	1855 813grt. 61.05×9.2×6.31 iron hull
B.	Robert Steele & Company, Greenock.
1855	Delivered as one of six similar sister ships.
1878	She completed the London–Port Chalmers voyage in ninety-three days and then sailed from New Zealand to the Unites States in ballast.
1878	15 October. Wrecked off Portland, Oregon.

City of Tanjore	1855 799grt. 59.16×8.75×6.31 iron hull
B.	Robert Steele & Company, Greenock.
1855	Delivered as one of six similar sister ships for the Indian service.
1879	Sold to T.C. Guthrie and then Guthrie, McDonald & Hood & Company, Glasgow.
1880	Owned by Prentout-Leblond & E. Boniface, Rouen, renamed Suzanne Boulet.
1891	Sold to Captain J. Gilhoux.

1895	Owned by A. Melling, Stavanger, renamed *Nor.*
1897	Purchased by Pangani Gesellschaft, Berlin, renamed Deutschland.
1898	On tow on the Pangani River, the rope broke and she went aground. She was salvaged and sold to Zanzibar interests.
1904	Broken up at Bombay.

City of Canton	1857 908grt. 60.17×9.51×6.34 iron hull
B.	Robert Steele & Company, Greenock.
1857	August. Delivered as one of six similar sister ships for the Indian service.
1877	Sold to J. & R. Wilson, Glasgow.
1892	Owned by M. Tutton, Swansea, renamed *Ffynone.*
1903	Sold to J.M. Thomsen, Norway, renamed *Undal.*
1906	Lost in the North Atlantic.

City of Delhi	1857 813grt. 54.47×9.72×6.64 iron hull
B.	Robert Steele & Company, Greenock.
1857	October. Delivered as one of six similar sister ships for the Indian service.
1867	January. Wrecked on Dungenness Point.

Ballengeich	1849 478grt.
B.	Barclay, Curle & Company, Glasgow.
1849	Delivered to J. Tod for the Clyde–USA–Calcutta service.
1851	On the emigrant service from the Clyde to Australia.
1855	Sold to Smith & Son for the Calcutta service.
1859	May. Wrecked on the Madras coast.

City of Perth	1857 466grt. 47.37×8.35×5.58
B.	Barclay, Curle & Company, Glasgow.
1857	Delivered
1867	Sold to Captain McPhail, Connell & Company, Glasgow.
1872	Sold to Thomas Dunlop and John Neil, Glasgow.
1876	Sold to A. Benecke, London. who sold her to French interests.

City of York	1859 569grt. 47.55×8.9×5.85
B.	Barclay, Curle & Company, Glasgow.
1859	Delivered.
1865	She was lost on a voyage from Calcutta to Glasgow.

City of Pekin	1858 893grt. 60.00×9.48×6.34 iron hull
B.	Barclay, Curle & Company, Glasgow.
1858	Delivered for the Smith & Sons service to the Far East.
1873	5 June. In collision off Cape de Verde, Cape Verde Islands and sank.

City of Lucknow	1858 869grt. 60.00×9.48×6.34 iron hull
B.	Alexander Stephen & Sons Limited, Glasgow.
1858	Delivered.
1861	9 February. Wrecked in Belfast Lough.

City of Madras (2)   1859   999grt.   63.7×9.75×6.67   iron hull
B.   Alexander Stephen & Sons Limited, Glasgow.
1859   Delivered.
1881   Purchased by Montgomerie & Workman, Glasgow, renamed *Duke of Connaught*.
1887   Sank following a collision.

City of Nankin   1859   986grt.   64.65×9.81×6.52   iron hull
B.   Barclay, Curle & Company, Glasgow.
1859   October. Delivered.
1881   Sold to Guthrie, McDonald & Hood & Company, Glasgow.
1883   Renamed *Keir*, owned by the Village Line.
1896   Purchased by Isaac Zagury, Liverpool.
1897   Sold to Andres Lupo, renamed *Andres Lupo*.
1908   Broken up.

City of Shanghai   1860   989grt.   64.77×9.81×6.52   iron hull
B.   Barclay, Curle & Company, Glasgow.
1860   October. Delivered.
1881   Sold to Captain Bramwell, owned by Bramwell & Gardener, Glasgow, renamed *Nith*.
1893   Purchased by John I. Jacobs, London.
1900   Lost on a voyage from Florida to Sydney.

City of Calcutta (2)   1860   984grt.   64.6×9.75×6.61   iron hull, 2 decks
B.   Alexander Stephen & Sons Limited, Glasgow.
1860   November. Delivered.
1881   Sold to Captain Charles Barrie, renamed *Calcutta*.
1895   16 September. She was abandoned off Staten Island, Cape Horn, on a voyage from Huanillos to London and Dundee.

City of Bombay   1862   990grt.   64.6×9.75×6.61   iron hull, 2 decks
B.   Alexander Stephen & Sons Limited, Glasgow.
1862   Delivered.
1882   Sold to Captain J. Rhind, Glasgow, renamed *Bombay*.
1884   Purchased by N. J. Ward & Son, Fleetwood.
1899   Sold to Carl Bech, Tvedestrand, Oslo, renamed *Norden*.
1907   1 March. Wrecked off the Seychelles.

City of Cashmere   1863   979grt.   64.6×9.75×6.61   iron hull, 2 decks
B.   Alexander Stephen & Sons Limited, Glasgow.
1863   March. Delivered.
1882   15 January. Wrecked when she lost her anchor and drifted onto Ninety Mile Beach, Timaru, New Zealand.

City of Ningpo   1862   986grt.   62.18×9.87×6.49   949n.   iron hull
B.   Barclay, Curle & Company, Glasgow.

1862	July. Delivered.
1881	Sold to Captain J. Rhind, Glasgow, renamed *Kinloss*.
1888	Owned by Gustavo Bahr, Hamburg, renamed *Gustavo Adolfo* for the nitrate trade between Chile and Hamburg.
1900	Sold to H. Bischoff & Company, Bremen for the Bremen–United States service.
1904	Owned by J. A. Leschbrandt, Norway, renamed *Valhal*.
1910	Broken up in Holland.

City of Amoy	1863 986grt. 63.92×9.87×6.52 iron hull
1863	March. Delivered.
1872	8 September. Her cargo shifted on a voyage from the Clyde to San Francisco and she diverted to the Falkland Islands with a severe list.
1882	Sold to Bramwell & Gardener, Glasgow, renamed *Amoy*. Owner as Robert Bramwell of London.
1889	8 October. Wrecked off the Falkland Islands on a voyage from Paranagua to Valparaiso.

City of Paris	1862 990grt. 64.16×9.69×6.52
B.	Charles Connell & Company, Glasgow.
1862	Delivered.
1882	Purchased by George Traill & Sons, Glasgow, renamed *Kiandra*.
1888	Sold to H. Bischoff & Company, Bremen. Operated as a tramp ship.
1895	Rescued the crew of the United States sailing ship *Sentinel* in the Atlantic.
1902	April. She was lost with all hands on a voyage from Philadelphia.

City of Brussels	1863 990grt. 64.4×9.69×6.52
B.	Charles Connell & Company, Glasgow.
1863	May. Delivered.
1881	Sold to Hugh Hogarth, Ardrossan, renamed *Brussels*.
1891	Purchased by Shaw, Savill & Company, London.
1903	Owned by the Niger Company, London.
1904	July. Hulked on the River Niger, West Africa.

City of Berlin	1864 1,011grt. 64.92×9.69×6.52 2 decks
B.	Charles Connell & Company, Glasgow.
1864	October. Delivered. The first vessel in the fleet over 1,000 tons.
1881	Sold to T.C. Guthrie & Company, Glasgow, renamed *Dalswinton*.
1884	March. Fire broke out in her cargo of coal and she was lost.

City of Vienna	1866 990grt. 64.92×8.53×6.52
B.	Charles Connell & Company, Glasgow.
3.1866	March. Delivered.
1881	Sold to T.C. Guthrie & Company, renamed *Dunscore*.
1894	Owned by James Currie & Company, Leith, renamed *Carrick*.
1896	Abandoned off the coast of Australia.

City of Florence   1867   1,198grt.   69.16×10.48×6.83   1,162n.
B.   Charles Connell & Company, Glasgow.
1867   January. Delivered.
1895   Her voyage from Vancouver to Antwerp via Cape Horn took 184 days and at
                     one point she was given up as lost.
1900   19 March. Wrecked at Half Moon Bay, California, on a voyage from Iquique to
                     San Francisco with a cargo of nitrate.

City of Venice   1867   1,199grt.   70.29×10.48×6.83   1,160n.
B.   Charles Connell & Company, Glasgow.
1867   April. Delivered for the Calcutta service.
1871   6 October. Wrecked on Rodrigues Island, east of Mauritius on a voyage from
                     the Clyde to Bombay.
1871   7 November. The ship broke up and the crew were taken to Mauritius.

City of Lahore   1864   988grt.   61.57×9.69×6.83
B.   Alexander Stephen, Glasgow.
1864   March. Delivered.
1883   Sold to T.C. Guthrie & Company, Glasgow, renamed *Durisdeer*.
1895   Wrecked on Oyster Bank.

City of Foochow   1864   1,034grt.   65.04×9.9×6.52   1,034n.   iron hull
B.   Barclay, Curle & Company, Glasgow.
1864   March. Delivered.
1876   13 November. In collision with *City of Seringapatam* off La Palma.
1877   1 April. Wrecked off Flinder's Isle, Bass Strait on a voyage from Sydney to
                     California.

City of Benares (2)   1865   1,182grt.   68.4×10.42×6.86   1,150n.   iron hull, 2 decks
B.   Barclay, Curle & Company, Glasgow.
1865   July. Delivered.
1881   Sold to G. Traill & Sons, Glasgow, renamed *Ruthin*.
1890   Owned by C.H.H. Winters, Bremen.
1910   Sold to T.H. Poulsson, Stavanger, renamed *Laugen*.
1911   Sunk by ice in the Baltic, raised and broken up.

City of Seringapatam   1866   1,190grt.   68.58×10.42×6.86   iron hull, 2 decks
B.   Barclay, Curle & Company, Glasgow.
1866   January. Delivered.
1876   13 November. In collision with *City of Foochow* off La Palma Island. Seven of
                     her crew were lost and she was towed into Puerto Cruz, Tenerife, minus her
                     mizzen mast.
1876   21 December. On a voyage from London to Melbourne she was wrecked off
                     Bona Vista Island, Cape Verde Islands. All the crew were rescued.

City of Athens   1867   1,198grt.   67.94×10.42×6.95   1,163n.   iron hull, 2 decks
B.   Robert Steele & Company, Greenock.

1867	Delivered.
1893	March. On a race with five sailing ships from San Francisco to Cobh, the City of Athens came first.
1900	Purchased by Johan Johanson, Lysaker, Oslo, and renamed *Athena*.
1909	23 November. Wrecked at Morant Bay, Jamaica.

City of Glasgow (2)   1867   1,168grt.   69.49×10.36×6.92   1,131n.   iron hull, 2 decks

B.	Barclay, Curle & Company.
1867	February. Delivered.
1874	Chartered to the New Zealand Shipping Company.
1874	3 January. Left Belfast for Dunedin, a voyage that took seventy-five days.
1900	Sold to Johan Johanson, Lysaker, and renamed *Albania*.
1907	17 May. She was abandoned on a voyage from New Caledonia to Europe with a cargo of nickel ore.

City of Delhi (2)   1867   1,199grt.   69.4×10.61×9.75   iron hull, 2 decks

B.	Barclay, Curle & Company.
1867	July. Delivered with an iron hull with wooden bulwarks.
1900	Sold to Johan Johanson, Lysaker, renamed *Ailsa*.
1906	2 January. On fire and abandoned off Rockall.

City of Edinburgh (2)   1868   1,206grt.   70.1×10.79×6.83   iron hull, 2 decks

B.	Barclay, Curle & Company.
1868	January. Delivered.
1874	20 November. In collision with the *French Empire* at Sandheads, Calcutta. Both vessels were lost.

City of Dover   1868   1,199grt.   70.1×10.79×6.83   iron hull, 2 decks

B.	Barclay, Curle & Company.
1868	Delivered.
1874	Sold.
1875	Wrecked off Ireland.

City of Lucknow (2)   1869   1,195grt.   70.44×10.82×6.77   iron hull, 2 decks

B.	Barclay, Curle & Company.
1869	March. Delivered.
1883	Completed a voyage from Adelaide to London in 75 days.
1884	January. In collision with *Simla*, which later sank with a loss of twenty lives. London to San Francisco in 109 days.
1889	Purchased by Knohr & Burchard, Hamburg, renamed *Reinbek*.
1896	Owned by E. Terrizano, Genoa, Italy, renamed *Agostino Terrizano*.
1907	Sold to Angelo Bertorello, Sampierdarena, Italy.
1909	Broken up at Genoa.

City of Hankow   1869   1,195grt.   67.97×10.73×6.8   iron hull, 2 decks

| B. | Alexander Stephen & Sons, Glasgow. |
| 1869 | June. Delivered. |

1873	Captain G. Napier was washed overboard and killed near Ascension Island.
1971	London–Calcutta–London in 191 days.
1874	November. Lizard–Melbourne in seventy days and beat Cutty Sark by three days. London–San Francisco in ninety-six days.
1900	Sold to G.J. Robertson, Sydney.
1903	Hulked at Thursday Island, Torres Straits, and later became a pontoon.

City of Madrid 1869 1,191grt. 70.59×10.76×6.77 iron hull, 2 decks

B.	Charles Connell & Company, Glasgow.
1869	September. Delivered.
1888	Purchased by S. Goldberg & Sons, Swansea, renamed *Agnes Lilian*.
1898	Owned by J.A. Henschien, Lillesand, Norway.
1915	Broken up in Norway.

City of Corinth 1870 1,219grt. 71.69×10.82×6.8 iron hull, 2 decks

B.	Barclay, Curle & Company.
1870	February. Delivered.
1889	8 March. Sank off the Isle of Wight following a collision with the *Trafalgar*.

City of Sparta 1870 1,193grt. 71.38×10.67×6.83 iron hull, 2 decks

B.	Alexander Stephen & Sons, Glasgow.
1870	March. Delivered as the final 'City' ship to be built by Alexander Stephen & Company.
1889	Sold to S. Goldberg & Sons, Swansea, renamed *Florence Stella*.
1906	Owned by J.B. Linaae, Sandefjord, renamed *Staut*.
1912	Purchased by A. Gordon-Firing.
1917	Sunk by bombs from the German raider *Moewe*.

City of York (2) 1869 1,194grt. 67.87×10.91×6.61

B.	Randolph, Elder & Company, Glasgow.
1869	September. Delivered as a member of the City of Athens class, but with an added poop.
1899	13 July. Wrecked off Rottnest Cove, Fremantle with a cargo of timber and wooden doors. She was on a voyage from San Francisco and twelve crew were lost.

City of Perth (2) 1866 1,188grt. 70.86×10.79×8.29 iron hull

B.	Charles Connell & Company, Glasgow.
1866	May. Delivered for the Calcutta service as a frozen-meat carrier.
1872	16 January. Left Calcutta on a voyage to New York which took seventy-nine days.
1882	14 May. Blown ashore at Timaru during a gale, in which *Benvenue* was wrecked and her crew came aboard *City of Perth*. She then grounded and nine of her crew were lost. She was later sold locally, refloated and towed to Port Chalmers to be repaired.
1883	Purchased by the New Zealand shipping Company, renamed *Turakina*. She completed fifteen round voyages for that company and was their last sailing ship.
1895	14 February. Overtook New Zealand Shipping Company's Ruapehu in the South Atlantic.

| 1899 | Sold to Alexander Bech, Norway, renamed *Elida*. |
| 1914 | May. Broken up. |

City of Oxford	1870 2,319grt. 99.39×11.00×8.44 1,497n. 12k. iron hull, 3 decks
E.	Sgl. screw, 2 cyl. comp. inv., 200 hp, 60 psi. By builder.
P.	80.
B.	Barclay, Curle & Company.
1870	10 October. Launched as George Smith's first steamer. Placed on the Indian service via the Suez Canal.
1870	13 December. Maiden voyage Glasgow–Bombay–Calcutta.
1881	Sold to the Clan Line, renamed *Clan Macduff*.
1881	21 October. On a voyage from Liverpool to Bombay she was lost in the Irish Sea, 40 miles from Cork. Thirty-two of her crew were lost.

City of Cambridge	1870 2,329grt. 99.52×11.00×8.44 1,497n. 12k. iron hull, 3 decks
E.	Sgl. screw, 2 cyl. comp. inv., 200 hp, 60 psi. By builder.
B.	Barclay, Curle & Company.
1870	10 December. Launched.
1876	New boilers fitted.
1881	Sold to the Clan Line, renamed *Clan Maclean*.
1890	28 March. Collided with Matamada Rock as she was entering Galle Harbour, Ceylon. She was repaired at Colombo.
1893	Tpl. exp. engines fitted by Bow, Mclachlan & Company, Paisley.
1903	13 August. On a voyage from Glasgow and Liverpool to Bombay she was wrecked 6 miles north of Cape St Vincent, Portugal.

City of Poonah	1870 2,283grt. 99.27×11.00×8.44 1,456n. 12k. iron hull, 3 decks
E.	Sgl. screw, 2 cyl. comp. inv., 200 hp, 60 psi. By builder.
B.	Charles Connell & Company, Glasgow.
1870	24 November. Launched.
1871	January. Delivered for the Indian service.
1878	Purchased by the Temperley Line, renamed *Clyde*.
1878	9 May. London–Quebec–Montreal service. Then she was on a six-month charter to the Government to transport troops to Cape Town.
1879	7 April. Wrecked on Dyer's Island, Cape Colony.

City of Mecca	1871 2,290grt. 99.27×11.00×8.44 1,436n. 12k. iron hull, 3 decks
E.	Sgl. screw, 2 cyl. comp. inv., 200 hp, 60 psi. By builder.
B.	Charles Connell & Company, Glasgow.
1871	22 March. Launched.
1871	May. Delivered for the service to India.
1881	Sold to the Clan Line, renamed *Clan Macleod*.
1883	Owned by Robert M. Sloman, renamed *Procida*.
1900	20 December. Sold to the Admiralty for use as a coal hulk at Simonstown, South Africa.
1901	Renamed *Nubian*, then *C370*.
1913	Broken up at Morecambe.

City of Manchester (2)   1873   3,126grt.   114.15×11.73×8.96   2,046n.   12k.   iron hull, 3 decks

E.	Sgl. screw, 2 cyl. comp. inv. 400 nhp, 65 psi. By builder.
B.	Barclay, Curle & Company.
1873	Delivered for the Liverpool–Calcutta service. Voyage time of thirty-three days outward and thirty-one days home.
1885	On a voyage from Calcutta to London with a cargo of sugar and cotton she was lost off Ushant. All crew and passengers were saved.

City of Carthage   1873   2,651grt.   109.82×11.22×8.05   1,717n.   iron hull, 2 decks

E.	Sgl. screw, 2 cyl. comp. inv., 350 nhp, 70 psi. By J.& J. Thompson.
B.	Charles Connell & Company, Glasgow.
1873	October. Delivered.
1876	She sailed from Calcutta to the United Kingdom in twenty-nine days.
1890	Sold to N. McLean & Sons, Glasgow, renamed *Straits of Magellan*.
1898	Broken up.

City of Canterbury 1875   3,212grt.   115.73×11.64×8.9   2,100n.   9½k.   iron hull, 3 decks

E.	Sgl. screw, 2 cyl. comp. inv., 440 NHP, 58 psi. By builder.
P.	39.
B.	Barclay, Curle & Company.
1875	January. Delivered.
1897	August. Shipped a record 17,000 chests of tea from Calcutta.
1897	She was ready to sail the next day, grounded and was lost at Hooghly River, Calcutta.

City of Venice (2)   1875   3,372grt.   115.67×11.64×8.9   2,229n.   9½k.   iron hull, 3 decks

E.	Sgl. screw, 2 cyl. comp. inv., 440 nhp, 58 psi. By builder.
P.	39.
B.	Barclay, Curle & Company.
1875	Delivered.
1879	Acted as a transport and headquarters ship for Sir Garnet Wolseley during the Zulu War.
1879	3 July. Ulundi Chief Cetawayo and his wives were taken prisoner aboard with the body of Prince Imperial Bonaparte.
1887	Quadruple expansion engines and new boilers fitted by J. Howden, Glasgow.
1899–1900	Boar War transport.
1901	Owned by Ellerman Lines.
1905	Transferred to Papayanni Line. Fred Swift as managers.
1908	March. Stranded at San Stephano de Cadore, Italy.
1912	27 January. Sold and broken up in Italy.

City of Khios   1878   3,241grt.   116.28×11.73×8.9   2,283n.   9½k.   iron hull, 3 decks

E.	Sgl. screw, 2 cyl. comp. inv., 440 nhp, 58 psi. By J. Howden & Company, Glasgow.
P.	39.
B.	J. Howden & Company, Glasgow.
1878	Delivered.

1901	Transferred to Ellerman Lines.
1904	Transferred to Papayanni, Fred Swift as managers.
1914	4 August. Seized by the Turks at Smyrna.
1915	April. Sunk as a block ship across the entrance to Smyrna Harbour during the Dardanelles campaign.
1919	Broken up.

City of London (2)   1876   3,212grt.   116.31×11.83×8.83   2,056n.   12k.   iron hull, 3 decks

E.	Sgl. screw, 2 cyl. comp. inv., 449 nhp. By J.& J. Thomson, Glasgow.
B.	Charles Connell & Company, Glasgow.
1876	January. Delivered.
1885	Re-boilered.
1900	January. Purchased by Wee Bin & Company, Singapore, renamed *Hong Bee*.
1913	Owned by Ho Hong Steam Ship Company, Singapore (formally Wee Bin & Company).
1917	Employed as a transport around India and East Africa.
1926	Broken up at Singapore.

City of London (2) loading cargo at Birkenhead.

City of Edinburgh (3)   1876   3,230grt.   116.28×11.73×8.83   2,060n.   12k.   iron hull, 3 decks

E.	Sgl. screw, 2 cyl. comp. inv., 449 nhp. By J.& J. Thomson, Glasgow.
B.	Charles Connell & Company, Glasgow.
1876	Delivered.
1886	Triple expansion engines installed by J. & J. Thomson, Glasgow.
1889	Transferred to the City Line.
1900	January. Purchased by Wee Bin & Company, Singapore, renamed *Hong Wan 1*.
1913	Transferred to Ho Hong Steam Ship Company.
1921	21 January. Stranded near Green Island, Swatow.
1926	Broken up.

City of Agra 1879   3,274grt.   117.5×11.79×8.72   2,133n.   12k.   iron hull, 3 decks
E.   Sgl. screw, 2 cyl. comp. inv., 500 nhp, 70 psi. By J.& J. Thomson, Glasgow.
B.   Charles Connell & Company, Glasgow.
1879   May. Delivered.
1897   3 February. Sailed from Liverpool to Calcutta with seventy-five people on board.
1897   22 February. Wrecked during a gale in Aron Bay, 6 miles east of Cape Vilano,
              Finisterre. Thirty-two crew and two stowaways survived.

City of Calcutta (3)   1881   3,836grt.   121.92×12.83×9.17   2,555n.   10k.   iron hull, 3 decks
E.   Sgl. screw, 2 cyl. comp., 583 nhp. By J.& J. Thomson, Glasgow.
B.   Charles Connell & Company, Glasgow.
1881   Delivered.
1889   Transferred to the City Line.
1901   August. Transferred to Ellerman Lines and sold to Wee Bin & Company, Singapore,
              renamed *Hong Moh*.
1913   Transferred to Ho Hong Steam Ship Company.
1916   5 January. Mined off Aden but managed to limp to port.
1921   3 March. On a voyage from Singapore to Amoy she was wrecked off Swatow,
              China.

City of Benares (3)   1882   1,574grt.   78.94×11.64×7.01   1,525n.   iron hull, 2 decks
B.   Barclay, Curle & Company.
1882   September. Delivered as the largest sailing ship in the fleet.
1891   17 September. Arrived at Port Stanley, Falkland Islands with weather damage after a
              mutinous crew turned her back from Cape Horn.
1900   Purchased by G. Revell, Nystad, Finland.
1911   1 October. On a voyage from Passage West and Cobh to Sundsvall she was wrecked
              in the West Kapelle.

City of Madras (3)   1882   1,577grt.   79.25×11.7×7.01   1,527n.   Rig, iron hull, 2 decks
B.   Barclay, Curle & Company.
1882   November. Delivered as the final sailing ship.
1900   Purchased by Hatfield, Cameron & Company, Glasgow, renamed *Wemyss Bay*.
1903   Wrecked on the Pacific coast of Mexico at Mazatlan.

City of Oxford (2)   1882   3,959grt.   121.92×13.17×9.08   2,603n.   12k.   Rig, iron hull, 3 decks
E.   Sgl. screw, 2 cyl. comp., 650 hp, 80 psi. By builder.
B.   Barclay, Curle & Company.
1882   June. Delivered.
1891   Tpl. exp. and high-pressure boilers installed by Barclay, Curle & Company.
1901   August. Purchased by Ellerman Lines.
1903   Transferred to Papayanni for the Alexandria route, Fred Swift as managers.
1914   28 October. Sold to the Admiralty and rebuilt by Harland & Wolff at Belfast as the
              dummy battleship HMS *St Vincent*, renamed *St Vincent* and later renamed *Special
              Services Ship No. 1*.
1915   January. Based at Scapa Flow and patrolled the North Atlantic.
1915   17 July. Became a kite balloon ship.

| 1919 | Returned to Ellerman ownership, placed with Bucknall Line. |
| 1924 | Broken up by Olivia & Company, Italy. |

City of Cambridge (2)   1882   3,788grt.   121.92×12.83×9.02   2,482n.   13½k.   iron hull, 3 decks
E.	Sgl. screw, 2 cyl. comp., 650 hp, 80 psi. By J. & J. Thomson, Glasgow.
P.	80 (saloon).
B.	Workman, Clark & Company, Belfast.
1882	August. Delivered as the first ship built away from the Clyde.
1900	Transferred to the Admiralty as a Boer War transport, becoming *Number 15*.
1901	16 January. In company of HMS *Tarter* she rescued the crew of the cruiser *Sybille*, which had been blown ashore at Lambert's Bay, South Africa.
1901	August. Returned to Ellerman services.
1903	Transferred to Papayanni Line for the Mediterranean services with City Line as managers.
1915	28 March. Twenty-five miles north-west by north from Bishops Rock she was attacked and fired at by a German submarine. She returned the fire and escaped.
1915	8 November. Attacked by a submarine in the Mediterranean and escaped.
1917	3 July. Torpedoed and sunk after attack by the German submarine UC-67, 10 miles north of the Algerian coast.

City of Bombay (2)   1885   4,492grt.   123.14×14.6×9.02   2,941n.   13½k.   iron hull, 3 decks
E.	Sgl. screw, 2 cyl. comp., 650 hp, 80 psi. By J. & J. Thomson, Glasgow.
P.	80 (saloon).
B.	Workman, Clark & Company, Belfast.
1885	August. Delivered as the first ship to exceed 4,000 tons.
1901	August. Owned by Ellerman Lines.
1903	Completed three voyages for the Allan Line on the Glasgow–Liverpool–Philadelphia service. The same charter took place in 1906 and 1907.
1904	Chartered by Lunn & Company, London, to transport Russian troops between Odessa and Vladivostok during the Russo–Japanese War.
1908	May. Broken up in Holland.

City of Dublin (2)   1888   3,267grt.   110.26×13.01×8.05   2,155n.   12k.   steel hull, 2 decks
E.	Sgl. screw, tpl. exp., 325 nhp, 160 psi. By J. & J. Thomson, Glasgow.
B.	Workman, Clark & Company, Belfast.
1888	January. Delivered as the first steel hull.
1900	Sold to Edmund Haselhurst & Company, London. Renamed *Clavering* for the Clavering Steam Ship Company.
1907	31 January. Lost off the Tees.

City of Dundee   1890   3,427grt.   110.26×12.19×8.53   2,572n.   12k.   steel hull, 2 decks
E.	Sgl. screw, tpl. exp., 325 nhp, 160 psi. By J. & J. Thomson, Glasgow.
B.	J. Howden & Company, Glasgow.
1890	Delivered.
1901	August. Owned by Ellerman Lines, Papayanni service, City managed.
1908	4 October. She sank following a collision in fog with Elder & Fyffe's *Matina* in

St George's Channel, on a voyage from Liverpool to Algiers and Alexandria. The captain and two crew were lost.

City of Perth (3)   1890   3,427grt.   110.26×12.19×8.53   2,578n.   12k.   steel hull, 2 decks
E.   Sgl. screw, tpl. exp., 325 nhp, 160 psi. By J. & J. Thomson, Glasgow.
B.   J. Howden & Company, Glasgow.
1890   Delivered.
1901   August. Owned by Ellerman Lines.
1917   12 June. Torpedoed and sunk by U-70, 195 miles south-south-west of Fastnet. Eight crew lost their lives.

City of Vienna (2)   1890   4,672grt.   125.67×14.23×8.93   2,979n.   14k.
E.   Sgl. screw, tpl. exp., 653 nhp. By J. & J. Thomson, Glasgow.
P.   100 (first), 250 (third).
B.   Workman, Clark & Company, Belfast.
1899   7 December. Launched.
1890   February. Delivered. Employed as a Boer War troopship.
1899–1902   Boer War transport *No. 36.*
1901   August. Owned by Ellerman Lines.
1902   Prison ship in the Boer War.
1906   Chartered to Allan Line for three voyages on the Glasgow–Liverpool–Philadelphia service.
1913   August. Purchased by the National Steam Navigation Company Limited, Greece, renamed *Thessaloniki.* Converted to carry 50 first-class, and 50 second- and emigrant-class passengers.
1914   16 February. Maiden voyage Piraeus–Kalamata–Patras–Palermo–New York service.
1915   22 December. Engines failed 500 miles from Sandy Hook, New York. Passengers were transferred to *Patris* which took the ship in tow.
1916   4 January. Engine room flooded and the vessel was scuttled.

City of Sparta (2)   1897   5,179grt.   131.06×15.3×8.69   3,339n.   13k.
E.   Sgl. screw, tpl. exp., 471 nhp. By builder.
P.   80 (first), 16 (second).
B.   Workman, Clark & Company, Belfast.
1896   9 October. Launched.
1897   Delivered.
1901   August. Owned by Ellerman Lines.
1913   Managed by Ellerman & Bucknall for the South African service.
1915   United Kingdom–Far East service via India and Rangoon.
1920   25 October. Transferred to Bucknall's New York–Suez Canal–Calcutta service.
1924   All passenger accommodation removed.
1931   Broken up at Port Glasgow.

City of Corinth (2)   1898   5,443grt.   131.06×15.3×8.69   3,491n.   13k.
E.   Sgl. screw, tpl. exp., 471 nhp. By builder.
P.   80 (first), 16 (second).
B.   Workman, Clark & Company, Belfast.

1898	22 February. Launched.
1901	August. Owned by Ellerman Lines.
1912	September. Purchased by Cie. de Nav. Sud-Atlantique, renamed *Sequana*.
1912 23	November. Maiden voyage Bordeaux–South America.
1916	Managed by Chargeurs Reunis.
1917	8 June. Torpedoed and sunk by UC-72 near Ile d'Yeu.

City of Athens (2)   1899   5,159grt.   131.06×15.3×8.69   3,571n.   13k.

E.	Sgl. screw, tpl. exp., 471 nhp. By builder.
P.	80 (first), 16 (second).
B.	Workman, Clark & Company, Belfast.
1899	Delivered.
1901	Owned by J.R. Ellerman.
1912–14	Operated on the Bucknall service.
1917	10 August. Twenty miles north-west of Cape Town she struck a mine that had been laid by the raider *Wolf II*, and nineteen crew were lost. The majority of those on board were saved by South African Railway's tug *Ludwig Wiener*. The captain had his certificate suspended for six months as he had sailed into a known mined area.

City of Lucknow (3)   1896   3,669grt.   106.83×13.81×5.46   2,371n.   10k.

E.	Sgl. screw, tpl. exp., 220 nhp, 160 psi, 2 sgl. blrs. By builder.
B.	Barclay, Curle & Company, Glasgow.
1896	November. Delivered as *Guyana* for Caw Prentice, Clapperton & Company, Glasgow.
1898	Owned by City Line Limited, renamed *City of Lucknow*.
1900	Owned by George Smith & Sons.
1901	August. Owned by J.R. Ellerman.
1914	August. Requisitioned by the Admiralty as a troopship for the British Expeditionary Force to France.
1916	30 April. Torpedoed and sunk by U-21, 60 miles east of Malta.

Maplemore / *City of Edinburgh* (4)   1899   7,803grt.   139.9×16.00×9.45   5,842n.   10½k.

E.	Sgl. screw, tpl. exp., 608 nhp, 2 dbl. & 1 sgl. blr. By D. Rowan & Sons, Glasgow.
B.	Charles Connell & Company, Glasgow.
1899	February. Delivered as *Maplemore* for Mentmore Limited, William Johnston & Company, Liverpool as managers. Employed as a cattle carrier on the Baltimore–Liverpool route.
1900	Operated as a troopship and to carry horses to South Africa during the Boer War.
1901	September. Owned by the City Line, later renamed *City of Edinburgh*.
1914	August. Requisitioned for the transport of troops, Liverpool–France.
1915	2 July. Torpedoed and damaged by U-39.
1929	May. Broken up.

City of Delhi (3)   1901   4,443grt.   117.5×14.84×8.23   2,826n.   10k.

E.	Sgl. screw, tpl. exp., 311 nhp, 80 psi. By builder.
B.	Barclay, Curle & Company, Glasgow.
1901	Delivered.

| 1923 | 27 August. Sold to N.G. Metaxas, Cephelonia, Greece, renamed *Margarita*. |
| 1925 | 8 October. Lost on the Great Fish Point, South Africa, between Durban and Port Elizabeth. All crew were lost. |

City of Madrid (2)   1901   4,901grt.   123.99×14.87×8.96   3,135n.   11½k.

E.	Sgl. screw, tpl. exp., 552 nhp, 180 psi, 2 dbl. blrs. By builder.
B.	Workman, Clark & Company, Belfast.
1901	July. Delivered to City Line Limited.
1927	Purchased by Soc. Anon Commercials Italo-Cilena, Genoa, renamed *Nitro*.
1932	Broken up in Italy.

City of Benares (4)   1902   6,984grt.   140.36×16.85×9.45   4,321n.   11½k.

E.	Sgl. screw, tpl. exp., 521 nhp. By builder.
P.	47 (first), 44 (second).
B.	Workman, Clark & Company, Belfast.
1901	29 October. Launched.
1902	February. Delivered to Ellerman Lines, George Smith as managers.
1914	8 August. Operated as a troopship for the British Expeditionary Force.
1919	16 January. Operated on the first post-war sailing of the American & Indian Line.
1927	Employed on the American & Manchurian Line New York–Far East service.
1933	February. Broken up at Blyth.

City of Manchester (3)   1903   5,551grt.   128.32×15.7×8.96   3,563n.   10k.

E.	Sgl. screw, tpl. exp., 424 nhp. By builder.
B.	Barclay, Curle & Company, Glasgow.
1902	13 December. Launched.
1903	Delivered to Ellerman Lines, with W.S. Workman as managers.
1921	December. Operated the first Middlesbrough–European Ports–Far East service.
1933	19 March. Arrived at Genoa and broken up at La Spezia.

City of Calcutta (4)   1903   7,512grt.   143.77×17.13×9.72   4,786n.   11½k.

E.	Sgl. screw, tpl. exp., 546 nhp. By builder.
P.	128 (first), 18 (second).
B.	Workman, Clark & Company, Belfast.
1903	17 March. Launched for Ellerman Lines, George Smith as managers.
1914–18	Operated as an Indian Expeditionary Force troopship from Bombay to Marseilles.
1918	3 October. Twenty-five miles south-west of Bardsey Island she was in collision with Elder Dempster's *Burutu*, which sank within nine minutes with a loss of 148 lives. Fifty survivors were picked up by *City of Calcutta*.
1924	26 October. Operated on Bucknall's American & Indian service from New York.
1934	November. Sold to ship-breakers in Japan, renamed *Calcut*.
1935	17 January. Arrived at breakers in Japan.

City of York (3)   1904   7,844grt.   147.83×17.16×9.75   4,935n.   12k.

E.	Sgl. screw, tpl. exp., 599 nhp. By builder.
P.	137 (first), 28 (second).
B.	Workman, Clark & Company, Belfast.

1903	17 December. Launched.
1904	April. Delivered to Ellerman Lines, managed by G. Smith & Sons.
1921	17 August. In service on the American & Indian Line service from New York to India.
1936	September. Purchased by Pedder & Mylchreest, London, renamed *City* to be broken up in Italy. She was later resold and was scrapped in Japan.

City of Karachi 1905 5,547grt. 126.06×15.7×8.9 3,563n. 11k.
E.	Sgl. screw, 4 cyl. quad. exp., 402 nhp. By builder.
P.	70 (first), 24 (second).
B.	Workman, Clark & Company, Belfast.
1905	Delivered to Ellerman Lines, George Smith as managers.
1913–14	On Bucknall's South Africa service.
1926	On the South Africa service.
1934	17 October. Sold to be broken up in Japan, renamed *Karachi*.

City of Glasgow (3) 1906 6,457grt. 135.03×16.34×9.23 4,112n. 11k.
E.	Sgl. screw, 4 cyl. quad. exp., 481 nhp. By builder.
P.	102 (first), 45 (second).
B.	Workman, Clark & Company, Belfast.
1906	Delivered to Ellerman Lines, George Smith & Sons as managers.
1914	August. Operated as a British Expeditionary Force troopship.
1918	1 September. Torpedoed and sunk by UB-118, 21 miles east-by-north of Tuskar Rock, twelve people were lost.

City of London (3) 1907 8,815grt. 154.23×17.62×9.9 5,693n. 15k.
E.	Sgl. screw, 4 cyl. quad. exp., 660 nhp, 215 psi, 2 dbl., 2 sgl. blrs. By builder.
P.	272 (first), 64 (second).
B.	Workman, Clark & Company, Belfast.
1906	November. Launched. She was built with a long bridge deck, long forecastle and long poop, Nos 2 and 4 hatchways being in the comparatively short well decks. Above the bridge was a second upper bridge deck, closed in except at the fore end where its sides were open, forming a short promenade. This opening extended further aft on the starboard side than on the port. Above this was a long deckhouse, with No. 3 hatchway between its fore end and the bridge. The ship's machinery consisted of a set of quadruple-expansion engines driving a single screw. There were two double-ended and two single-ended cylindrical boilers providing steam at 215 lbs per sq. in. At full speed she burned about 80 tons of coal a day, and 930 tons were carried in permanent bunkers. Accommodation was provided for 272 first-class and 64 second-class passengers with the first class having the whole midships of the ship to themselves. Most of the cabins contained bedsteads instead of bunks and some cabins *de luxe* were provided. A swimming pool was rigged on the after deck when the weather permitted. The second-class passengers had their accommodation in and above the poop. After the First World War a pair of tall ventilators were fitted just forward of the funnel and an extra boat was carried on each side of a short length of deck, a large house was

	built on top of the poop house and she was given a yard on the foremast and a gaff on the main.
1907	February. Delivered for the Bombay service.
1909	Recorded a voyage of eighteen days nineteen hours from Bombay to London.
1916	January. Requisitioned by the Admiralty and converted into an Armed Merchant Cruiser, eight 6-inch guns and two 6 pounders fitted. Operated in the Far East patrolling the South China coast and the Sunda Strait looking for German raiders.
1919	Returned to builder.
1919	5 July. Sailed on the Indian service.
1923	Calcutta–Liverpool in twenty-three days.
1931–35	Operated on Ellerman & Bucknall's South African service and later to India.
1939	November. Requisitioned as a troopship with a capacity for 1,400 troops.
1940	In collision with *Menelaus* in fog in a North Atlantic convoy and both vessels were damaged.
1940	25 December. Attacked by the German cruiser *Admiral Hipper*, west of Sierra Leone. *Admiral Hipper* was attacked by HMS *Berwick* and terminated the attack. *City of Derby* and *City of Canterbury* were in the same convoy.
1941	April. Landed troops at Suda Bay during the Greek campaign and later evacuated over 3,700 troops from Crete to Alexandria. Her master received the DSC.
1946	January. Decommissioned.
1946	13 May. Arrived at Dalmuir to be broken up.

City of Paris (2)	1907 9,191grt. 150.33×17.59×9.9 5,935n. 15k.
E.	Sgl. screw, 4 cyl. quad. exp., 660 nhp, 215 psi, 2 dbl., 2 sgl. ended blrs. By builder.
P.	272 (first), 64 (second).
B.	Barclay, Curle & Company.
1907	10 August. Launched.
1907	Delivered to Ellerman Lines, George Smith & Sons as managers. Liverpool–Bombay service.
1911	Liverpool–Bombay service of nineteen days one hour.
1915	Requisitioned as a troopship and later took Government officials to India.
1917	4 April. On a voyage from India to Marseilles she was torpedoed by U-52, 46 miles south-by-east of Cap d'Antibes. The German submarine then sank her with a second torpedo. Four lifeboats were later found with forty-one bodies in them and a total of 122 lives were lost.

City of Poona	1912 7,467grt. 137.77×17.25×9.51 4,766n. 12k.
E.	Twin screw, 2×4 cyl. quad. exp., 451 nhp. By Wallsend Slipway & Engineering Company, Newcastle.
P.	88 (first), 50 (second).
B.	Swan Hunter & Wigham Richardson, Newcastle.
1912	21 January. Launched as the first twin-screw vessel in the fleet.
1929	9 September. Operated on the American & Indian Line from New York to India.
1934	November. Broken up in Japan.

City of Exeter	1914 9,447grt. 148.35×17.95×9.93 6,023n. 12k.
E.	Twin screw, 2×4 cyl. quad. exp., 584 nhp, 225 psi. By builder.
P.	180 (first), 62 (second).
B.	Workman, Clark & Company, Belfast.
1914	1 April. Launched.
1914	July. Delivered to Ellerman Lines, George Smith & Sons as agents. First cruiser stern passenger ship in the fleet, and fitted with a removable funnel for the Manchester Ship Canal service. Built with a long bridge with an upper bridge erection open at its fore end and above that the navigating bridge on a short deck and the boat deck abaft of No 3 hatchway. There were five holds and six hatchways, No. 3 hold being able to be used as a deep tank. Cargo was worked by fifteen derricks and steam winches. Subdivision was by eight main bulkheads. The eight lifeboats were under Welin davits, while two smaller boats were carried on the poop under ordinary round bar davits. The twin screws were driven by quadruple expansion engines constructed by the builders. Steam was provided by two double-ended boilers and one single-ended, coal burning at 225 lbs psi. The consumption was 70 tons a day and the bunker capacity was 1,890 tons. She carried 180 first- and 62 second-class passengers in accommodation described as 'being exceptionally good without being luxurious, comfortable and homely, similar to that of a good class family hotel'.
1914	August. Operated as an Indian Army troopship.
1915	In service with Ellerman & Bucknall.
1915	7 May. Chased by a submarine off Queenstown but escaped unharmed. *City of Exeter*, *Etonian* and the tanker *Narragansett* were answering the distress calls from the Cunard liner *Lusitania* but had to abandon the search when two submarines were sighted near them.
1917	Under the Liner Requisition Scheme in which her voyages and cargoes were directed by the Government.
1917	11 June. Collided with a mine 200 miles from Bombay but managed to get to port safety.
1919	Returned to service.
1933	On Ellerman & Bucknall service to east African and South African ports, although occasionally returning to the Indian service when required.
1940	1 May. After passing the German Merchant Cruiser *Atlantis*, disguised as the *Kashii Maru*, she radioed and reported her as a suspicious vessel. *Atlantis* had decided to let the *City of Exeter* proceed as she did not have room to accommodate her passengers. The master of the *City of Exeter* reported the sighting of *Kashii Maru* and as a result the *Atlantis* had to adopt another disguise and pose as the Dutch motor ship *Abbekerk*.
1939	Chartered by the British Government to take a diplomatic delegation to Russia.
1942	Suffered a small fire at Bombay.
1946	Transported King Zog of Albania and family back from Britain to Port Said.
1950	25 March. Sailed on her last round voyage from Birkenhead to Bombay and Karachi.
1950	11 July. Left the Mersey in tow of Steel & Bennie's *Brigadier* and *Strongbow* for Dalmuir.

City of Oran.

City of Oran   1915   7,784grt.   141.88×17.71×9.66   5,048n.   11½k.
E.   Sgl. screw, tpl. exp., 628 nhp, 220 psi, 3 sgl. blrs. By Central Marine Engine
               Works, West Hartlepool.
B.   William Gray & Company Limited, West Hartlepool.
1915   September. Delivered, owned by the City of Oran Steam Ship Company.
1916   31 December. Attacked and escaped from a German U-boat in the English
               Channel.
1920   Transferred to Montgomerie & Workman Limited, W.S. Workman as managers.
1933   Managed by the City Line.
1936   Transferred to Ellerman Lines Limited.
1943   2 August. In convoy CB21 she was torpedoed by U-196 off Mozambique.
1943   3 August. Sunk by escort vessels.

City of Birmingham (2)   1917   6,182grt.   119.18×16.52×8.8   4,002n.   11k.
E.   Sgl. screw, tpl. exp., 581 nhp, 220 psi, 3 sgl. blrs. By Central Marine Engine Works,
               West Hartlepool.
B.   William Gray & Company Limited, West Hartlepool.
1917   September. Delivered to Ellerman Lines and requisitioned for government
               service.
1922   Transferred to City Line, George Smith & Sons as managers.
1940   16 August. Left Fife in a convoy and collided with a mine off Spurn Head.

City of Bagdad   1919   7,506grt.   143.07×17.8×9.84   4,710n.   12k.
E.   Sgl. screw, tpl. exp., 710 nhp, 220 psi, 4 sgl. blrs. By builder.
B.   Tecklenborg AG, Geestemunde.
1919   Completed as *Gierfels* for DD-G 'Hansa'. Handed to the Shipping Controller,
               G. Thompson & Company, Glasgow as managers.
1920   Owned by Montgomerie and Workman Limited, W.0S. Workman as managers,
               renamed *City of Bagdad*.
1927   Managed by George Smith & Sons.
1933   Transferred to W.S. Workman as managers.
1936   Owned by Ellerman Lines Limited.
1940   11 July. Sunk by the German Raider *Atlantis*, 400 miles west of Addu Atol in the
               Indian Ocean.

City of Lucknow (4)   1908   7,248grt.   134.56×16.06×9.02   4,520n.   12k.
E.   Twin screw, 2× tpl. exp., 750 nhp, 213 psi, 4 sgl. blrs. By builder.
P.   89 (first), 28 (second).
B.   A. Reiherstieg, Hamburg.
1908   19 November. Launched as *Heluan* for DD-G 'Kosmos', Hamburg.
1920   Owned by the City of Oran Steam Ship Company, renamed *City of Lucknow*.
1921   21 October. Operated on Bucknall's American & Indian Line New York to India
                service.
1926   24 November. Sold to Hamburg America Line, renamed *Heluan*.
1931   November. Broken up at Osaka.

City of Valencia 1908   7,329grt.   134.84×16.06×9.02   4,539n.   12k.
E.   Twin screw, 2×tpl. exp., 750 nhp, 213 psi, 4 sgl. blrs. By builder.
P.   89 (first), 28 (second).
B.   A Reiherstieg, Hamburg.
1908   14 January. Launched as *Roda* for DD-G 'Kosmos', Hamburg.
1920   Owned by City Line Limited, W.S. Workman as managers, renamed *City of
                Valencia* for the Karachi service.
1921   18 November. Operated on the American & Indian Line service.
1933   Laid up at Liverpool.
1934   February. Broken up at Blyth.

City of Milan   1907   4,222grt.   118.2×15.5×7.68   2,558n.   11k.
E.   Sgl. screw, tpl. exp., 473 nhp, 213 psi, 3 sgl. blrs. By builder.
B.   Flensburger S.G., Flensburg.
1907   2 March. Launched as *Plauen* for Deutsch-Australische D-G, Hamburg.
1914   August. At the start of the First World War she was at Hamburg.
1917   Converted into an auxiliary cruiser by the German Navy, work abandoned.
1918   17 December. Returned to owners.
1919   13 April. Operated by the Shipping Controller with Watts, Watts & Company as
                managers.
1921   Purchased by Ellerman Lines, renamed *City of Milan*, owned by City Line
                Limited.
1930   Sold to the Cia. Colonial de Nav., Lisbon, renamed *Ganda*.
1941   20 June. Torpedoed and sunk by U-123, west of Cape St Vincent.

City of Cambridge (3)   1920   7,058grt.   138.38×17.74×10.52   4,557n.   11k.
E.   Sgl. screw, 4 cyl. quad. exp., 647 nhp, 225 psi, 3 sgl. blrs. By builder.
B.   Workman, Clark & Company, Belfast.
1920   Delivered to City Line Limited, W.S. Workman as managers.
1934   6 October. Wrecked on Pratas Reef in the China Sea.

City of Simla   1921   9,468grt.   145.3×17.74×9.54   5,955n.   11k.
E.   Twin screw, 4 drg steam turb., 1,243 nhp, 225 psi, 5 sgl. blrs. By Central Marine
                Engine Works, West Hartlepool.
P.   260 (first).
B.   William Gray & Company Limited, West Hartlepool.

1921	November. Delivered to City Line Limited, George Smith as managers, with a removable funnel top for the Manchester Ship Canal service. Maiden voyage to Yokohama, then to India.
1925	Operated on the Bucknall service to South Africa.
1932–33	Laid up on the River Clyde.
1940	21 September. Torpedoed and sunk by U-138 off the Outer Hebrides in convoy OB 216. The convoy sailed from the Clyde to the United States and four ships were sunk by U-138.

City of Simla.

City of Nagpur (2).

City of Nagpur (2)	1922 10,146grt. 149.00×18.07×12.19 6,280n. 14k.
E.	Sgl. screw, 4 cyl. quad. exp., 1,038 nhp, 230 psi, 5 sgl. blrs. By builder.
P.	350.
B.	Workman, Clark & Company, Belfast.
1922	30 May. Launched.
1922	12 September. Delivered to Ellerman Lines as the first ship in the fleet over 10,000 tons. City Line Limited as managers.
1922	12 October. Maiden voyage Glasgow–Liverpool–Bombay then to the Japan service.

1933	Laid up at Bombay.
1934	Operated on the South Africa service.
1936–39	Operated summer cruises to the Norwegian Fjords.
1938	Passenger accommodation refurbished by William Gray & Company Limited, West Hartlepool.
1939	September. Final summer cruise cancelled.
1941	29 April. On her fifth wartime voyage she was torpedoed and sunk by U-75, 900 miles west of Fastnet. There were 300 passengers, including naval, military and RAF personnel, 106 women and 44 children, and 215 European and Indian crew on board. The first torpedo hit the engine room and the vessel immediately began to list. Order was maintained and Captain Lloyd directed all hands into their respective boats, then to lie off whilst he remained on the bridge and a volunteer gun crew manned the Bofors gun. Fifteen minutes later a second torpedo opened up the forward holds and the enemy submarine surfaced. The Bofors crew went into action but the vessels list was increasing too rapidly to make accurate firing possible. The submarine's gun replied and a shell tore through the funnel, another crashed into the glass dome over the salon and machine-gun fire forced the gun crew to take to the boats. The vessel was soon ablaze from the bridge aft, and it was only then that Captain Lloyd dropped over the side on a rope and onto a raft to watch his ship sink. One passenger and ten crew were lost. The lifeboats remained together for three days until spotted by a Catalina flying boat which directed HMS *Hurricane* to the rescue. *Hurricane* later picked up 504 survivors. Captain Lloyd was awarded the OBE for his conduct but it was several months before he was well enough to receive it at Buckingham Palace. He was later appointed the first commodore of the City Line.

City of Paris (3)   1922   10,840grt.   149.74×18.07×9.94   6,855n.   14k.

E.	Sgl. screw, 3 drg steam turb., 1,315 nhp, 225 psi, 5 sgl. blrs. By Wallsend Slipway Company, Newcastle.
P.	230 (first), 100 (second).
B.	Swan Hunter & Wigham Richardson, Newcastle.
1921	She was designed with two overall decks and a shelter deck, six holds and hatchways and eight main bulkheads. Above the shelter deck was a long promenade deck with a boat deck above in two parts, divided by the gap for No. 3 hatchway. She was a single screw vessel driven by a set of double reduction geared turbines of impulse-reaction type, both the ahead and astern HP and LP turbines being in series. Five single-ended boilers provided steam at 225 lbs per sq.inch. Fitted with superheaters and forced draft they had four furnaces each, a total heating surface of 15,765 sq.ft. and burned coal at the rate of 90 tons per day, with permanent bunkers holding 1,212 tons of coal. Her original accommodation was for 230 first- and 100 second-class passengers, while third-class could be berthed in two of the upper 'tween decks if required. However, the numbers were soon altered to 255 first- and 44 second-class.
1921	September. Ran trials and was then fitted out and completed at Penhoet, St Nazaire, because of a joiner's strike at the builders. Delivered three months late.
1922	February. Delivered. Maiden voyage UK–Japan, then on the India service. Black hull.
1924	Operated on cruises to the northern capitals in Ellerman's Wilson colours. Grey hull later.

City of Paris (3).

1932	Laid up at Garloch.
1936	Operated on the South African service.
1939–45	Requisitioned as a troopship.
1939	16 September. Collided with a mine in the River Thames, which did considerable damage, although she made port and was repaired. This was the first damage to a British ship caused by this type of mine.
1940	16 June. Transported 600 Senegalese troops from Kontonu to Bordeaux.
1940	20 June. Reinforcements were too late and France collapsed, and she then transported the troops to Dakar.
1940	September. Left the Clyde for South Africa with 100 children on board to be evacuated.
1940–41	September–February. Troop-carrying to the Middle East via the Cape with accommodation for 1,500 troops.
1942	February. Sent to Bombay and from there to Singapore with Australian troops and a detachment of nurses, in a large convoy. However, Singapore fell and she was diverted to the East Indies. The Battle of the Java Sea followed and she was again diverted, this time to Adelaide, for fear of a Japanese invasion of Australia. She then ran between Australia, Ceylon and India.
1942	4 June. Arrived at Bombay. She was painted in red, white and blue stripes when she carried the Japanese delegation from Bombay to Lourenco Marques. She was painted with the word 'Diplomatic' in 4ft letters on her side. There were also deck markings fore and aft for the benefit of aircraft, and at night these marks were floodlit. It was reported that 'her Japanese passengers behaved excellently and on disembarking handed a letter to the master thanking him for the consideration shown and for their safe and pleasant voyage.' This was much appreciated by the master and crew but it was an embarrassment to the Japanese Government, who announced that there had actually been brutality shown to its nationals while on passage on a British ship.
1943	Returned to troop-carrying duties in the Indian Ocean, between Australia, India and Africa. During the year she covered 56,000 miles and carried 21,500 troops.
1944	Converted to a personnel ship for the Pacific Fleet Train. However, the war ended before this work could be completed.
1945	September. Used as an accommodation ship at Hong Kong for the men engaged in restoring the dockyard to a workable condition.

1946	Operated as a troopship and painted with a white hull, broad blue band and yellow funnel.
1947	January. Refitted by builder for the Ellerman & Bucknall service. Passenger accommodation was renewed and improved for 168 passengers in single and double rooms, all with hot and cold running water. A new lounge at the fore end of the promenade deck and a bar and veranda café at its aft end was fitted. Eleven single *de luxe* rooms were also fitted on the deck.
1955	Final voyage Lourenco Marques–Rotterdam–London–Hull–Middlesbrough.
1956	25 February. Arrived at Newport to be broken up by J. Cashmore & Company. She was thirty-four years old and the last survivor of the group of sister ships. *City of Simla* was torpedoed in 1940, *City of Nagpur* in 1941 and *City of Canterbury* was scrapped in 1953. The slightly later *City of Hong Kong* had been sold in 1951 and broken up four years later.

City of Canterbury (2)   1922   8,421grt.   136.67×17.19×9.51   5,290n.   13k.

E.	Sgl. screw, 4 cyl. quad., 4,250 ihp at 81 rpm, 230 psi, 4 blrs. By Wallsend Slipway Company, Newcastle.
P.	120 (first), 48 (second).
B.	Swan Hunter & Wigham Richardson, Newcastle.
1922	February. Delivered to City Line for the Indian service, W.S. Workman as managers. Black hull. She was built with two overall decks, a long forecastle and combined bridge and poop. She had ten main bulkheads and seven holds and hatchways, with a promenade deck amidships and bridge and boat deck above. Her single screw was driven by a quadruple-expansion engine with cylinders 26¾, 38½, 55½ and 80 inches diameter, and a stroke of 51 ins. At 81 rpm. it produced 4,250 ihp. There were four single-ended boilers working at 230 lbs per sq.inch and burning coal at the rate of about 70 tons per day. Passenger accommodation was for 90 first, 40–80 first/second interchangeable and 48 second class. This included a dining room, lounge, smoking room and nursery.
1924	Occasionally she sailed inbound from Bombay–Durban–Cape Town–UK.
1930	Fitted with a Metropolitan Vickers impulse electric exhaust turbine which increased her power by 23 per cent, giving her a service speed of 14 knots. She returned to the Indian service but with occasional voyages on the Ellerman & Bucknall routes.

City of Canterbury (2).

1940	Requisitioned by the Admiralty as a troopship to carry 1,500 people.
1940	25 December. As Commodore ship in the convoy with 1,500 troops on board destined for the Middle East, she was attacked by the German heavy cruiser *Admiral Hipper*. The *Admiral Hipper* left the scene when she was fired upon by HMS *Berwick*.
1941	February. Loaded anti-aircraft personnel and 1,500 marines at Durban and took them to Crete.
1941	May. Carried the Greek crown jewels and two Greek princesses from Suda Bay in Crete to Alexandria after the capitulation of Greece to Germany. On board were also the survivors of twelve ships that had been sunk. She carried 1,000 Italian prisoners of war, with 70 guards to Durban and was then employed on troop-carrying duties along the east coast of Africa.
1942	January. Transported troops from Durban to Singapore. She lay at Durban for a time acting as a temporary barracks for Royal Naval ratings. She then made further voyages with prisoners from Berbera to Mombasa, arriving there with a fire in her bunkers.
1942	February. On arrival at Singapore she was attacked by eighteen Japanese bombers. Following further attacks on her as she evacuated 2,000 refugees, both military and civil, landing them all in Batavia. Captain Percival and Mr Hetherington, the chief officer, were awarded the OBE and MBE respectively. She left Batavia with 500 naval survivors of sunken warships as commodore ship of a convoy for Colombo. She was later sent to Bombay for overhaul and repair of the damage sustained during her time at Singapore.
1942	Requisitioned as a repatriation ship exchanging Japanese and Allied civilians at Lourenco Marques, and from there she sailed for Australia and took Australian troops to the Middle East, then on to Bombay.
1943	Left Bombay with a full complement of United States troops for Khorramshahr and after discharging them she went to Basrah and embarked Indian troops for Bombay.
1943	June. Took on 900 troops who were training for the Sicily, landings at Suez for Alexandria. She carried them to the invasion and then proceeded to Malta for more troops.
1943–44	Operated in the Mediterranean.
1944	May. Returned to the Clyde.
1944	9 June. Embarked 1,300 troops at Woolwich for the Normandy beaches and landed them at Arromanches. Following service at the Omaha and Utah beaches.
1944	July. She sailed to the Clyde and was returned to the Ellerman Lines for the India service.
1945	Chartered from Ellerman to carry troops between India and Burma.
1947	Overhaul at her builders on the Tyne and converted to burn oil fuel. All her public rooms were redesigned and refurbished, and larger staterooms were provided for 127 first-class passengers, with various grades of cabins. A bronze plaque commemorating her war service was put up in the smoke room.
1947	May. Returned to service.
1953	1 June. Sold to be broken up.

City of Venice (3)   1924   8,762grt.   138.74×17.71×9.54   5,492n.   14k.
E.   Sgl. screw, 4 cyl. quad. exp., 230 psi, 4 sgl. blrs. By builder.

P.   133 (first), 32 (second).
B.   Workman, Clark & Company, Belfast.
1924   6 February. Launched.
1924   April. Delivered to Ellerman Lines for the Indian service, George Smith & Sons as managers.
1924   September. Transferred to the American & Indian service from New York to Calcutta.
1932   Fitted with Bauer-Wach LP exhaust turbine driving a generator-motor geared to the shaft. Laid up at Liverpool.
1936   Took Princess Mary, Princess Royal and Lord Lascelles to Cyprus.
1943   24 June. Sailed from the Clyde in convoy KMS 18B.
1943   4 July. Torpedoed by U-375 off Cape Tenez, in the Mediterranean and set on fire on way to Operation Husky, the invasion of Sicily. The South American Saint Line vessel *St Essylt* and Lamport & Holt's *Devis* were also sunk.

City of Hong Kong   1924   9,606grt.   143.32×18.74×9.81   6,071n.   12½k.
E.   Sgl. screw, 4 cyl. quad. exp., 837 nhp, 225 psi, 4 sgl. blrs. By builder.
P.   104 (first).
B.   Earle's Shipbuilding & Engineering Company, Hull.
1923   Laid down as *Colorado* for Ellerman's Wilson Line.
1923   11 December. Launched as *City of Hong Kong* for Ellerman Lines. An order for a sister ship was cancelled.
1924   15 May. Trials.
1924   May. Delivered to the City Line for the Indian service.
1926   Managed by Ellerman & Bucknall and placed on the South African service.
1930   Low-pressure exhaust turbine driving a reversible electric generator was fitted. This increased her power by around a third and fuel consumption was reduced from 73 to 66 tons a day and her service speed increased to 13½ knots.
1930   26 November. Returned to service on the New York to Calcutta route. Later transferred to Ellerman & Bucknall.
1936   Transferred to the City Line.
1939–45   Requisitioned as a troopship.
1946   Operated to Bombay. In collision with *Rippingham Grange* at Port Said.

City of HongKong.

1951	August. Purchased by Fratelli Grimaldi Armatori, Genoa, renamed *Centauro* for the Central America service.
1953	Major overhaul at Genoa.
1955	February. On a voyage from Naples to Hampton Roads she docked at Bermuda to refuel. During a storm she lost both anchors and went aground. She was refloated by two tugs and taken in tow to Hampton Roads by the *Foundation Francis*.
1955	March. Sailed from Hampton Roads for Ceuta–Bagnoli–Genoa.
1955	29 April. Laid up at Genoa.
1955	15 June. Left in tow for Savona, where she was broken up.

City of Delhi (4)   1925   7,443grt   137.31×17.86×9.78   4,731n.   12½k.

E.	Sgl. screw, 4 cyl. quad. exp., Baucer–Wach exhaust turb. drg to shaft by hydraulic coupling, 225 psi, 3 sgl. blrs. By Central Marine Engine Works, West Hartlepool.
B.	William Gray & Company Limited, Wear Shipyard, Sunderland.
1925	July. Delivered to Ellerman Lines, W. S. Workman as managers.
1956	Sold to British Iron & Steel Limited, London.
1957	May. Broken up on the Firth of Forth, by P. & W. McLellan Limited.

City of Mandalay   1925   7,049grt.   135.09×17.65×9.72   4,511n.   14k.

E.	Sgl. screw, tpl. exp., 644 nhp. By Wallsend Slipway Company, Newcastle.
B.	Swan Hunter & Wigham Richardson, Newcastle.
1925	January. Delivered to Ellerman Lines, W.S. Workman as managers. Later operated on Ellerman & Bucknall services with a black hull.
1939	17 October. She was Ellerman's first Second World War loss when she was torpedoed and sunk by U-46, off Cape Finisterre as part of Convoy HG3. The convoy was attacked by four German U-boats, U-46, U-37, U-45 and U-48, and it was believed to be the first time they had attacked a convoy as a pack.

City of Mandalay.

City of Dieppe 1929 7,958grt. 141.88×17.74×9.81 4,850n. 14k.

E.	Sgl. screw, 4 cyl. quad. exp. with LP drg turb. and hydraulic coupling to shaft. By Central Marine Engineering Works, West Hartlepool.
B.	B. William Gray & Company Limited, West Hartlepool.
1929	June. Delivered to Ellerman Lines, City Line as managers. Builders' 1,000th ship.
1934	Lengthened to 152.95 and fitted with a Maier bow. Speed increased to 16 knots.
1937	Transferred to Ellerman & Bucknall.
1941	She was stationed at Freetown as a store-ship for the Royal Navy, relieving *City of Tokio*. The growth on the hulls of the store-ships resulted in them being unfit for further service and when they returned to the United Kingdom they were normally broken up.
1943	Sailed from Liverpool to the East Indies Fleet.
1944	January. Took up station at Trincomalee, Ceylon.
1945	January. Sailed to Australia to join the British Pacific Fleet which was assembling in Sydney Harbour.
1945	6 April. Arrived at San Pedro Bay in the Philippines with supplies for the convoy. In charge of the Fleet Train was Rear Admiral Fisher, flying his flag on HMS *Lothian* (ex *City of Edinburgh*).
1945	June. Returned to Sydney for replenishments.
1945	25 August. Left Manus after providing stores to ships anchored in the bay.
1945	2 September. Arrived Tokyo Bay, being present when General MacArthur accepted the Japanese surrender on board USS *Missouri*. She was berthed alongside the harbour wall with the hospital ship *Tjitjalengka* at the next berth.
1945	September. Sailed to Sasebo, close to Nagasaki and then made a rendezvous with the British Task Force.
1945	15 September. Joined the Task Force en route to Shanghai with HMS *Belfast* as flagship with Captain R.M. Dick, flying the flag of Rear Admiral. RN Services.
1945	19 September. The twenty-six vessels in the fleet began the voyage up the Whangpoo River to Shanghai.
1945	21 September. Arrived at Shanghai, moored opposite the Bund and later tied up alongside Pootung Wharf. Shanghai was returned to Chinese sovereignty while she was berthed in the city.
1945	October. Sailed for Hong Kong.
1956	March. Sold to Eastman Shipping Company, Nassau, renamed *Eastman*.
1959	Broken up.

City of Benares (5) 1936 11,081grt. 155.14×19.11×10.54 7,758n. 15k.

E.	Sgl. screw, geared turb. 6,000 shp. By Cammell Laird & Company Limited.
P.	219 (first).
B.	Barclay, Curle & Company.
1936	5 August. Launched.
1936	15 October. Delivered as the only two-funnelled ship in the fleet. She was designed with a total of five decks of which three were overall length, the shelter deck, upper and main decks. Above these were the promenade and boat decks amidships, and a forecastle. An orlop deck was fitted in No. 1 hold. There were nine main bulkheads, the foremost one, the collision bulkhead, being up to the shelter deck and others up to the upper deck. The single screw was driven by

Parsons impulse-reaction turbines, sgl. reduction geared to the shaft. Five single-ended cylindrical boilers working at 275 lbs psi supplied the steam. Fitted with superheaters, they gave 180°C at the engines. Under forced draught, they were coal burning but they and the various bunkers and tanks were so arranged and fitted as to be readily converted to oil fuel. The forward funnel was a dummy and contained the emergency generator and fuel tanks, and exhaust draught fans. Uptakes from all five boilers led to the aft funnel. She had accommodation for 219 first-class passengers. The covered promenade deck had large Beclawat windows and a dance space was provided, with a special children's room on the shelter deck. The lounge and ballroom were on the promenade deck, with the card room. Aft of that was an entrance hall and veranda café with a swimming pool between the mainmast and No. 5 hatchway. This had underwater floodlighting and could also be covered over to form additional dance space for dancing on deck. On the upper deck a number of passenger rooms were followed by the dining saloon, kitchens, bakeries and more cabins. Aft of No.6 hatchway were the firemen's and seaman's accommodation and the main deck was mainly for store rooms and cargo, with stewards quarters aft. Aft of No.2 hatchway were a library and writing room, passenger cabins, children's room and playground and aft, the crew's galleys.

BARCLAY CURLE
GLASGOW:

ELLERMAN PASSENGER LINER
"CITY OF BENARES"

FOUR BUILDING BERTHS
700' 0' LONG
MODERN APPLIANCES
GRAVING DOCK PROPRIETORS
MODERN REPAIR
AND FITTING OUT
WORKS
DEEP WATER WHARVES
MARINE STEAM ENGINES
DOXFORD DIESELS
WERKSPOOR DIESELS

BUILDERS OF FIRST CLASS PASSENGER LINERS, CARGO SHIPS, OIL TANKERS, COASTERS, ETC.

**HEAD OFFICE & SHIPYARD—
CLYDEHOLM SHIPYARD**
GLASGOW, W.4.

LONDON OFFICE—21 RUSSELL SQUARE, W.C. I.

Barclay Curle advertisement featuring *City of Benares*, 1942.

1936	10 October. Ran trials on the Clyde, reached 17¾ knots.
1936	16 October. Left the Clyde for Liverpool.
1936	24 October. Maiden voyage Liverpool–Bombay via Marseilles and Suez.
1940	12 September. With 209 crew, 6 convoy staff and 191 passengers she left Princes Landing Stage at Liverpool and anchored in the River Mersey.
1940	13 September. Sailed at 18.00 as the commodore ship of a nineteen-ship convoy, with one destroyer and two sloops.
1940	17 September. At 01.00 the escorts left the convoy and at 22.05 she was hit by a torpedo from U-48, 600 miles from land. She started to settle by the stern, listing to port and the captain ordered to abandon ship. All lifeboats were launched but several turned over. *City of Benares* sank at 22.45 with a loss of 248 lives. Seventy-seven of these were children who were being sent to Canada under the Government's 'Children's Overseas Evacuation Board'.
1940	18 September. HMS *Hurricane* rescued 105 survivors but five died later on the ship.
1940	25 September. A Sunderland flying boat of the Royal Australian Navy, on patrol in the Atlantic, sighted a lifeboat containing 47 people, including six children. The aircraft later dropped food to the survivors. The destroyer HMS *Anthony* picked the forty-five survivors up at 17.00 and they were taken to Greenock. There were 145 survivors and of these 88 were crew and 57 passengers.

City of Karachi (2)   1937   7,139grt.   141.52×18.04×9.51   15k.

E.	Sgl. screw, 3 srg Parsons Marine turb. By builder.
B.	Barclay, Curle & Company.
1937	19 October. Launched.
1938	Delivered to City Line.
1941	13 April. Attacked by bombers at Volo, Crete, during the evacuation of the island and beached next day. The Ellerman & Papayanni vessel Destro attempted to assist with anti-aircraft fire but *City of Karachi* sank.

City of Karachi.

City of Edinburgh (5)   1938   8,036grt.   157.21×19.02×9.54   3,965n.   15k.

E.	Twin screw, 2×3 srg turb., 1,867 nhp, 265 psi, 6 sgl. blrs. By builder.
B.	Cammell Laird & Company Limited, Birkenhead.
1938	14 April. Launched.
1938	11–12 August. Trials.
1938	August. Delivered to Ellerman Lines, with City Line Limited as managers. USA–Australia–New Zealand service.
1941	While berthed at Takordai, she caught fire and was towed out to sea, as there was a possibility that she would capsize and block the port. The fire was eventually brought under control.
1942	16 February. Sailed from the Clyde with ammunition, bombs and Matilda, Crusader and Valentine tanks, twelve of which were stowed on deck. During bad weather some of the tanks broke loose and the ship had to return to the Clyde.
1942	23 March. Sailed from the Clyde in convoy with the cruiser HMS *Repulse* as escort.
1942	18 May. Arrived at Suez, berthing at Port Said the following day.
1942	29 May. Sailed for Haifa after discharging her cargo.
1942	31 May. Loaded her cargo of benzene, coal, kerosene, ammunition and bombs, flour, barley and wheat.
1942	12 June. Crew supplemented by eighty-four officers and men of the Royal Navy and the Royal Air Force, and she left Haifa in convoy for Malta.
1942	13 June. Convoy joined by ships from Port Said and Alexandria and other warships. It was attacked by ten enemy aircraft which continued for the rest of the day, throughout the night and the following day. HMS *Hermione* was sunk with the loss of eight-two lives.
1942	16 June. Convoy arrived at Alexandria and it was decided to abandon the voyage to Malta. The additional personnel left the ship and the cargo was discharged.
1942	26 November. In convoy KMF4 she carried troops for Operation Torch from the Clyde. D. Robertson was a soldier on the Donaldson Line *Letitia*, which was a member of the convoy KMF4 and he later reported that:

We went down river to the Clyde anchorage where we remained until late on Friday evening. Troops were brought on board by tender, the last arriving on the Smeaton, of Belfast, not long before we proceeded seawards at 23.00 hours. We got our last sight of land on the following morning, in the haze away to port, probably the Donegal coast. Ships from the Clyde merged with the others from Liverpool to form the full convoy, a follow up to Operation Torch. The convoy consisted of the City of Edinburgh, Ajax, Gloucester, Pardo, Elizabeth Bakke, City of Pretoria, Llanstephan Castle and H.M.S. Helvig from Gibraltar. Samaria, Dempo, Derbyshire, Otranto and Monarch of Bermuda for Oran, Letitia, Samuel Chase, Reina del Pacifico, Stratheden, Durban Castle, Batory and Duchess of Bedford for Algiers, Sobieski and Antenor for Philippeville, Tanatside, Quickmatch and Redoubt, corvettes Exe and Swale and the sloops Egret and Banff. Hurricane left the convoy on November 29th. On December 1, the Egret sighted an unknown merchantman which was found to be the Italian ship Cortelazzo. Sixty prisoners, including some Germans, were taken from her following which she was sunk by Redoubt. Owing to bad weather on December 2, the City of Edinburgh was forced to heave-to, but was able to make her way independently to Gibraltar, arriving December 5.

1943	1 January. Ordered to proceed to Algiers for discharge.
1943	20 January. Arrived back at Gibraltar to wait for a large American convoy of 40 ships for New York under the escort of USS *Brooklyn*, USS *Texas*, the French battleship *Richelieu* and two French destroyers.
1943	12 March. Arrived at Liverpool after an unescorted voyage from New York.
1943	September. Requisitioned by the Admiralty and converted into a landing ship headquarters for the Pacific Operations. Fitted with additional radar, wireless communications and two twin 4-inch guns, six sets of oerlikon AA guns and six Landing Craft Vehicles, three each side on davits. She carried a crew of 450.
1944	July. She was renamed HMS *Lothian* and became the command ship to Force X, and joined the United States 7th Fleet.
1944	3 August. Force X left the Clyde for the Pacific via New York and Panama. HMS *Lothian* had 750 on board and was commanded by Rear Admiral A.G. Tolbot DSO.
1944	1 September. While berthed a Balboa there was an armed mutiny involving 103 men. It was the only armed mutiny in the Royal Navy since the nineteenth century and it was brought under control by the Royal Marines, who were armed. The men received suspended court martial sentences and remained on duty.
1944	29 September. She joined the United States 7th Fleet at Langemack Bay, New Guinea and became part of the Philippines invasion fleet. She was later sent to Sydney.
1945	23 February. Arrived at Sydney and became flagship to the Rear Admiral Fleet Train (RAFT), D.B. Fisher CB, CBE, ADC.
1945	29 May. Prepared as headquarters ship for the British invasion forces for South-East Asia.
1945	3 September. Arrived at Singapore following the Japanese surrender, then sailed to Hong Kong and Shanghai to evacuate British civilians and prisoners of war.
1946	February. Sailed from Trincomalee to Britain for decommissioning. In her twenty-two months with the Royal Navy she had steamed over 67,000 miles, and of the 750 men who left the Clyde on her only thirty completed the commission.
1947	6 May. Returned to Ellerman Lines at Port Sunlight on the Mersey.
1947	Overhauled and transferred to Ellerman & Bucknall Line.
1961	7 April. Sold to the Hong Kong Salvage & Towage Company, renamed *Castle Mount*.
1961	3 July. Broken up at Hong Kong.

City of Calcutta (5)   1940   8,063grt.   157.18×19.02×9.54   3,977n.   15k.

E.	Twin screw, 2×3 srg turb., 1,867 nhp, 265 psi, 6 sgl. blrs. By builder.
B.	Cammell Laird & Company Limited, Birkenhead.
1940	August. Delivered as the fifth ship of the City of Cape Town class.
1941	28 February. Winston Churchill was concerned about the safety of the ship, writing:

City of Calcutta, due Loch Ewe March 2, is reported to be going to Hull, arriving March 9. This ship must on no account be sent to the East Coast. It contains 1,700 machine guns, 44 aeroplane engines and no fewer than 14,000,000 cartridges. These cartridges are absolutely vital to the defence of Great Britain which has been so largely confided by the Navy to the Army and the Air Force. That it should be proposed to send such a ship round to the East Coast, with all the additional risk, is abominable. I am sending a copy of this minute to the Minister of Transport.

1952	Managed by Ellerman & Bucknall Line.
1952	17 March. Suffered a small fire in one of the holds.
1961	16 December. Purchased by Grosvenor Shipping Company, Hong Kong, renamed *Grosvenor Pilot*.
1962	Renamed *Castle Mount* for her final voyage and broken up at Hong Kong.

City of Calcutta (4).

City of Bristol (2).

City of Bristol (2)   1943   8,459grt.   150.27×19.6×10.33   4,321n.   15k.

E.	Twin screw, 2×3 turb. By Wallsend Slipway & Engineering Company, Newcastle.
B.	Swan Hunter & Wigham Richardson, Newcastle.
1943	January. Delivered.
1952	15 November. Suffered a small fire on one of her holds.
1961	Purchased by the Far Eastern Navigation Corporation, renamed *Tung Lee*.
1962	September. Deleted from Lloyds List.
1964	Broken up.

City of St Albans	1943 7,264grt. 134.63×17.37×10.61 4,456n. 11k.
E.	Sgl. screw, tpl. exp., 2,500 bhp at 76 rpm, 240 psi. By General Motors Corporation, Hamilton, Ohio.
B.	Bethlehem Fairfield Corporation, Baltimore.
1943	December. Delivered as *Frederick Banting* on charter to the Ministry of War Transport. City Line as managers.
1947	Owned by City Line, renamed *City of St Albans*.
1959	19 November. Sold to Soc. di Nav. Magliveras, Panama, renamed *Marineri*.
1967	Sold to Dolphin Shipping Company, Famagusta, renamed *Liberias*.
1969	March. Broken up at Onomichi, Japan.

City of Durham (4)	1945 7,253grt. 151.64×19.63×8.78 4,121n. 15k.
E.	Sgl. screw, 2 drg turb., 2 blrs. By Richardsons, Westgarth, West Hartlepool.
B.	Cammell Laird & Company Limited, Birkenhead.
1945	March. Delivered to City Line.
1962	23 August. Sold to Waywiser Navigation Corporation, Taiwan, renamed *Yonlee*.
1965	Broken up at Taiwan.

City of Oxford (4)	1948 7,593grt. 146.39×18.84×9.3 4,427n. 15½k.
E.	Sgl. screw, 3 sgl. Parsons reduction geared turb., 7,200 shp at 115 rpm, 275 psi, 2 Babcock & Wilcox blrs. By builder.
B.	John Brown & Company, Clydebank.
1948	24 June. Launched.
1948	December. Delivered to City Line. First of a class of ten ships.
1976	Sold to Union Brothers Marine Corporation SA, Panama, renamed *Union Arabia*.
1977	Managed by the Arabian Establishment for Trade, Saudi Arabia.
1978	4 January. Arrived at Kaohsiung.
1978	20 February. Demolition commenced.

City of Birmingham (3)	1949 7,599grt. 146.39×18.84×9.3 4,430n. 15½k.
E.	Sgl. screw, 3 sgl. Parsons reduction geared turb., 7,200 shp at 115 rpm, 275 psi, 2 Babcock & Wilcox blrs. By builder.
B.	John Brown & Company, Clydebank.
1948	18 November. Launched.
1949	3 May. On trials the same day as the *City of Liverpool*.
1971	Laid up at Barry Docks.
1971	9 October. Arrived at Castellon to be broken up.

City of Perth (5)	1949 7,547grt. 147.86×18.84×9.3 4,407n. 15½k.
E.	Sgl. screw, 3 sgl. Parsons reduction geared turb., 7,200 shp at 115 rpm, 275 psi, 2 Babcock & Wilcox blrs. By Parsons Marine Steam Turbines, Wallsend.
B.	Caledon Shipbuilding & Engineering Company, Dundee.
1949	June. Delivered to City Line.

| 1967 | 22 November. Sold to Astro Aspirante Cia Nav. SA, Piraeus, renamed *Elenif*. |
| 1968 | 3 January. Struck a wreck at Alexandria, beached and broke in two. Abandoned. |

City of Manchester (5)   1950   7,583grt.   147.92×18.84×9.3   4,413n.   15½k.

E.	Sgl. screw, 3 sgl. Parsons reduction geared turbines, 7,200 shp at 115 rpm, 275 psi, 2 Babcock & Wilcox blrs. By Wallsend Slipway & Engineering Company, Wallsend.
B.	Thompson & Sons, Sunderland.
1950	March. Delivered to City Line.
1971	10 June. Sold to Kavo Cia Naviera SA, Panama, renamed *Kavo Yerakes*.
1971	11 November. Arrived at Kaohsiung to be broken up by Tung Cheng Steel and Iron Works.

City of Manchester (5).

City of Karachi (4)   1951   7,320grt.   147.77×18.84×9.14   4,192n.   14k.

E.	Sgl. screw, 2 srg turb., 1,210 nhp, 2 blrs. By builder.
P.	4.
B.	William Denny & Brothers, Dumbarton.
1950	10 November. Launched.
1951	15 March. Delivered to City Line.
1971	November. While berthed at Karachi during the East and West Pakistan civil war she was attacked, and her Indian crew members were taken prisoner. The officers took the ship to Bombay.
1972	11 May. Sold to Navieros Progresivos SA, Panama, renamed *Kavo Kolones*.
1974	10 January. Arrived at Kaohsiung to be broken up by Chin Ho Fa Steel and Iron Company.

City of Ripon (3)   1956   7,713grt.   154.59×20.1×8.62   4,033n.   15k.
E.   Sgl. screw, oil, 6 cyl. 2S.SA Doxford, 8,000 bhp. By Vickers Armstrong Limited, Barrow.
B.   Vickers Armstrong Limited, Walker-on-Tyne.
1956   March. Delivered to City Line.
1973   1 January. Transferred to Ellerman City Liners Limited.
1978   May. Sold to Ben Line, renamed *Benvannoch*.
1979   7 February. Arrived at Kaohsiung to be broken up by Kao Feng Iron & Steel Company.

City of Colombo (2)   1956   7,739grt.   154.59×20.1×8.62   4,056n.   15k.
E.   Sgl. screw, oil, 6 cyl. 2S.SA Doxford, 8,000 bhp. By builder.
B.   Barclay, Curle & Company, Glasgow.
1955   7 October. Launched.
1956   February. Delivered to City Line.
1973   1 January. Transferred to Ellerman City Liners Limited.
1977   August. Sold to Ben Line, renamed *Benmhor*.
1979   7 February. Arrived at Kaohsiung to be broken up by Gi Yuen Steel Enterprise
             Company.

Salmo / City of Athens (4)   1967   1,523grt.   93.88×13.92×5.08   708n.   12k.
E.   Sgl. screw, oil, 6 cyl. type ALSSDM 4S.SA, 2,580 nhp at 280 rpm. Direct reversing
             and turbocharged. By Mirrlees National Limited, Stockport, bow thruster.
B.   Henry Robb Limited, Leith.
1966   12 December. Launched as *Salmo* for Ellerman's Wilson Line.
1967   March. Delivered.
1973   1 January. Transferred to Ellerman City Liners Limited.
1974   Renamed *City of Athens*, registered at Hull.
1978   The 'S' class was replaced by the City of Plymouth class. Purchased by Red
             Cascade Shipping Company SA, Panama, renamed *Aldebaran II*.
1980   Owned by Spyrthem Shipping Company, Cyprus, renamed *Argiro*.
1988   Sold to Amin Shipping Services Limited, St Vincent, renamed *Ameen*.
1988   23 January. Arrived at Gadani Beach and broken up.

Salerno / City of Corinth (5)   1965   1,559grt.   93.81×13.92×5.08   703n.   12k.
E.   Sgl. screw, oil, 6 cyl. type ALSSDM 4S.SA, 2,580 nhp at 280 rpm. Direct reversing
             and turbocharged. By Mirrlees National Limited, Stockport, bow thruster.
B.   Henry Robb Limited, Leith.
1965   November. Delivered as *Salerno* for Ellerman's Wilson Line.
1973   1 January. Transferred to Ellerman City Liners Limited.
1974   Renamed *City of Corinth*, registered at Hull.
1978   Sold to Perivale Maritime Incorporated, renamed *Pyrgos Star*.
1981   Owned by Pallada Marine Limited, Cyprus, renamed *Paxi*.
1986   Sold to Medfleet Kavadas Limited, San Lorenzo, Honduras, renamed *Lefkas Sun*.
1988   Sold to Kiriaki Shipping Company Limited, St Vincent, renamed *Kiriaki II*.
1988   Renamed *Geniki*, same owners.
1998   Renamed *Selamat Berjaya*, owned by Perkapalan Dai Zhun Sen. Ber., Malaysia.
2001   Purchased by Sun Flora Shipping SA, Cambodia, renamed *Pertama*.
2006   7 July. At Singapore, sold to Bangladash ship-breakers.

Sorrento / City of Sparta (3)   1967   1,523grt.   93.81×13.92×5.08   708n.   12k.

E.	Sgl. screw, oil, 6 cyl. type ALSSDM 4S.SA, 2,580 nhp at 280 rpm. Direct reversing and turbocharged. By Mirrlees National Limited, Stockport, bow thruster.
B.	Henry Robb Limited, Leith.
1967	24 May. Launched as *Sorrento* for Elerman's Wilson Line.
1973	1 January. Transferred to Ellerman City Liners Limited.
1974	Renamed *City of Sparta*, registered at Hull.
1978	Sold to Gracechurch Line Limited, London, renamed *Gracechurch* for a Runcorn–Mediterranean service.
1983	Owned by Protac Shipping Limited, Gibraltar, renamed *Weybridge*. Owned by Interlines SA.
1983	Renamed *Wayfarer*.
1986	Renamed *Five Stars*, owned by Sinbad Maritime Limited, Malta.
1989	Sold to St Vincent and Grenadines interests.
1992	Sold to Shahmir Maritime Limited, Kingston, Jamaica, renamed *Sea Princess*.
1998	Renamed *Albatros*, same owners.
2001	Sold to Summit Services Limited Inc., St Vincent and Grenadines, renamed *Almarjan*.

Silvio / City of Patras   1968   1,523grt.   93.81×13.92×5.08   708n.   12k.

E.	Sgl. screw, oil, 6 cyl. type ALSSDM 4S.SA, 2,580 nhp at 280 rpm. Direct reversing and turbocharged. By Mirrlees National Limited, Stockport, bow thruster.
B.	Henry Robb Limited, Leith.
1967	30 November. Launched as *Silvio* for Ellerman's Wilson Line.
1968	January. Delivered.
1973	1 January. Transferred to Ellerman City Liners Limited.
1974	Renamed *City of Patras*, registered in Hull.
1978	Sold to Gulf Maritime Company, Takoradi, Ghana, renamed *City of Tema*. Later owned by Meridian Oceanic Services Lines, Ghana.
1988	Owned by Teer Shipping Company, Cyprus, renamed *Lemissa*.
1988	Renamed *Shazli*, owned by Independent Maritime SA, St Vincent.
1989	13 September. Arrived at Bombay and broken up.

Sangro / City of Ankara   1968   1,523grt.   93.81×13.92×5.08   708n.   12k.

E.	Sgl. screw, oil, 6 cyl. type ALSSDM 4S.SA, 2,580 nhp at 280 rpm. Direct reversing and turbocharged. By Mirrlees National Limited, Stockport, bow thruster.
B.	Henry Robb Limited, Leith.
1968	May. Delivered as *Sangro* to Ellerman's Wilson's Line.
1973	1 January. Transferred to Ellerman City Liners Limited.
1974	Renamed *City of Ankara*, registered in Hull.
1978	Sold to Singapore Enterprises Limited, Panama, renamed *Rezeki*.
1979	Purchased by P.T. Abadi Lines, Indonesia.
1990	Owned by P.T. Pelayaran Meratus, Indonesia, renamed *Melina II*.
1997	Sold to Indonesian interests, renamed *Kalimantan Pacific*.
2007	6 May. Beached at Chittagong and broken up.

Dilkara   1971   13,151grt.   199.02×28.71×20.14   6,875dwt.

E.	18 cyl. Pielstick diesel.

B.   Eriksbergs Mekaniska Verkstad AB, Gothenburg.
1971   October. Delivered to ACTA for the Pacific Australia Direct service, with Ellerman
            Lines, Blue Star Line and Port Line each having a third share.
1971   29 December. Arrived at Sydney on her maiden voyage.
1986   29 December. Arrived at Ankom Chin Tai Steel and Iron Limited, Kaohsiung to be
            broken up.

Rapallo / City of Limassol   1960   3,402grt.   111.61×16.59×6.39   1,453n.   13½k
E.   Sgl. screw, oil, 7 cyl. Sulzer 2S.SA, 3,500 bhp. By G. Clark & North East Marine
            (Sunderland) Limited.
B.   Henry Robb Limited, Leith.
1960   April. Delivered to Ellerman's Wilson Line as *Rapallo*.
1968   4 July. Assisted and towed *Tactician* into Punta Delgada, following a fire on the
            Harrison Line vessel.
1973   1 January. Transferred to Ellerman City Liners Limited.
1974   Renamed *City of Limassol*, registered in Hull.
1977   May. Sold to Associated Levant Lines (SAL), Lebanon, renamed *Beiteddine*.
1986   14 July. Arrived at Aviles to be broken up.

City of Exeter (3)   1974   9.014grt.   141.00×20.48×8.85   6,383n.   15k.
E.   Sgl. screw, oil, 5 cyl. Sulzer 2S.SA, 7,500 bhp. By Hawthorn Leslie Engineering
            Works, Newcastle.
B.   Austin & Pickersgill Limited, Sunderland.
1974   4 July. Launched.
1974   October. Delivered to P&O Steam Navigation Company as *Strathdare*.
1976   Renamed *City of Exeter* for a joint service with P&O.
1980   Sold to Monodora Shipping Corporation, Greece, renamed *Phoevos*.
1982   Purchased by the Islamic Investment Shipping Company, SA, Panama, renamed
            Safina-e-Barket chartered to the Pan-Islamic Steam Ship Company, Karachi.
1986   Charter completed, renamed *Nour*.
1995   February. Sold and renamed *Zenith*, owned by Carter Marine Limited, Cyprus.
1996   21 June. Arrived at Zarate with cracks in her shell plating suffered after a voyage
            from Richards Bay.

City of Exeter (3).

1998	December. Renamed *Nikolaos S* by Third Element Enterprises Shipping Limited, Cyprus.
1999	23 December. Arrived at Haldia and broken up.

City of Winchester (4)   1976   7,691grt.   150.65×21.04×8.03   4,494n.   16k.

E.	Sgl. screw, oil, 6 cyl. 2S.SA, MAN K6Z 70/120E type, 8,976 bhp at 145 rpm. By builder. Controlled from bridge.
B.	Bremer Vulkan, Vegesack.
1976	3 March. Launched.
1976	June. Delivered to Ellerman City Liners for the East African and Arabian Gulf services. She was designed with five holds forward and a grain capacity of 23,000 cub. m. All of the holds contained 'tween decks and No. 3 hold had the facility to be used as a liquid cargo or ballast tank. The forward three holds were served by a 12.5-ton crane, while the remaining two holds were served by a heavy mast wih derricks.
1981	Sold to Solco Incorporated, Piraeus, owned by The Architug Corporation, renamed *Arc Odysseus*.
1989	Sold to Tweendeck V. K/S, Norway, renamed *Nortween Slevik*.
1991	Renamed *Slevik*, same owners.
1994	Owned by Union Shipping Limited, Hong Kong, renamed *Lady Sharon*.
1998	Sold to Coral Maritime Limited, Malta, renamed *Harmony Dove*.
2001	26 May. Arrived at Alang and broken up.

Arc Odysseus, ex-*City of Winchester* (4).

City of York (5)   1976   7,691grt.   150.65×21.04×8.03   4,494n.   16k.

E.	Sgl. screw, oil, 6 cyl. 2S.SA, MAN K6Z 70/120E type, 8,976 bhp at 145 rpm. By builder. Controlled from bridge.
B.	Bremer Vulkan, Vegesack.
1976	29 April. Launched. She was designed with five holds, served by three 12½-ton tower cranes, two 12½-ton conventional derricks, one 60/20-ton swinging derrick and one 30/13-ton swinging derric. She was fitted to take containers on deck and lift 322 standard containers in the holds. She was also strengthened longitudinally for heavy loads and to carry a large amount of ballast water so that she could undertake light ship passages. Also designed with full bridge control of the main machinery, which could be operated with the engine room unmanned. She

incorporated a built-in incinerator for refuse disposal, a fresh water sanitary system and a fully equipped laundry.

1976	July. Delivered and owned by Lloyds Leasing Limited on charter to Ellerman City Liners.
1976	August. Maiden voyage to Kuwait, Dammam, Doha and Umm Said in the Persian Gulf.
1986	Operated by Bend Shipping Company, Cyprus. Owned by Starco Shipping Company, Limassol, renamed *Vicman*.
1988	Sold to Joy Marine Company, Greece, renamed *Joy*.
1991	Purchased by Pal Joy Marine Company Limited, Cyprus, renamed *Pal Joy*.
1992	Owned by World Independence SA, Greece, renamed *Emerald*.
1995	Sold to Kronos Shipping Company Limited, Malta, renamed *Felicita*.
1998	9 December. Arrived at Alang and broken up.

City of
Canterbury (4).

City of Canterbury (4)   1976   7,691grt.   150.65×21.04×8.03   4,494n.   16k.

E.	Sgl. screw, oil, 6 cyl. 2S.SA, MAN K6Z 70/120E type, 8,976 bhp at 145 rpm. By builder. Controlled from bridge.
B.	Bremer Vulkan, Vegesack.
1976	September. Delivered to Ellerman City Liners, owned by Barclays Export Finances Company, London.
1981	11 July. Arrived at Immingham on her last voyage for Ellerman and laid up.
1981	August. Sold to Drilco Incorporated, Piraeus, renamed *Arc Aeolos*. Owned by the Architug Corporation.
1990	Owned by Tweendeck VI K/S, Norway, renamed *Nortween Sletter*.
1991	Renamed *Hibiscus Trader* then *Sletter*, same owners.
1993	Sold to Norship (HK), Hong Kong, renamed *Lady Juliet*.
2000	9 November. Arrived at Chittagong and broken up.

City of Edinburgh (6)   1973   58,284grt.   289.57×32.34×13.02   34,387n.   26½k.

E.	Twin screw, 2×2 steam turb., 88,000 shp. By GEC Turbine Generators Limited, Manchester.
B.	Howaldswerke-Deutsche Werft, Hamburg.
1973	5 March. Launched for Ben Line Steamers Limited, Ellerman had a 20 per cent share in the ship.

1973	November. Delivered and owned by Bernard Street Holdings, London. Ellerman Lines colours.
1992	January. Renamed *Benarty* and sold to the East Asiatic Company.
1993	May. Owned by Maersk Line, renamed *Maersk Edinburgh*.
1993	September. Renamed *Edinburgh Maersk*.
1999	January. Owned by Lily Navigation Corporation (Danaos Shipping Company Limited), renamed *Edinburgh*.
2002	13 May. Sailed from Busan for Xingang and broken up.

City of Durban (3)   1978   53,790grt.   258.5×32.31×13.03   34,895n.   21½k.

E.	Twin screw, oil, 2x8 cyl. Man, 51,360 bhp at 122 rpm. By Masch, Augsburg Nurnberg. Two controllable-pitch bow thrusters.
B.	A. G. Weser, Bremen.
1977	16 September. Launched for Ellerman Harrison Container Line Limited.
1978	6 February. Delivered to Ellerman Lines & Charente Shipping Company.
1983	Chartered to Overseas Container Line, renamed *Portland Bay*.
1984	Renamed *City of Durban*.
1986	Transferred to Associated Container Lines (Australia), renamed *ACT 8*.
1990	Reverted to *City of Durban*.
1996	Renamed *Pegasus Bay*.
2002	19 October. Arrived at Jiangyin and broken up by the Jiangyin Changiang Shipbreaking Factory, China.

City of Plymouth   1978   1,559grt.   104.17×16.77×5.56   1,084n.   14½k.

E.	Sgl. screw, oil, 3 cyl. 2S.SA, 6,000 bhp. By Doxford Engines Limited, Sunderland, bow thruster.
B.	Appledore Shipbuilders Limited, Appledore, Devon.
1978	November. Delivered to Ellerman City Liners, owned by Finance for Ships Limited. She was the first of five purpose-built sister ships designed for the 'Ellerman / Strath and Ellerman / Prince Mediterranean' container services. She incorporated a new main engine specially developed for Ellerman City Liners by Doxfords. Designated 58JS3, the three-cylinder opposed-piston crosshead oil engine developed 5,500 bhp at 220 rpm, directly driving a four-blade propeller. The new engine was designed to produce savings due to lower fuel consumption, lower running and maintenance costs and the ability to burn cheaper lower grade residual fuels. She was able to carry 300 twenty-foot or 139 forty-foot containers in the holds and on deck. Accommodation for the crew of fourteen was of a very high standard with all cabins having their own toilet and shower and most having extended bunks enabling partners to be carried.
1987	Owned by Cunard–Ellerman Limited.
1993	May. Renamed *Cervantes*.
1996	Renamed *City of Lisbon*.
1998	April. Renamed *Pacheco*.
2007	December. Became *Pacheco 1*.
2009	August. Renamed *Sarah Hanem*.
2009	20 August. Foundered off the Yemeni coast.

City of Perth / City of Lisbon (2) 1978 1,559grt. 104.17×16.77×5.56 1,084n. 14½k.

E.	Sgl. screw, oil, 3 cyl. 2S.SA, 6,000 bhp. By Doxford Engines Limited, Sunderland, bow thruster.
B.	Appledore Shipbuilders Limited, Appledore, Devon.
1978	23 June. Floated.
1979	February. Delivered to Ellerman City Liners, owned by Investors for Industry plc.
1983	Laid up at Chatham.
1986	Renamed *City of Lisbon*.
1987	Owned by Cunard–Ellerman Limited.
1989	Sold to Cyprian interests, renamed *Erka Sun*.

City of Lisbon (2).

City of Hartlepool / City of Manchester (6) 1,559grt. 104.17×16.77×5.56 1,084n. 14½k.

E.	Sgl. screw, oil, 3 cyl. 2S.SA, 6,000 bhp. By Doxford Engines Limited, Sunderland, bow thruster.
B.	Appledore Shipbuilders Limited, Appledore, Devon.
1979	3 February. Floated.
1979	29 March. Named by Mrs J.W. Cameron, wife of the president of J.W.Cameron & Company Limited, the brewing operation owned by Ellerman Lines, which was based in Hartlepool. She was the first *City of Hartlepool* in the fleet.
1979	May. Delivered to Ellerman City Liners, owned by Container Rentals Limited.
1984	Renamed *Laxfoss* on charter to the Iceland Steam Ship Company.
1985	January. Renamed *City of Manchester*.
1987	Owned by Cunard–Ellerman Limited.
2007	June. Renamed *City*.
2008	September. Renamed *Zeeland*.
2009	December. Sold to North Bulkers SA, Panama, renamed *Golden Bay*.
2011	8 October. Arrived at Chittagong.
2011	13 October. Beached and broken up.

City of Ipswich 1979 1,559grt. 104.17×16.77×5.56 1,084n. 14½k.

E.	Sgl. screw, oil, 3 cyl. 2S.SA, 6,000 bhp. By Doxford Engines Limited, Sunderland bow thruster.

B.	Appledore Shipbuilders Limited, Appledore, Devon.
1979	9 May. Floated.
1979	July. Delivered to Lloyd's Leasing Limited on charter to Ellerman City Lines.
1981	Renamed *Manchester Fulmar*, on charter to Manchester Liners.
1983	Renamed *City of Ipswich*.
1984	Renamed *Liverpool Star*.
1987	Owned by Cunard–Ellerman Limited.
1991	November. Reverted to *City of Ipswich*.
1992	March. Owned by Pelia Shipping Company, SA, renamed *Pelmariner*.
1999	26 July. Collided with *Pel Ranger* off the Island of Bozcaada, near to the Dardanelles Straits. The crew of twelve were rescued when she sank.

City of Oxford (5)   1981   1,559grt.   104.15×16.77×5.56   1,084n.   14½k.

E.	Sgl. screw, oil, 3 cyl. 2S.SA, 6,000 bhp. By Doxford Engines Limited, Sunderland, bow thruster.
B.	Appledore Shipbuilders Limited, Appledore, Devon.
1981	6 March. Launched for Ellerman Lines plc.
1981	May. Delivered .
1983	Renamed *Bakkafoss* on charter to the Iceland Steamship Company.
1987	Owned by Cunard–Ellerman Limited.
1988	Renamed *Oxford*.
1993	April. Became *Norisia Malacca*.
1994	April. Renamed *Hyundai Malacca*.
1996	May. *Hub Melaka*.
1996	September. *Jts. Sentosa*.
2005	June. Sold to Systemindo Container Perdana, Jakarta, Indonesia, renamed *Systemindo Perdana*.

Robert Alexander & Company

Sun Shipping Company

Hall Line

Robert Alexander

James Alexander

Robert Alexander (2)

Liston Young

Stewarts

Sylph	1850	298grt. Barque rig
B.	Dumbarton.	
1850	Delivered for the Glasgow–Belfast–Valparaiso service.	
1861	Wrecked.	

New Margaret 1844   370grt.   33.28×8.17×5.64   Barque rig
B. Whitehaven.
1850 Purchased by James Alexander for the China trade.
1874 Broken up.

Helena 1841   265grt.   Rig
B. Nova Scotia.
1841 Delivered.
1846 Sold to Edmunds & Son, Dublin.
1851 Purchased by James Alexander for services from Liverpool.

Great Britain 1843   467grt.
B. Poole.
1843 Delivered.
1853 Purchased by Robert Alexander, managed by James Alexander and Robert Alexander.
1861 Managed by Alexander & Young and later by R. Alexander & Company.
1867 Wrecked.

Annie Hall 1853   280grt.
B. Prince Edward Island.
1853 Delivered.
1856 Purchased by Robert Alexander for the Dublin–New York and Glasgow–New York services, twenty-four passengers.
1858 Transferred to services from Liverpool, James and Robert Alexander as managers.
1861 Managed by Alexander & Young and later by R. Alexander & Company.
1867 Wrecked.

Echunga 1853   1,118grt.
B. M Cochran, Moncton, New Brunswick.
1853 Delivered to William Johnston.
1855 Purchased by James Alexander and employed as a Crimean War transport and supply ship.
1857 Sold to William Johnston and then to Taylor & Company, Liverpool.
1862 Purchased by Potter & Company, Glasgow. Lengthened to 52.42×10.97.
1874 Broken up.

Courier 1836   369grt.   Barque rig
B. Sunderland.
1849 Lengthened to 33.59×8.11×5.42.
1855 Purchased by Liston Young & Company, London. Robert Alexander as agent in Liverpool and part owner. Operated from Liverpool.
1858 Sold to Williams & Company, Liverpool.

Panola   1851   893grt.   Rig
B.   Quebec.
1851   Delivered.
1855   Purchased by Robert Alexander for the India service.
1859   Abandoned at sea on a voyage to Liverpool.

Star of the South 1853   1,252grt.   Rig
B.   James Nevins, St John, New Brunswick.
1853   Delivered to M de Mill, St John.
1855   Purchased by James Alexander, R. Alexander & Company as managers.
1857   Sold to Ramsey & Company, Liverpool for the Australian service.

Morning Star   1854   1,327grt.   Rig
B.   F. & J. Ruddick, St John.
1854   Delivered to Alexander & Company.
1859   Sold to Fernie Brothers, Liverpool.
1880   7 May. She was lost on a voyage from Quebec to Liverpool, crew saved.

Magoola   1854   549grt.
B.   New Jersey.
1854   Delivered.
1855   Purchased by James Alexander.
1883   Broken up.

Starlight   1854   366grt.
B.   United States of America.
1854   Ordered by Robert Alexander, owned by Robert and James Alexander.
1855   January. Delivered for the United States–India service, later from Liverpool.
1859   Owned by H. Churchill, Liverpool.
1866   Broken up.

Kheronese   1855   1,409grt.   iron hull, 2 decks
B.   Robert Hickson & Company, Belfast.
1855   4 October. Launched for the Liverpool, Newfoundland & Halifax Steam
                    Navigation Company (James and Robert Alexander were shareholders).
1856   April. Requisitioned as a troopship in the Crimean War.
1856   23 August. Maiden voyage Liverpool–Canada–Portland–Maine. Lost propeller
                    on the inward voyage and continued under sail.
1857   Purchased by the North Atlantic Steam Navigation Company. Transferred to
                    become an Indian Mutiny transport, Robert Alexander as managers.
1859   Owned by Weir, Cochrane & Company, Liverpool, managers of the North
                    Atlantic SN Co.
1863   Sold to Robert Duncan & Company.
1863   23 January. Liverpool–New York service.
1866   Became a barque rig, engines removed.
1889   Purchased by Dutch interests.
1891   22 July. Suffered a serious fire at Montevideo.

Egeria	1859 1,066grt. Barque
B.	Fisher, New Brunswick.
1859	Delivered.
1861	Sold to Alexander & Young for the India, Australia and South American triangular service.
1877	Laid up.

Elizabeth Fry	1861 1,094grt. Barque
B.	Fisher, New Brunswick.
1861	July. Delivered as a sister ship to *Egeria*.
1862	Managed by Alexander & Young.
1868	Owned by Sun Shipping Company.
1871	Sold to Bickell & Company, Liverpool for the India service.
1872	Purchased by P. Dale & Company, North Shields for the UK–New Orleans service.
1885	Broken up.

Cornwallis	1862 1,214grt. iron hull, 1 deck
B.	Thomas Vernon & Sons, Liverpool.
1862	June. Delivered to Liston Young & Company, Robert Alexander was part owner.
1872	Sold to Balfour, Williamson, Liverpool.

Bavelaw	1862 1,027grt. Rig
B.	Thomas Vernon & Sons, Liverpool.
1862	July. Delivered to Robert Alexander, Alexander & Young as managers.
1868	Sold to S. Vaughan, Glasgow.
1879	Purchased by W. Dixon, Newcastle upon Tyne.
1881	23 February. Lost on a voyage from New York to London.

Bolingbroke	1863 1,255grt.
B.	Morton, Leith.
1863	Delivered to Liston Young & Company, Robert Alexander as partner.
1869	Wrecked.

Robert Lees	1863 1,239grt. 1,200n. Rig
B.	Thomas Vernon & Sons, Liverpool.
1863	April. Delivered to Liston Young & Company, London. Operated from Liverpool with R. Alexander as managers.
1880	Purchased by J.H. Worthington.
1881	Renamed *Roscrana*.
1886	Abandoned at sea.

Dragon	1864 696grt. Rig
B.	M. Pearse & Company, Stockton.
1864	September. Delivered to T. Haviside for the India service, Liston & Young as managers.
1879	Sold to S.D. Grant.
1882	Purchased by Major Pratt.

1888	Sold to Ship Dragon Company, London, F.M.Tucker as managers.
1889	Broken up.

Bayard	1864 1,028grt. Rig
B.	Thomas Vernon & Sons, Liverpool.
1864	April. Delivered to Alexander & Young for the Glasgow–Calcutta–Burma service.
1868	Transferred to Sun Shipping Company as their first ship.
1881	Sold to Foley & Company.
1893	Owned by Norwegian interests.
1911	Hulked at Calcutta.

Malleney	1868 1,026grt. Rig
B.	Thomas Royden & Sons, Liverpool.
1868	June. Delivered to James Alexander, R. Alexander as managers.
1872	Purchased by Horatio N. Hughes, Liverpool for the India service.
1888	Wrecked.

Runnymede	1868 700grt. Barque rig
1868	March. Delivered to Redfern, Alexander & Company, London.
1884	Purchased by H. Joyau, Nantes.
1889	Owned by Madam Vivienne Cazer, Port Aven, Finisterre.
1902	Broken up.

Haddington	1846 1,271grt. 1,206n. iron hull, 2 decks
B.	Thomas Vernon & Sons, Liverpool.
1846	Delivered to the P&O Steam Navigation Company for the Calcutta service via the Suez Canal.
1846	5 December. Maiden voyage Southampton–Calcutta via the Cape route.
1854	Converted to a ship rig at Blackwall.
1854	12 August. Returned to service as a stores supply ship and cadet training ship.
1871	26 March. Sold to T. Haviside, London. Liston Young & Company as managers. Operated on the London–China service.
1882	Sold to E.B. Hatfield & Company for the London–Calcutta service.
1885	Purchased by E. A. Kinnear, London.
1888	Destroyed by fire off Iquique.

Lord Palmerston	1862 1,057grt.
B.	New Brunswick.
1862	Delivered.
1865	Purchased by Alexander & Young.
1869	Lost at sea.

Thermutis	1864 310grt.
B.	Quayle & Company.
1864	March. Delivered to Cunningham & Company, Liverpool for the UK–Galveston service.
1870	Purchased by Alexander & Company.

Port of London advertisement.

Vernon   1864   1,319grt.   Rig
B.   Thomas Vernon & Sons, Liverpool.
1864   October. Delivered for the Glasgow–Australia–San Francisco–Cape Horn–
              Glasgow service.
1880   Sold to Thompson, Anderson & Company, Liverpool.

Estepona   1872   1,049grt.   676n.
E.   Sgl. screw, 2 cyl. comp. inv., 120 nhp, 60 psi. By builder.
B.   A. & J. Inglis & Company, Glasgow.
1872   September. Delivered to Liston Young & Company, London for the service from
              the Clyde to Spain.
1879   Sold to Ramsey & Sawyer, Hull.
1881   Major engine repair by Massey & Sawyer.
1882   Broken up.

Marlborough 1862   879grt.   Rig, iron hull
B.   Pile, Spence & Company, West Hartlepool.
1862   August. Delivered to Mills & Brothers, Stockton.
1873   Purchased by Liston Young & Company, London.

Scotia   1856   921grt.   Barque rig.
B.   Quebec.
1856   Delivered.
1865   Owned by Hamilton, Greenock.
1868   Purchased by A.F. MacKay, Liverpool.
1873   Owned by J. Alexander & Company.
1878   Sold to R.W. Muir, W. Harrison as managers.
1882   Owned by T. Howatt, Liverpool.
1884   Broken up.

Haddon Hall 1868   1,491grt.   1,416n.   Rig, iron hull, 2 decks
B.   Thomas Royden & Sons, Liverpool.
1868   September. Delivered to Sun Shipping Company, Glasgow, Alexander & Young as
              managers. The first 'Hall' ship.
1878   Sold to Liston Young & Company, Liverpool.
1880   Purchased by J.J. de Wolff & Company, Liverpool.
1913   1 February. On a voyage from Liverpool to Cape Town she went ashore at Port
              Morison, Cape Colony.

Locksley Hall 1869   1,356grt.   69.18×10.97   Rig, iron hull, 2 decks
1869   Delivered to Sun Shipping Company, Glasgow for the India service.
1881   Sold to Lowden, Edgar & Company, Liverpool.
1887   27 August. On a voyage from San Francisco she was being towed in the Mersey
              and was in collision with the *Regulus* and sank. As she was across the top of the
              Mersey rail tunnel she could not be dynamited. She was eventually lifted, beached
              at Tranmere and repaired. She was sold to R. Singlehurst & Company,

Liverpool, who owned the Red Cross Line and renamed *Carvoeira*. She was placed on their service to Brazil and later became a hulk on the Amazon.

1901	Became part of the Booth Steamship Company.
1922	Broken up.

Rokeby Hall	1863 1,004grt. Rig, iron hull, 2 decks
B.	Thomas Vernon & Sons, Liverpool.
1863	August. Delivered.
1868	Transferred to Liston Young & Company.
1875	Purchased by Balfour, Williamson & Company, Liverpool.
1913	Broken up.

Eaton Hall	1870 1,860grt. 1,779n. Rig, iron hull, 2 decks
B.	Thomas Royden & Sons, Liverpool.
1870	March. Delivered to Sun Shipping Company.
1874	20 April. Left Liverpool for Melbourne. The voyage took seventy-two days and then sixty-three days to San Francisco.
1874	30 October. Arrived back in Liverpool.
1875	Sold to Balfour, Williamson & Company, Liverpool.
1908	August. On a voyage from New South Wales to Valparaiso she lost a mast in a cyclone. Became a hulk at the Society Islands.

Knowsley Hall	1873 1,860grt. 1,774n.
1873	September. Delivered for the Australian service.
1879	14 June. Left London for Lyttleton and disappeared with fifty-three passengers and thirty-five crew.
1879	17 June. Passed Start Point, never heard of again.

Mistley Hall	1874 1,867grt. 1,772n.
B.	R. & J. Evans & Company, Liverpool.
1874	May. Delivered to Sun Shipping Company.
1878	Sold to William Herron.
1882	Transferred to Herron, Dunn & Company. Captain C.G. Dunn came into the partnership.
1887	Company became Globe Shipping Company, later C.G. Dunn & Company.
1900	Sold to Enrico Beraldo, Recco, Genoa, renamed *Ascensione*.
1905	Broken up.

Rydal Hall	1874 1,771grt. 1,682n.
B.	R. & J. Evans & Company, Liverpool.
1874	February. Delivered to Sun Shipping Company.
1876	17 October. On a voyage from Cardiff to San Francisco, with a cargo of coal she went ashore on Cape Pillar, near Punta Arenas, nine of her crew lost. She was salvaged, repaired and sold to Brazilian interests.

Rydal Hall	1871 2,114grt. 100.74×10.48×7.41 9k. iron hull, 2 decks
E.	Sgl. screw, 2 cyl. simple, 250 nhp, 60 psi, 2 sgl. blrs. By builder.

B.	London & Glasgow Company, Glasgow.
1871	July. Delivered to Sun Shipping Company as their first steamer with a sgl. exp. engine.
1874	Sold to the West Indian & Pacific Steam Navigation Company, renamed *Chilean*.
1885	Converted to tpl. exp. engines by Harland & Wolff, Belfast.
1888	Sold to Carlisle & Company (London) limited.
1890	Purchased by MacBeth & Gray, Belfast.
1894	January. Abandoned at sea.

Branksome Hall 1875 2,086grt. 101.00×10.42 1,347n. 10k.

E.	Sgl. screw, 2 cyl. comp. inv., 1,600 ihp, 80 psi. By builder.
B.	London & Glasgow Company, Glasgow.
1875	November. Delivered to Sun Shipping Company.
1881	Sold to Cia Transatlantica Espanola. Renamed *Panama* for the New York–Havana service.
1898	She was captured by USS *Mangrove* during the American Spanish War as used as a transport.
1898	10 December. Ceded to the United States.
1899	Converted by the Morse Shipyard for the US Army Corps of Signals to lay cables between the Philippines. On the voyage from New York to Manila via the Suez Canal, she was forced to put into Gibraltar for boiler repairs. She was wrecked on the first project at Corregidor, Manila Bay while laying cables.

Trentham Hall 1876 2,101grt. 101.04×10.42 1,359n. 10k.

E.	Sgl. screw, 2 cyl. comp., 1,600 ihp, 80 psi. By builder.
B.	London & Glasgow Company, Glasgow.
1876	January. Delivered.
1881	Sold to Cia. Transatlantica, Spain, renamed *Mexico* for the New York–Havana service.
1901	Sank.

Childwall Hall 1876 2,017grt. 101.13×10.42 1,361n. 10k.

E.	Sgl. screw, 2 cyl. comp. inv., 1,600 ihp, 80 psi. By builder.
B.	London & Glasgow Company, Glasgow.
1876	March. Delivered.
1877	Sold to James Wood of James Wood & Sons, Liverpool.
1878	April. Wrecked.

City of Baltimore 1855 2,292grt. 100.8×11.89×7.92 1,444n. 11k.

E.	Sgl. screw, 2 cyl. comp. inv., 300 nhp, 70 psi. By J. Jack Rollo & Company, Liverpool.
B.	Tod & McGregor.
1855	20 January. Launched for the Inman Line. Chartered during the Crimean War as a transport.
1855	20 March. Maiden voyage Liverpool–Marseilles.
1856	23 April. On the North Atlantic service to Philadelphia.

1866	Compound engines and new boilers fitted.
1866	November. Returned to service.
1874	Purchased by Robert Alexander for the Sun Shipping Company for the India service.
1882	Sold to Spanish interests, renamed *Fivaller*, then *Benicarlo* owned by J. Ripolles, Valencia.
1892	Broken up.

Marina	1870 1,358grt. 73.39×9.94×7.25 86in. 10k.
E.	Sgl. screw, 2 cyl. comp. inv., 135 hp. By builder.
P.	20 (first), 240 (third).
B.	Barclay, Curle & Company, Glasgow.
1870	25 October. Launched for Donaldson Brothers.
1870	10 December. Maiden voyage Glasgow–River Plate.
1873	Sold to the Brazil Steam Ship Company (Alexander, Radcliffe & Company).
1878	Owned by the Hall Line, Alexander, Radcliffe & Company as managers.
1881	Sold to Rocco Piaggio & Sons, Genoa, renamed *Maria*.
1885	Owned by Navigazione Generale Italiana, renamed *Paraguay*.
1910	Sold to S.A. Nazionale di Servizi Marittimi.
1921	Purchased by G. Randazzo, Palermo, renamed *Torrero* for a Palermo–South American service.
1928	Sold to Angelo Bertorello, Genoa.
1929	Broken up at Genoa.

Rydal Hall (3)	1878 2,708grt. 110.39×11.28×8.05
E.	Sgl. screw, 2 cyl. comp. By builder.
B.	London & Glasgow Company, Glasgow.
1878	February. Delivered to Sun Shipping Company.
1888	Sold to Navigazione Generale Italiana, renamed *Nilo*.
1911	Purchased by Soc. Nazionale di Servizi Marittimi, Palermo.
1916	Broken up.

Speke Hall	1878 2,672grt. 110.39×9.14×10.67
E.	Sgl. screw, 2 cyl. comp. inv., 135 hp. By J. & J. Thomson Limited, Glasgow.
B.	Charles Connell & Company, Glasgow.
1878	March. Delivered to Sun Shipping Company.
1885	3 June. On a voyage from Cardiff to Bombay with a cargo of coal she was lost in a cyclone, 180 miles from Aden. One member of the crew was saved, fifty-eight others were lost.

Wistow Hall	1878 2,674grt. 109.88×9.14×10.67
E.	Sgl. screw, 2 cyl. comp. inv., 135 hp. By J. & J. Thomson Limited, Glasgow.
B.	Charles Connell & Company, Glasgow.
1878	Delivered.
1886	Sold to Nav. Gen. Italiana, Genoa, renamed *Bosforo*.
1910	Transferred to Soc. Anon Nazionale di Servizi Marittimi. Palermo for the India service.
1920	Broken up.

Bretton Hall 1881   2,421grt.   99.75×11.03×7.77   1,918n.

E.   Sgl. screw, 2 cyl. comp., 300 nhp, 75 psi. By J.& J. Thomson Limited, Glasgow.

B.   Charles Connell & Company, Glasgow.

1881   Delivered.

1883   On charter to the Bucknall Line.

1885   6 December. Wrecked at Starkham Point, Devon. All fifty crew were saved.

Merton Hall 1881   4,053grt.   122.07×12.86×9.05   2,647n.   10k.

E.   Sgl. screw, 2 cyl. comp., 500 nhp, 80 psi. By builder.

B.   Gourlay Brothers, Dundee.

1881   28 December. Launched for Sun Shipping Company, Alexander & Radcliffe as managers.

1889   Sold to Donaldson Brothers, Glasgow, renamed *Amarynthia*.

1889   7 May. First sailing Glasgow–Canada.

1894   Grounded at Montreal.

1902   4 January. Final sailing to St John, New Brunswick.

1902   March. Arrived at Genoa to be broken up.

Werneth Hall 1882   4,100grt.   122.22×12.8×9.05   2,690n.   10k.

E.   Sgl. screw, 2 cyl. comp., 500 nhp, 80 psi. By J.& J. Thomson, Glasgow.

B.   Charles Connell & Company, Glasgow.

1882   Delivered.

1899   Transferred to Hall Line.

1901   June. Laid up at Liverpool.

1902   March. Sold to Macbeth & Company, Glasgow.

1906   March. Owned by G.E. Olsen, Arendal, renamed *Coronel*.

1907   Broken up.

Kirby Hall   1882   2,691grt.   100.55×12.19×7.89   1,759n.   10k.

E.   Sgl. screw, 2 cyl. comp., 300 nhp, 80 psi. By builder.

B.   London & Glasgow Company, Glasgow.

1882   November. Delivered to Kirby Hall Steam Ship Company, R. Alexander & Company as managers.

1896   Sold to Charles Burrell & Son, renamed *Aquileja* for the Austro-Americana Steam Ship Company, Trieste.

1900   Service taken over by Cosulich & Company, Trieste.

1903   Cerutti Brothers as managers.

1904   Broken up.

Aston Hall   1882   3,568grt.   109.72×12.98×8.53   2,323n.   10k.

E.   Sgl. screw, 2 cyl. comp., 400 nhp, 85 psi. By builder.

B.   Gourlay Brothers, Dundee.

1882   September. Delivered to Sun Shipping Company.

1899   Transferred to Hall Line Limited.

1901   June. Sold to J.R. Ellerman, Hall Line Limited, R. Alexander & Company as managers.

1909   Broken up in Turkey following a collision in the Bosphorous.

Eden Hall	1883 3,610grt. 109.72×12.98×8.53 2,332n. 10k.
E.	Sgl. screw, 2 cyl. comp., 400 nhp, 85 psi. By builder.
B.	Gourlay Brothers, Dundee.
1883	April. Delivered to Sun Shipping Company.
1899	Owned by Hall Line.
1901	June. Sold to J.R. Ellerman.
1911	Transferred to Westcott & Laurence Line, London, J.R. Westcott as managers.
1928	January. Broken up.

Rydal Hall (4)	1889 3,315grt. 106.53×12.83×8.53 2,139n. 10k.
E.	Sgl. screw, 2 cyl. tpl. exp., 400 nhp, 85 psi. By builder.
B.	Caird & Company, Greenock.
1889	December. Delivered to Sun Shipping Company.
1899	Owned by Hall Line Limited.
1901	June. Torpedoed and sunk by UC-75, near Eastbourne, twenty-three of her crew lost their lives.

Netherby Hall	1890 3,316grt. 106.53×12.83×8.53 2,139n. 10k.
E.	Sgl. screw, 2 cyl. tpl. exp., 400 nhp, 85 psi. By builder.
B.	Caird & Company, Greenock.
1890	March. Delivered to Sun Shipping Company.
1898	Sold to L. Dixon & Sons, Belfast, renamed *Belfast*.
1915	Owned by Aristides Milonas, Corfu, renamed *Tharros*.
1922	Sold to the Oriental Shipping Company, Corfu, A.A. Caparis as managers.
1928	Purchased by Aristide Mylonas & Company, Piraeus.
1930	Broken up.

Wistow Hall (2)	1890 3,314grt. 106.53×12.83×8.53 2,139n. 10k.
E.	Sgl. screw, 2 cyl. tpl. exp., 400 nhp, 85 psi. By builder.
B.	Caird & Company, Greenock.
1890	January. Delivered to Sun Shipping Company.
1899	Owned by Hall Line Limited.
1901	June. Transferred to J.R. Ellerman.
1903	Operated on the South American service.
1912	18 January. Wrecked on Buchan Rocks, Aberdeenshire, fifty-four of her crew were lost. The loss of lives is recorded on a memorial stone at North Cruden and a plaque in St James' Episcopal Church, Aberdeen.

Stanley Hall	1894 4,104grt. 115.21×13.81×8.59 2,660n. 10k.
E.	Sgl. screw, 2 cyl. tpl. exp., 365 nhp, 180 psi. By builder.
B.	Palmers Company, Jarrow.
1894	March. Delivered to Sun Shipping Company.
1899	Owned by Hall Line Limited.
1901	June. Transferred to J.R. Ellerman.
1920	In service with Ellerman & Bucknall.
1928	22 April. Sold to Alloa Metal Industries, Alloa and broken up.

Haddon Hall (2)   1895   4,177grt.   115.82×13.81×8.87   2,677n.   10k.
E.   Sgl. screw, 2 cyl. tpl. exp., 365 nhp, 180 psi. By builder.
B.   Palmers Company, Jarrow.
1895   December. Delivered to Sun Shipping Company.
1899   Owned by Hall Line Limited.
1901   June. Transferred to J.R. Ellerman.
1913   1 February. On a voyage from Liverpool to Durban she was wrecked north
                          of Saldanha Bay, South Africa, on charter to Ellerman & Bucknall, sailing to
                          South Africa and India.

Hardwick Hall   1896   4,175grt.   115.82×13.81×8.87   2,676n.   10k.
E.   Sgl. screw, 2 cyl. comp., 400 nhp, 85 psi. By builder.
B.   Palmers Company, Jarrow.
1896   January. Delivered to Sun Shipping Company.
1899   Owned by Hall Line Limited.
1901   June. Transferred to J.R. Ellerman.
1903   18 October. On a voyage from Delagoa Bay to Calcutta she was wrecked on
                          Farquhar Island, north of Madagascar.

Trentham Hall (2) 1897   4,173grt.   115.82×13.81×8.87   2,662n.   10k.
E.   Sgl. screw, 2 cyl. comp., 365 nhp, 180 psi. By builder.
B.   Palmers Company, Jarrow.
1897   October. Delivered to Sun Shipping Company.
1899   Owned by Hall Line Limited.
1901   June. Transferred to J.R. Ellerman.
1917   26 May. Wrecked on Pluckington Bank in the Mersey, off Liverpool.

Worsley Hall   1886   3,489grt.   100.5×13.26×8.87   2,238n.   10k.
E   Sgl. screw, tpl. exp., 400 nhp, 150 psi. By builder.
B.   Palmers Company, Jarrow.
1886   August. Delivered to Sun Shipping Company with accommodation for forty
                          passengers.
1899   Owned by Hall Line Limited.
1901   June. Transferred to J.R. Ellerman.
1920   6 January. Purchased by Hydra Steam Ship Company (George M.
                          Chruassachi), London for the Black Sea trade.
1922   September. Evacuated Greek people from Smyrna during the Greco–Turkish
                          dispute.
1924   Broken up in Germany.

Methley Hall   1886   3,492grt.   100.5×13.26×8.87   2,242n.   10k.
E.   Sgl. screw, tpl. exp., 400 nhp, 150 psi. By builder.
B.   Palmers Company, Jarrow.
1886   October. Delivered to Sun Shipping Company.
1899   Owned by Hall Line Limited.
1901   June. Transferred to J.R. Ellerman.
1908   13 April. Arrived at Briton Ferry to be broken up.

Locksley Hall (2)	1888 3,957grt. 115.82×13.82×8.35 2,579n. 10k.
E.	Sgl. screw, tpl. exp., 550 nhp, 150 psi. By builder.
P	60.
B.	Palmers Company, Jarrow.
1888	January. Delivered to Sun Shipping Company.
1899	January. Sold to P&O Steam Navigation Company for the Far East trade. Renamed *Pekin* and requisitioned as a Boer War transport.
1906	Owned by Esafji Tajbhoy Borah, Bombay, renamed *Shah Nawaz*.
1909	Purchased by Hajaz Steam Navigation Company, Bombay to transport pilgrims to Jeddah, renamed *Najmi*.
1911	Broken up at Bombay.

Branksome Hall (2)	1888 3,839grt. 115.82×13.82×8.35 2,555n. 10k.
E.	Sgl. screw, tpl. exp., 550 nhp, 150 psi. By builder.
P	60.
B.	Palmers Company, Jarrow.
1888	February. Delivered to Sun Shipping Company.
1898	December. Sold to P&O Steam Navigation Company for the Far East trade. Renamed *Tientsin* and requisitioned as a Boer War transport.
1906	July. Owned by Esafji Tajbhoy Borah, Bombay, renamed *Shah Mazir*.
1908	Owned by Hajaz Steam Navigation Company, renamed *Fakhi*. Operated as a pilgrim ship, from Bombay to Jeddah for part of the year.
1911	Wrecked on Perim Island, Gulf of Aden. All those on board were saved.

Rufford Hall	1888 3,840grt. 115.82×13.82×8.35 2,580n. 10k.
E.	Sgl. screw, tpl. exp., 550 nhp, 150 psi. By builder.
P.	60.
B.	Palmers Company, Jarrow.
1888	March. Delivered to Sun Shipping Company.
1898	9 December. Sold to P&O Steam Navigation Company for the Far East trade, renamed *Nankin*.
1899	Requisitioned as a Boer War transport.
1904	Sold to M.Y. Kawasaki, Kobe, Japan, renamed *Kotohera Maru No 2*.
1907	Wrecked in the Soya Strait, north of Hokkaido and broken up.

Crewe Hall	1898 4,218grt. 115.82×14.42×8.9 2,691n. 10½k.
E.	Sgl. screw, tpl. exp., 404 nhp, 200 psi. By builder.
B.	Palmers Company, Jarrow.
1898	November. Delivered to Sun Shipping Company.
1899	Owned by Hall Line Limited.
1901	June. Transferred to J.R. Ellerman.
1929	2 October. Sold for £9,750 (£2 per ton), arrived at Newport to be broken up by J. Cashmore.

Pinemore	1898 6,306grt. 139.9×16.02×9.45 4,072n. 12k.
E.	Sgl. screw, tpl. exp., 608 nhp, 200 psi. By D. Rowan & Company, Glasgow.
P.	12.

B.	Charles Connell & Company, Glasgow.
1898	Delivered as Pinemore to William Johnstone to transport live cattle and general cargo on the North Atlantic trade.
1901	Purchased by J.R. Ellerman for the Antwerp–Canada service but sold the rights and the three ships back to Leyland Line.
1902	Owned by Frederick Leyland Limited, renamed *Oxonian*.
1928	Broken up.

Prome / Locksley Hall (3)   1893   3,580grt.   105.15×13.44×8.32   2,299n.   10½k.

E.	Sgl. screw, 329 nhp, 200 psi, 2 sgl. blrs. By builder.
B	William Denny & Brothers, Dumbarton.
1893	30 October. Launched.
1893	9 December. Delivered to the Burmah Steam Ship Company, P. Henderson as managers.
1901	Owned by Hall Line Limited, later renamed *Locksley Hall*. Employed from South Africa to India repatriating Indian troops from the Boer War.
1917	12 May. Torpedoed and sunk by U-32, 30 miles east-south-east of Malta, six of her crew lost their lives.
1917	13 May. Survivors were picked up and landed at Marsa Scirocco.

Merton Hall (2)   1889   4,327grt.   122.07×14.39×8.5   2,773n.   11k.

E.	Sgl. screw, tpl. exp., 435 nhp, 150 psi, 2 dbl. blrs. By builder.
B.	Palmers Company, Jarrow.
1889	16 May. Launched as *Knight Templar* for Greenshields, Cowie & Company, Liverpool. Owned by Knight Companion Steam Ship Company.
1891	Transferred to Knight Steam Ship Company.
1903	Sold to Ellerman Lines, renamed *Merton Hall*.
1918	11 February. On a voyage from New York to La Pallice with a cargo of steel, she was torpedoed by U-53, 30 miles off Ushant. Captain and fifty-seven crew were lost.

Knowsley Hall   1903   4,190grt.   113.69×14.23×8.44   2,705n.   10k.

E.	Sgl. screw, tpl. exp., 320 nhp, 180 psi, 2 sgl. blrs. By Wallsend Slipway Company, Newcastle.
B.	Swan Hunter & Wigham Richardson, Newcastle.
1903	Delivered to Hall Line, fitted with a removable funnel top and telescopic masts for the Manchester Ship Canal service.
1928	1 October. Sold to T.N. Epiphaniades, Piraeus, renamed *Wanda*.
1934	October. Broken up in Italy.

Crosby Hall   1903   4,052grt.   111.25×14.23×8.44   2,597n.   10k.

E.	Sgl. screw, tpl. exp., 320 nhp, 180 psi, 2 sgl. blrs. By Wallsend Slipway Company, Newcastle.
B.	Swan Hunter & Wigham Richardson, Newcastle.
1903	Delivered to Hall Line.
1927	7 January. Sold to D. G. Coucoubanis, Salonika, renamed *Georgios P*.
1944	June. Sunk as a block ship at Arromanches, as part of the Mulberry harbour on the Normandy beach head.

Branksome Hall (3) 1904   4,662grt.   114.21×14.23×8.44 2,728n.   10k.

E.	Sgl. screw, tpl. exp., 320 nhp, 180 psi, 2 sgl. blrs. By Wallsend Slipway Company, Newcastle.
B.	Swan Hunter & Wigham Richardson, Newcastle.
1904	Delivered to Hall Line.
1906	Operated by the Glen Line, McGregor Gow & Company, renamed *Glenavon*.
1910	Renamed *Branksome Hall* for Hall Line.
1917	17 June. Avoided a torpedo in the English Channel.
1917	2 November. Hit by a torpedo fired by UC-65 in the English Channel and beached, salvaged.
1918	14 July. Torpedoed and sunk by U-105, 68 miles off Marsa Susa, North Africa.

Newby Hall   1905   4,391grt.   114.3×14.39×8.44   2,841n.   10k.

E.	Sgl. screw, tpl. exp., 330 nhp, 180 psi, 2 sgl. blrs. By builder.
B.	Barclay, Curle & Company, Glasgow.
1905	7 April. Launched.
1905	Delivered to Hall Line.
1930	10 July. Sold to G. Andreou, Andros, renamed *Yiannis*.
1936	Renamed *Amiral Pierre*, owned by French interests.
1942	30 September. Scuttled off Madagascar by HMS *Hotspur* and HMS *Nizam*.

Langton Hall   1905   4,437grt.   115.06×14.48×8.44   2,882n.   10k.

E.	Sgl. screw, tpl. exp., 320 nhp, 180 psi, 2 sgl. blrs. By Wallsend Slipway Company, Newcastle.
B.	Swan Hunter & Wigham Richardson, Newcastle.
1905	Delivered to Hall Line.
1906	May. Operated the first Hamburg–UK–Marmagao sailing.
1915	30 November. Captured and sunk by gunfire from U-33, 112 miles east of Malta. It was Hall Line's first loss in the war.

Netherby Hall (2)   1905   4,461grt.   116.31×14.48×8.44 2,855n.   10k.

E.	Sgl. screw, tpl. exp., 320 nhp, 180 psi, 2 sgl. blrs. By Wallsend Slipway Company, Newcastle.
B.	Swan Hunter & Wigham Richardson, Newcastle.
1905	Laid down as *Netherby Hall* but completed as *Glenearn* for McGregor, Gow and Company.
1910	Renamed *Netherby Hall* for Hall Line.
1917	10 January. Captured by the German raider *Moewe*, 300 miles east-by-north of Pernambuco. There were 250 people on board and these were transfered to the *Hudson Maru*, which had been captured a week earlier. They were then released at Pernambuco.

Sutton Hall   1905   4,460grt.   114.42×14.45×8.44   2,870n.   10k.

E.	Sgl. screw, tpl. exp., 320 nhp, 180 psi, 2 sgl. blrs. By Wallsend Slipway Company, Newcastle.
B.	Swan Hunter & Wigham Richardson, Newcastle.
1905	Delivered to Hall Line.

1915	3 March. On Belgian relief work between Plymouth and Antwerp and carrying international colours, she was attacked by a German submarine. However, the torpedo failed to make contact with her and she was able to proceed.
1916–17	Loaned to the French Government.
1930	18 December. Sold to be broken up.

Sandon Hall 1906   5,134grt.   122.35×15.3×8.44   3,293n.   10k.

E.	Sgl. screw, tpl. exp., 320 nhp, 180 psi, 2 sgl. blrs. By Wallsend Slipway Company, Newcastle.
B.	Swan Hunter & Wigham Richardson, Newcastle.
1906	Delivered to Hall Line.
1918	1 January. With a cargo of stores and ammunition she was torpedoed and sunk by U-40, 22 miles north-east of Linosa. All crew were saved.

Locksley Hall (4) / *City of Agra* (2)   1903   4,808grt.   121.92×15.3×8.81   3,096n.   10k.

E.	Sgl. screw, tpl. exp., 379 nhp, 180 psi. By builder.
B.	Workman, Clark & Company, Belfast.
1903	Ordered as *Locksley Hall*, delivered as *City of Agra*, Hall Line.
1932	12 April. Sold to be broken up in Italy.

City of Agra (2).

Rufford Hall (2) / *City of Madras* (4)   1903   4,684grt   120.52×15.12×8.81   3,048n.   10k.

E.	Sgl. screw, tpl. exp., 379 nhp, 180 psi. By builder.
B.	Palmers Company, Jarrow.
1903	Laid down as *Rufford Hall*, delivered as *City of Madras*, Hall Line.
1931	9 September. Sold for demolition in Italy.

City of Karachi (3)   1905   5,547grt.   126.08×15.7×8.9   3,563n.   10k.

E.	Sgl. screw, tpl. exp., 379 nhp, 180 psi. By builder.
B.	Workman, Clark & Company, Belfast.
1905	8 March. Launched.
1905	June. Delivered to Hall Line with accommodation for sixty-nine first- and nineteen second-class passengers.
1908	Transferred to the management of George Smith & Sons for City Line services. Owned by Ellerman Lines.

| 1921 | 16 December. Operated on American & Indian Line's service from New York to India. |
| 1934 | 17 October. Sold to be broken up in Japan. |

Trafford Hall	1905 5,321grt. 121.07×15.24×8.84 3,437n. 11k.
E.	Sgl. screw, tpl. exp., 369 nhp, 180 psi. By builder.
P.	70 (first), 24 (second).
B.	Barclay, Curle & Company, Glasgow.
1905	28 October. Launched.
1912	Operated on Bucknall Steamship Lines service.
1914–18	On commercial service.
1919	24 February. Operated on the American & Indian Line service.
1929	On a voyage from Hamburg to South Africa she suffered a serious fire caused by spontaneous combustion in a synthetic wool shipment. It was particularly serious as it occurred in the South Atlantic, 2,000 miles from Cape Town. Water was sprayed onto the cargo for eight days until she reached port and the fire was kept under control. For his conduct on the occasion Captain D.L. Lloyd was awarded the silver medal of the Society for the Protection of Life from Fire.
1934	4 September. Sold to be broken up in Italy.
1934	28 September. Arrived at Trieste.

Trafford Hall.

Denbigh Hall	1906 4,943grt. 122.22×15.3×9.0 3,211n. 11k.
E.	Sgl. screw, tpl. exp., 353 nhp, 225 psi, 2 sgl. blrs. By builder.
B.	Barclay, Curle & Company, Glasgow.
1906	22 October. Launched.
1906	Delivered.
1914–18	Requisitioned as an Indian Government transport and supply ship. Carried coal outwards and returned with grain.
1918	18 May. On a voyage from Buenos Aires to the United Kingdom she was torpedoed and sunk by U-55, 90 miles south-west of Bishops Rock.

| *Thornton Hall / City of Carthage* (2)   1906   5,524grt.   122.22×16.06×9.0   3,211n.   11k. |
E.	Sgl. screw, tpl. exp., 353 nhp, 225 psi, 2 sgl. blrs. By builder.
B.	Barclay, Curle & Company, Glasgow.
1906	Laid down as *Thornton Hall*.

1906	23 June. Launched, delivered as *City of Carthage* for the Far East service.
1907	10 August. On a voyage from Philadelphia to Hiogo she was wrecked at Kamodasaki, Japan.

Walton Hall	1907 4,932grt. 122.22×15.3×9.0 3,203n. 11k.
E.	Sgl. screw, tpl. exp., 353 nhp, 225 psi, 2 sgl. blrs. By builder.
B.	Barclay, Curle & Company, Glasgow.
1907	30 January. Launched.
1907	Delivered.
1931	8 October. Arrived at Port Glasgow to be broken up.

City of Naples	1908 5,739grt. 127.5×16.24×9.26 3,714n. 11k.
E.	Sgl. screw, tpl. exp., 353 nhp, 225 psi, 2 sgl. blrs. By builder.
B.	Swan Hunter & Wigham Richardson, Newcastle.
1908	Delivered.
1926	16 June. On a voyage from Dunkirk to Yokohama she was wrecked on Zenisu Reef, Miyaki Island, Japan.

City of Colombo	1909 5,598grt. 129.54×16.49×9.42 3,901n. 11k.
E.	Sgl. screw, tpl. exp., 353 nhp, 225 psi, 2 sgl. blrs. By builder.
B.	Swan Hunter & Wigham Richardson, Newcastle.
1909	Delivered.
1917	1 August. Attacked by the German submarine U-155 and escaped after firing at her.
1917	4 August. Attacked again by an enemy submarine and escaped.
1918	October. Managed by City Line.
1921	March. Wrecked at Nova Scotia.

Claverhill / Croxteth Hall	1905 3,991grt. 109.12×15.03×5.55 2,435n. 10k.
E.	Sgl. screw, tpl. exp., 391 nhp, 180 psi, 3 sgl. blrs. By North East Marine Limited, Sunderland.
B.	Craig, Taylor & Company, Stockton.
1905	September. Delivered as *Claverhill* to Claverhill Steam Ship Company, London, E. Haselhurst as managers.
1909	Purchased by Hall Line and renamed *Croxteth Hall*.
1913	Sold to W. Crosby & Company, Melbourne, renamed *Ooma* for the Australia–Pacific Islands service.
1920	Registered in Suva.
1926	8 February. On a voyage from Sydney to Naura with coal and general cargo she was wrecked on Sydney Point, Ocean Island.

City of Chester	1910 5,413grt. 125.12×15.85×9.26 3,521n. 11k.
E.	Sgl. screw, tpl. exp., 362 nhp. By builder.
B.	Barclay, Curle & Company, Glasgow.
1910	25 April. Launched.
1910	Delivered to Hall Line
1924	Transferred to City Line services, managed by Graham Smith, owners Ellerman Lines Limited.

1932	Managed by City Line Limited.
1933	December. Sold to be broken up by Arnott & Young.
1934	30 January. Arrived at Dalmuir.

City of Chester.

City of Bombay (3)   1910   5,186grt.   122.28×15.48×9.05   3,355n.   11k.

E.	Sgl. screw, tpl. exp., 509 nhp. By builder.
B.	Palmers Company, Jarrow.
1910	September. Delivered to Hall Line.
1932	May. Broken up by Douglas & Ramsey at Glasgow.

City of Baroda   1911   5,032grt.   122.44×15.48×9.05   3,279n.   11k.

E.	Sgl. screw, tpl. exp., 362 nhp. By builder.
B.	Barclay, Curle & Company, Glasgow.
1911	March. Delivered to Hall Line, owned by Ellerman Lines Limited.
1917	4 June. Torpedoed and sunk by UC-53, 90 miles north-west of Tory Island. Six of her crew were lost.

City of Durham 1911   5,356grt.   124.05×15.67×9.05   3,460n.   11k.

E.	Sgl. screw, tpl. exp., 521 nhp. By builder.
B.	Palmers Company, Jarrow.
1911	February. Delivered.
1933	26 January. Sold and broken up in Italy.

City of Birmingham   1911   7,498grt.   137.77×16.98×9.6   4,839n.   12k.

E.	Sgl. screw, quad. exp., 756 nhp, 225 psi, 4 sgl. blrs. By builder.
P.	130 (first), 40 (second).
B.	Palmers Shipbuilding Company, Newcastle.
1911	November. Delivered to Hall Line for the Indian passenger service.
1914–16	Employed as an Indian Expeditionary Force troopship.
1916	27 November. Torpedoed and sunk by U-32 off Malta. On board were 170 passengers and a crew of 145. Four of her crew were lost when the ship was abandoned and the captain was picked up by the lifeboats after the ship had sunk. The survivors were rescued three hours later by the British hospital ship *Letitia*.

City of Lincoln	1911 5,867grt. 128.62×16.28×9.42 3,784n. 11k.	
E.	Sgl. screw, tpl. exp., 581 nhp, 220 psi. By builder.	
B.	Palmers Shipbuilding Company, Newcastle.	
1911	Delivered to Hall Line.	
1917	18 September. Torpedoed by UB-32 off the Scilly Isles. Towed into port, repaired.	
1934	25 January. Sold to be broken up in Italy.	

City of Lahore (2)	1911 6,948grt. 133.65×16.49×9.51 4,471n. 12k.	
E.	Sgl. screw, 4 cyl. quad. exp., 434 nhp, 180 psi. By Wallsend Slipway & Engineering Company Limited, Wallsend.	
P.	73 (first), 40 (second).	
B.	Swan Hunter & Wigham Richardson, Wallsend.	
1911	14 March. Launched.	
1919	7 November. Operated on the American & Indian Line service, Bucknall funnel, black hull.	
1922	1 December. Ran aground in fog on the Antrim coast, refloated the next day.	
1926	On a voyage from Rotterdam to the River Plate she collided with the *Agia Marina* in the English Channel.	
1927	October. Operated on the American & Indian Line service, Bucknall funnel.	
1932	Laid up in the Gareloch.	
1933	August. Sold and broken up at Troon.	

Melford Hall	1912 5,514grt. 125.33×16.7×8.84 3,506n. 12k.	
E.	Sgl. screw, tpl. exp., 369 nhp. By builder.	
B.	Barclay, Curle & Company, Glasgow.	
1911	23 December. Launched.	
1912	Delivered.	
1915	November. Inaugurated the Manchester–New York service.	
1917	22 June. On a voyage from Liverpool to Karachi and Bombay she was torpedoed and sunk by U-100, 95 miles north-by-west of Tory Island.	

City of Bristol	1912 6,741grt. 127.77×17.25×9.63 4,345n. 12k.	
E.	Sgl. screw, tpl. exp., 379 nhp. By builder.	
B.	Swan Hunter & Wigham Richardson, Wallsend.	
1912	Delivered to Hall Line.	
1936	1 December. Sold to Barry Shipping Company, renamed *St Woolos* for the Antwerp–River Plate service.	
1937	Sold under the 'scrap and build scheme'.	
1938	Broken up at Osaka.	

City of Dunkirk	1912 5,861grt. 128.23×16.52×9.23 3,759n. 11k.	
E.	Sgl. screw, tpl. exp., 379 nhp. By builder.	
B.	Barclay, Curle & Company, Glasgow.	
1912	25 September. Launched.	
1912	October. Delivered.	
1914–18	Operated in commercial service.	

1950	9 January. Sold to Luigi Monta fu Carlo, Genoa, renamed *Marilen*.
1953	May. Purchased by Minerva Imprese Marittimi, Genoa, renamed *Minerva*.
1959	Broken up at La Spezia.

City of Marseilles 1913 8,250grt. 143.04×17.37×9.78 5,284n. 14k.

E.	Twin screw, 2×4 cyl. quad. exp., 851 nhp, 225 psi, 4 sgl. blrs. By builder.
P.	169 (first).
B.	Palmers Shipbuilding Company, Newcastle.
1912	26 October. Launched.
1913	26 January. Maiden voyage Liverpool–New York–Port Said–Bombay, then Liverpool–Bombay.
1915	23 November. Attacked by a German submarine on a voyage from Liverpool to Bombay, escaped.
1916	November. Rescued 95 out of the 721 survivors from the P&O vessel *Arabia* which had been torpedoed 112 miles south-west of Cape Matapan.
1921	Operated on the American & Indian Line service to India.
1923	Trooping service to India.
1930	Replaced on this service by the Bibby Line *Lancashire*.
1940	6 January. Collided with a mine in the River Tay.
1943	22 January. On a voyage from Liverpool to Madras and Calcutta she stranded near Batticaloa, Ceylon. She was later refloated.
1947	Broken up.

City of Marseilles.

City of Norwich 1913 6,382grt. 132.4×16.67×9.51 4,346n. 12k.

E.	Sgl. screw, tpl. exp., 606 nhp, 220 psi, 3 sgl. blrs. By Central Marine Engineering Works, West Hartlepool.
P.	3.
B.	William Gray & Company, West Hartlepool.
1913	July. Delivered.
1955	22 February. Sold to T. Maglivers, Panama, renamed *Marinucci*.
1959	Broken up at Yokohama.

City of Corinth (3) 1913 5,870grt. 128.06×16.85×9.08 3,773n. 12k.

E.	Sgl. screw, tpl. exp., 391 nhp. By builder.

B.   Barclay, Curle & Company, Glasgow.
1913   14 October. Launched.
1913   Delivered.
1917   21 May. On a voyage from Singapore to London she was torpedoed and sunk by
            UB-31, 12 miles south-west of the Lizard, Cornwall.

City of Mysore   1914   5,294grt.   122.25×15.63×5.99   3,416n.   12½k.
E.   Sgl. screw, tpl. exp., 534 nhp, 2 sgl. blrs. By builder.
1914   Delivered.
1915   23 February. On a voyage from Calcutta to London and Dunkirk she was wrecked
            on Komuriya Reef, Ceylon.

City of Florence (2)   1914   5,399grt.   124.11×15.63×9.05   3,490n.   12k.
E.   Sgl. screw, tpl. exp., 547 nhp, 220 psi, 2 sgl. blrs. By builder.
B.   Palmers Shipbuilding Company, Newcastle.
1914   Delivered.
1917   20 July. Torpedoed and sunk by UC-17, 188 miles off Ushant in the North
            Atlantic.

Rufford Hall (3)   1914   5,506grt.   124.81×16.18×9.14   3,553n.   12k.
E.   Sgl. screw, tpl. exp., 390 nhp, 220 psi, 2 sgl. blrs. By Wallsend Slipway & Engineering
            Company Limited.
B.   Swan Hunter & Wigham Richardson, Newcastle.
1914   Delivered.
1915   6 October. On a voyage from New York to Honolulu and Vladivostok she was
            wrecked on the Tsugaru Strait, near Omazaki.

*City of
Rangoon.*

City of Rangoon   1914   6,633grt.   135.02×16.85×9.51   4,272n.   12k.
E.   Sgl. screw, tpl. exp., 617 nhp, 220 psi, 3 sgl. blrs. By Central Marine Engineering
            Works, West Hartlepool.
B.   William Gray & Company, West Hartlepool.
1914   June. Delivered.
1944   Sustained bottom damage, repaired.

1945	25 October. Purchased by the Ministry of War Transport, renamed *Oscar III*, managed by Hall Line. Sailed to the Far East with a cargo of coal.
1946	Coal store and later a hulk at Singapore.
1950	10 December. Arrived at Bombay to be broken up.

City of Vienna (3)   1914   6,111grt.   128.11×16.98×9.42   3,917n.   12k.

E.	Sgl. screw, tpl. exp., 424 nhp, 220 psi, 3 sgl. blrs. By builder.
B.	Workman, Clark & Company, Belfast.
1914	Delivered.
1918	2 July. On a voyage from Montreal to Halifax in ballast she was wrecked at Ketch Harbour, Sambro, Nova Scotia.

City of Winchester   1914   6,800grt.   136.92×17.31×10.15   12k.

E.	Sgl. screw, tpl. exp.,641 nhp, 220 psi, 3 sgl. blrs. By builder.
B.	Earle's Shipbuilding Company, Hull.
1914	Delivered.
1914	6 August. On her maiden voyage she was captured by the German light cruiser *Konigsberg*, 280 miles east of Aden sailing from Calcutta back to Britain with a cargo of tea. She was taken into Makalla, where the crew were transferred to the German vessel *Zeiten*.
1914	5 December. Following the discharge of her stores and coal the ship was taken out to sea and scuttled off Suda Island, Kuria Maria Islands. She was Ellerman Lines' first war loss.

City of Newcastle   1915   7,280grt.   139.14×17.19×9.45   4,462n.   12k.

E.	Sgl. screw, tpl. exp., 616 nhp, 220 psi, 3 sgl. blrs. By Central Marine Engineering Works, West Hartlepool.
B.	William Gray & Company, West Hartlepool.
1914	16 December. Damaged by German bombing while she was being fitted out at Hartlepool.
1915	19 January. Delivered and requisitioned as a transport for the Indian Expeditionary Force.
1917	April. Operated under the Liner Requisition Scheme.
1926	Twenty-nine Muslim crew refused to sail on a voyage to Philadelphia as the cook was Buddhist.
1940	Experienced storm damage and was forced into Cape Town for repairs.
1943	July. Operated as a stores ship for the invasion of Sicily. Damaged by aerial bomb attack at Augusta.
1951	May. Sold to Soc. Nav. Magliveras, Panama, renamed *Marinucci*.
1952	11 August. Arrived at La Spezia to be broken up.

City of Hankow (2)   1915   8,420grt.   141.85×17.74×9.69   5,869n.

E.	Sgl. screw, quad. exp.,738 nhp, 220 psi, 3 sgl. blrs. By Central Marine Engineering Works, West Hartlepool.
B.	William Gray & Company, West Hartlepool.
1915	Delivered.
1922	Owned by the Oran Steam Ship Company, Hall Line as managers.

1924	Owned by Montgomerie & Workman Limited, operated by City Line and managed by Hall Line.
1936	Owned by Ellerman Lines Limited, Hall Line as managers.
1942	18 December. Wrecked at Saldanha Bay, South Africa.

City of Hankow (2).

City of Canton (2).

City of Canton (2)   1916   6,982grt.   142.16×17.34×9.48   4,471n.

E.	Sgl. screw, 2 turb., srg, 751 nhp, 220 psi, 3 sgl. blrs. By Wallsend Slipway & Engineering Company Limited, Wallsend.
B.	Swan Hunter & Wigham Richardson, Newcastle.
1916	September. Delivered to Hall Line.
1943	16 July. Torpedoed and sunk by U-178 off Beira. The survivors were in the life-rafts for seven days without food or water before they were rescued.

City of Manila   1916   8,340grt.   144.78×17.74×9.69   4,834n.

E.	Sgl. screw, quad. exp. drg LP turbines connected by hydraulic coupling, 859 nhp, 220 psi, 3 sgl. blrs. By Central Marine Engineering Works, West Hartlepool.
B.	William Gray & Company, West Hartlepool.
1916	June. Delivered.
1942	19 August. In convoy SL 118 she was torpedoed and sunk by U-406 off the Azores.

Langton Hall (2) / *City of Cardiff*   1918   5,661grt.   127.86×16.58×9.08   4,211n.

E.	Sgl. screw, tpl. exp., 552 nhp, 220 psi, 3 sgl. blrs. By North East Marine Limited, Newcastle.
B.	Craig, Taylor & Company, Stockton.
1918	January. Delivered with removable funnel top for Manchester Ship Canal service.
1926	Renamed *City of Cardiff*, Hall Line.
1932–33	Laid up in the Gareloch with *City of Carlisle*, *City of Chester*, *City of Eastbourne*, *City of Harvard*, *City of Lahore*, *City of Mobile*, *City of Nagpur* and *City of Paris*.
1942	28 August. Torpedoed off Cape Finisterre by U-566 in convoy SL 119. She was abandoned and sank the following day.

City of Cardiff.

City of Nagpur   1914   8,331grt.   141.82×17.76×9.63   14½k.

E.	Sgl. screw, 4 cyl. quad. exp., 492 nhp. By builder.
P.	222 (first), 92 (second).
B.	Workman, Clark & Company, Belfast.
1914	Delivered for the Indian service.
1917	23 August. On a voyage from Durban to Bombay she was wrecked on Danea Shoal, Delagoa Bay, South Africa. All 195 on board were saved.

City of Cairo   1915   7,882grt.   137.13×16.98×9.54   5,042n.   12k.

E.	Sgl. screw, 4 cyl. quad. exp., 774 nhp, 3,900 ihp, 225 psi, 3 sgl. blrs. By builder.
P.	133 (first), 43 (second).
B.	Earle's Shipbuilding Company, Hull.
1914	2 October. Launched.
1915	January. Delivered.
1927	6 March. Operated on the American & Indian service to Calcutta and Rangoon.
1942	1 November. Departed Cape Town at 6 a.m., carrying 101 passengers, of whom 28 were women and 19 children. Also aboard were ten gunners from the Army and Royal Navy. She was unescorted and maintained a course approximately 45 miles from the African coast. Unfortunately she was making excessive smoke and only capable of a speed of 12 knots.

City of Cairo.

1942	6 November. Five hundred miles south of St Helena and five days out of Cape Town she was torpedoed by U-68 at 8.30 p.m. Three passengers and eighteen of the crew lost their lives and a second torpedo damaged all but two lifeboats after they had been launched.
1942	19 November. Three of the lifeboats, containing the captain and 154 survivors were rescued by the *Clan Alpine*. They reported that there were three other boats, but following an unsuccessful search *Clan Alpine* landed the survivors at St Helena. Later that day another lifeboat with 47 survivors was rescued by *Bendoran* and taken to Cape Town.
1942	12 December. Three survivors were picked up by the German blockade vessel *Rhakotis*, but one died later.
1942	27 December. One boat with only two survivors on board, the third officer and a female passenger, was sighted by the Brazilian Navy minelayer *Caravelas*. They had been in the boat for fifty-one days and had got within 80 miles of the Brazilian coast and were landed at Recife. The third officer was later awarded the MBE, but was killed when *City of Pretoria* was torpedoed and sunk by U-172 on 4 March the following year. Margaret Gordon, the female passenger, was awarded the BEM. Of the 311 people on board, 104 had died, including 79 crew members, 3 gunners and 22 passengers, with 207 surviving. Six people died in the sinking, 91 in the boats and seven after being rescued.
1943	1 January. Rhakotis was scuttled off Cape Finisterre after being followed by the cruiser HMS *Scylla*.
1984	14 September. Sixteen survivors of the attack by U-68 met the captain of the submarine on HMS *Belfast* in London. Captain Karl Friedrich Merten made a special journey from his home in Waldshut, near the Swiss–German border. It was the first occasion that the survivors had met as a group since the incident.

Hermiston	1901 4,389grt. 114.18×14.66×8.5 2,831n. 10k.
E.	Sgl. screw, tpl. exp., 360 nhp, 180 psi, 3 sgl. blrs. By D. Rowan & Company, Glasgow.
B.	R. Duncan & Company, Port Glasgow.
1901	Delivered as *Hermiston* to Borderdale Shipping Company, Glasgow, J. Little as managers.
1917	War loss replacement for Ellerman Lines, owned by the City of Oran Steam Ship Company.

1919	Purchased by E. Engelis, Piraeus, renamed *Athena*.
1922	Renamed *Charalambos* for Alex G. Yannoulato, Greece.
1838	Broken up.

Borderer	1904 4,372grt. 114.1×14.9×8.5 2,835n. 10k.
E.	Sgl. screw, tpl. exp., 418 nhp, 180 psi, 3 sgl. blrs. By Clyde Shipbuilding & Engineering Company, Port Glasgow.
B.	R. Duncan & Company, Port Glasgow.
1904	December. Delivered to Border Union Steam Ship Company, Glasgow, J. Little as managers.
1917	Operated by Ellerman & Papayanni Line, owned by Joshua Nicholson Steam Ship Company, Liverpool, H.H. Mc Allester as managers.
1921	Transferred to Hall Line.
1929	Sold to Reederei Eugen Friederich, Bremen, renamed *Emmy Friederich*.
1939	1 November. Scuttled after being followed by a British naval vessel.

City of Winchester (2)	1917 7,891grt. 139.02×17.65×9.54 5,164n. 12½k.
E.	Sgl. screw, 2 turbines, 736 nhp, 200 psi, 2,900 ihp, 3 sgl. blrs. By builder.
B.	Palmers Shipbuilding Company, Newcastle.
1917	October. Delivered.
1918	15 April. Torpedoed by UC-77 but escaped and returned to port.
1941	8 September. Torpedoed and sunk by U-103, west of Dakar.

City of Adelaide	1917 8,389grt. 131.98×17.49×9.2 4.179n. 12k.
E.	Sgl. screw, 2 turbines, 736 nhp, 200 psi, 2,900 ihp, 3 sgl. blrs. By Central Marine Engineering Works, West Hartlepool.
B.	William Gray & Company, West Hartlepool.
1917	April. Delivered.
1918	11 August. As several members of her crew were ill she left her convoy to dock at Malta. She was torpedoed and sunk by U-63, 60 miles east-north-east of Malta, four of her crew lost their lives. HMS *Asphodel* picked up the survivors.

City of Adelaide (2).

City of Corinth (4)   1918   5,318grt.   119.18×16.52×8.81   3,424n.   12k.

E.	Sgl. screw, tpl. exp., 581 nhp, 200 psi, 2,900 ihp, 3 sgl. blrs. By Central Marine Engineering Works, West Hartlepool.
B.	William Gray & Company, West Hartlepool.
1918	January. Delivered.
1940	21 December. Damaged by bombs and incendiaries during an air raid at Liverpool.
1942	17 November. Torpedoed and sunk by U-508 at Trinidad.

City of Brisbane   1918   7,138grt.   141.3×17.92×9.42   4,527n.   12k.

E.	Sgl. screw, tpl. exp., 885 nhp, 200 psi, 2,900 ihp, 3 sgl. blrs. By Wallsend Slipway & Engineering Company, Wallsend.
B.	Swan Hunter & Wigham Richardson, Newcastle.
1918	Delivered.
1918	15 August. Torpedoed and sunk by UB-57 in the English Channel, near Newhaven. All of the crew were saved.

Melford Hall (2) / *City of Johannesburg*   1920   5,669grt.   127.16×16.7×8.84   3,583n.

E.	Sgl. screw, tpl. exp., 885 nhp, 200 psi, 2,900 ihp, 3 sgl. blrs. By builder.
B.	Barclay, Curle & Company, Glasgow.
1920	23 May. Launched.
1920	Delivered as *Melford Hall*.
1926	15 October. Renamed *City of Johannesburg*.
1942	23 October. On a voyage from Calcutta to the United Kingdom via Cape Town she was torpedoed and sunk off East London by U-504.

City of Pekin (2)   1920   6,960grt.   134.96×17.89×8.84   4,426n.

E.	Sgl. screw, 2 turb., 736 nhp, 200 psi, 2,900 ihp, 3 sgl. blrs. By builder.
B.	Palmers Shipbuilding Company, Newcastle.
1920	December. Delivered.
1930	10 April. On a voyage from Vladivostok to Dairen she struck a rock and sank at Brook Island off Korea.

City of Adelaide (2)   1920   6,589grt.   137.37×17.49×9.2   4,178n.

E.	Sgl. screw, 2 turb., 736 nhp, 200 psi, 2,900 ihp, 3 sgl. blrs. By Central Marine Engineering Works, West Hartlepool.
B.	William Gray & Company, West Hartlepool.
1920	November. Delivered.
1944	30 March. On a voyage from Karachi to Britain she was attacked by gunfire and torpedoed by the Japanese submarine I-8. She was Ellerman Lines' final war loss.

City of Brisbane (2)   1920   7,138grt.   141.3×17.92×9.42   4,527n.

E.	Sgl. screw, tpl. exp., 885 nhp, 200 psi, 2,900 ihp, 3 sgl. blrs. By Wallsend Slipway & Engineering Company, Wallsend.
B.	Swan Hunter & Wigham Richardson, Newcastle.
1920	June. Delivered.
1940	2 August. Bombed by German aircraft off Long Sands in the Thames Estuary. She was set on fire, sank and broke in two. Eight members of her crew were lost.

City of Lucknow (5) 1917 8,293grt. 144.78×17.74×9.66 4,973n. 12k.

E.   Sgl. screw, 4 cyl. quad. exp., 758 nhp, 225 psi, 3 sgl. blrs. By Central Marine
                       Engineering Works, West Hartlepool.

B.   William Gray & Company, West Hartlepool.

1917   June. Delivered to the Oran Steam Ship Company, Hall Line as managers.

1917   21 December. Torpedoed and sunk by UB-50, 50 miles north-east of Cani Rocks,
                       Tunisia.

City of Shanghai (2) 1917 5,528grt. 127.56×16.76×8.96 3,748n. 12k.

E.   Sgl. screw, tpl. exp., 565 nhp, 220 psi, 2 sgl. blrs. By builder.

B.   Earle's Shipbuilding Company, Hull.

1917   August. Delivered.

1941   10 May. On a voyage from Rosyth to Cape Town via the Suez Canal and Turkey,
                       off St Paul's Rocks 980 miles from Pernambuco, she was torpedoed and sunk by
                       U-103. The Union Castle vessel *Rochester Castle* rescued the survivors from one of
                       the lifeboats after two days, and the crew in the second lifeboat were found by an
                       Argentine vessel after five days. They were all landed at Pernambuco.

City of Shanghai (2).

Croxteth Hall (2) 1917 5,872grt. 126.22×16.00×8.99 3,741n. 11k.

E.   Sgl. screw, tpl. exp., 556 nhp. 220 psi, 2 sgl. blrs. By builder.

B.   Palmers Shipbuilding Company, Newcastle.

1917   July. Delivered to the Barcelona Steam Ship Company, Hall Line as managers.

1917   17 November. Sunk off Bombay by a mine.

City of Baroda (2) 1918 7,129grt. 132.1×17.43×9.33 4,500n. 12½k.

E.   Sgl. screw, tpl. exp., 447 nhp, 220 psi. By builder.

P.   113 (first).

B.   Barclay, Curle & Company, Glasgow.

1918   26 June. Launched as the final Hall Line passenger vessel for the Calcutta service.
                       She had been laid down as a cargo ship.

1927   3 February. Operated on the American & Indian service.

1943   2 April. On a voyage from London to Durban and Colombo via Walvis Bay, off
                       Luderitz Bay, South Africa, she was torpedoed and sunk by U-509. One member of
                       her crew and thirteen passengers were lost.

City of Baroda (2).

City of Florence (3).

City of Florence (3)   1918   6,826grt.   136.79×17.13×9.57   4,391n.   12k.

E.	Sgl. screw, tpl. exp., 621 nhp, 220 psi, 3 sgl. blrs. By Central Marine Engineering Works, West Hartlepool.
B.	William Gray & Company, West Hartlepool.
1918	February. Delivered.
1956	When she arrived at Liverpool on her final voyage she had a stateless Ceylonese stowaway on board. He had been on the ship for several years as he was not allowed to land at any port. However, when the ship was sold to F. Theodorides a resident's permit was granted to the stowaway for six months. Renamed *Mount Olympus*.
1959	Broken up in Japan.

Kioto   1918   4,397grt.   105.92×14.2×7.44   2,777n.

E.	Sgl. screw, tpl. exp., 384 nhp, 220 psi, 2 sgl. blrs. By builder.
B.	William Gray & Company, West Hartlepool.
1918	April. Purchased by Hall Line.
1942	15 September. Torpedoed and sunk by U-514 in the North Atlantic.

City of Melbourne   1919   6,630grt.   125.73×16.92×10.48   4,125n.   12k.

E.	Sgl. screw, tpl. exp., 597 nhp, 180 psi. By J. Dickinson & Sons, Sunderland.
B.	J. L. Thompson, Sunderland.
1919	June. Delivered to Hall Line.
1942	13 May. Torpedoed and sunk by U-156 off the Leeward Islands.

Romeo / City of Guildford   1919   5,157grt.   121.92×15.94×8.69   3,236n.   11k.

E.	Sgl. screw, tpl. exp., 517 nhp, 180 psi, 3 sgl. blrs. By Central Marine Engineering Works, West Hartlepool.
B.	William Gray & Company, West Hartlepool.
1919	17 March. Launched as *War Midge*, as a standard B-type hull.
1919	June. Delivered as *Romeo* to Hall Line.
1928	Renamed *City of Guildford*.
1943	27 March. Torpedoed and sunk by U-593 off Madeira.

Merton Hall (3) / *City of Salford*   1905   4,988grt.   119.69×14.6×8.62   3,134n. 10k.

E.	Sgl. screw, tpl. exp., 380 nhp, 180 psi. By Wallsend Slipway & Engineering Company, Wallsend.
P.	850 (emigrants).
B.	Swan Hunter & Wigham Richardson, Newcastle.
1905	17 June. Launched as *Santa Cruz* for the Hamburg Süd-Amerika Line.
1905	14 September. Maiden voyage Hamburg–La Plata–Rosario.
1914	August. Renamed *Sperrbrecher 7* for the German Navy.
1918	Delivered back to Hamburg Süd-Amerika Line.
1919	26 March. Owned by the British Shipping Controller, managed by MacVicar, Marshall & Company
1921	Purchased by Hall Line, renamed *Merton Hall*.
1926	Renamed *City of Salford*.
1933	November. Broken up by Douglas & Ramsey, Glasgow.

Branksome Hall (4)   1905   4,467grt.   117.93×15.79×7.59   2,808n.   11k.

E.	Sgl. screw, 4 cyl. quad. exp., 440 nhp, 213 psi, 2 sgl. blrs. By builder.
B.	Swan Hunter & Wigham Richardson, Newcastle.
1905	September. Delivered to DD-G 'Hansa', Bremen, renamed Arensburg.
1919	March. Responsibility of the British Shipping Controller, manager G. Heyn & Sons, Belfast.
1920	Owned by Ellerman Lines, Hall Line, renamed *Branksome Hall*.
1933	Collided with Southend Pier, uneconomic to repair.
1933	31 July. Arrived to be broken up in Italy.

Croxteth Hall (3)   1909   4,243grt.   111.86×14.54×8.32   2,621n.   11k.

E.	Sgl. screw, tpl. exp., 327 nhp, 185 psi. By Bremer Vulkan, Vegesack.
B.	Rickmers AG, Bremerhaven.
1909	14 August. Launched.
1909	11 September. Delivered as *Etha Rickmers*, as one of twelve sister ships.
1914	31 July. When the First World War began she was at Sevastopol and was captured as a war prize, renamed *Kaca*. She was employed as a floating workshop for the Black Sea fleet.
1918	Employed to repatriate German troops from Turkey to Wilhelmshaven.
1920	Responsibility of the British Shipping Controller, to Hall Line as managers, renamed *Croxteth Hall*.
1929	28 February. Wrecked in fog near the Wandelaar Lightship, Blankenberghe, Belgium.

City of Westminster   1916   6,094grt.   143.41×18.93×7.71   3,771n.   12k.

E.	Sgl. screw, tpl. exp., 701 nhp, 200 psi. By builder.
B.	Flensburger SG, Flensburg.
1916	Delivered as *Rudelsburg* to DD-G 'Hansa', Bremen.
1919	Responsibility of the British Shipping Controller, Andrew Weir & Company as managers.
1920	To the Oran Steam Ship Company, Hall Line as managers, renamed *City of Westminster*.
1923	10 October. On a voyage from Port Natal to Belfast and Rotterdam she was wrecked on the Runnelstone, Cornwall.

City of Genoa   1906   6,365grt.   125.45×15.45×8.72   4,008n.   12k.

E.	Twin screw, 2× tpl. exp., 625 nhp, 220 psi, 4 sgl. blrs. By builder.
P.	96 (first), 62 (second), 80 (third).
B.	Blohm & Voss, Hamburg.
1905	8 November. Launched as *Gertrud Woermann* for the Woermann Line.
1906	25 January. Maiden voyage on the Hamburg–West Africa service.
1907	25 April. Purchased by Hamburg America Line, renamed *Windhuk* on a joint service with Woermann Line to West Africa.
1914	4 August. Used as a depot ship at Hamburg.
1919	1 April. Responsibility of the British Shipping Controller, Elder Dempster as managers.
1921	Sold to Ellerman Lines, H.H. MacAllester as managers. Hall Line service to Africa, renamed *City of Genoa*.
1928	Purchased by Cia. Colonial, Loanda, renamed *Joao Belo*.
1950	5 July. Sold to be broken up at Thornaby.

City of Genoa.

City of Sydney   1914   5,775grt.   137.49×15.63×7.74   3,486n.   12½k.

E.	Sgl. screw, tpl. exp., LP turbine drg by hydraulic coupling, 872 nhp, 223 psi, 4 sgl. blrs. By builder.
B.	J.C. Tecklenborg AG, Geestemunde.
1914	12 March. Launched as *Freiburg* for Deutsche Austalienische DG, Hamburg.
1914	4 August. Interned at Soerabaja.
1919	22 July. Responsibility of the British Shipping Controller, British India Line as managers.

1921	Sold to Montgomerie & Workman, H.H. MacAllester as managers. Operated on the Hall Line service, renamed *City of Sydney*.
1923	Purchased by Deutsche Australienische, owned by DD-G 'Kosmos', Hamburg, renamed *Luneburg*.
1926	The Kosmos fleet was taken over by the Hamburg America Line.
1939	30 September. Renamed *Sperrbrecher IX*.
1940	30 July. Renamed *Sperrbrecher 9*.
1944	1 July. Scuttled at La Pallice across the harbour mouth.
1946	Raised and beached.
1948	Broken up.

City of Glasgow (4)   1920   5,321grt.   119.27×16.52×8.81   3,401n.   12k.

E.	Sgl. screw, 2 drg steam turb., 632 nhp, 225 psi, 3 sgl. blrs. By Central Marine Engineering Works, West Hartlepool.
B.	William Gray & Company, West Hartlepool.
1920	September. Delivered.
1956	July. Sold to Westport Shipping, London, renamed *Marianne*.
1958	Broken up.

City of Christiania.

City of Christiania   1921   4,940grt.   115.85×16.15×8.69   3,031n.   12k.

E.	Sgl. screw, tpl. exp., 550 nhp, 225 psi, 3 sgl. blrs. By builder.
B.	Earle's Shipbuilding Company, Hull.
1921	August. Delivered.
1957	October. Broken up.

City of Pittsburg   1921   7,377grt.   141.94×17.86×9.69   4,719n.   12k.

E.	Sgl. screw, 3 drg turb., 759 nhp, 225 psi, 3 sgl. blrs. By builder.
B.	Palmers Shipbuilding Company, Newcastle.
1921	January. Delivered.
1942	January. Stranded at the entrance to Alexandria harbour. Cargo was salvaged but the ship broke her back and was declared a total loss.

City of Tokio 1921   6,993grt.   134.87×17.98×9.63   4,426n.   12k.

E.	Sgl. screw, 3 srg steam turb., 746 nhp, 225 psi, 3 sgl. blrs. By Palmers, Newcastle.
B.	Craig, Taylor & Company, Stockton.
1921	September. Delivered.
1940	Stores ship at Freetown, Sierra Leone.
1941	Replaced at Freetown by *City of Dieppe*.
1951	7 June. Arrived at Dalmuir to be broken up.

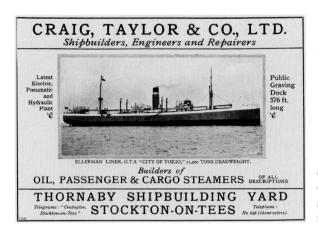

Craig, Taylor & Company Limited advertisement featuring *City of Tokio*.

City of Evansville   1922   6,528grt.   132.04×17.46×9.17   4,141n.   12k.

E.	Sgl. screw, tpl. exp., 617 nhp, 225 psi, 3 sgl. blrs. By Central Marine Engineering Works, West Hartlepool.
B.	William Gray & Company, West Hartlepool.
1922	October. Delivered.
1926	Low-pressure turbines added, hydraulic coupling, 729 nhp.
1932	March. First British merchant ship to pass under Sydney Harbour Bridge.
1940	July. Repatriated 1,500 troops to Morocco and 1,400 British people were brought home.
1951	A fire occurred in her cargo of jute and was quickly extinguished.
1957	31 October. Sold to Pan Norse Steam Ship Company, renamed *Dorca*.
1959	Broken up at Keelung.

City of Athens (3)   1923   6,558grt.   137.37×17.49×9.2   4,187n.   12k.

E.	Sgl. screw, tpl. exp., 665 nhp, 225 psi, 3 sgl. blrs. By Central Marine Engineering Works, West Hartlepool.
B.	William Gray & Company, West Hartlepool.
1923	July. Delivered.
1927	Low-pressure turbines added, hydraulic coupling, 728 nhp.
1942	8 October. On a voyage from Takoradi to Cape Town she was torpedoed and sunk by U-179 off Cape Town.

City of Eastbourne   1923   5,563grt.   128.59×16.52×8.78   3,509n.   12k.

E.	Sgl. screw, tpl. exp., 665 nhp, 225 psi, 3 sgl. blrs. By Central Marine Engineering Works, West Hartlepool.

B.	William Gray & Company, West Hartlepool.
1923	May. Delivered to Ellerman Lines, H.H. MacAllester as managers.
1928	22 March. Radio officer heard the last message from *Asiatic Prince* when 1,800 miles from Los Angeles.
1930	New turbine fitted with electric drive to a motor on the shaft.
1932	Laid up at Gareloch on the Clyde. She rotated with other ships of the fleet.
1939–45	Operated on commercial service during the Second World War.
1952	Grounded for a short while on the Indian coast, little damage to hull,
1953	21 November. Purchased by Francesco Pittaluga, Genoa, renamed *Ninin Pittaluga*.
1959	Broken up at La Spezia.

City of Singapore 1923 6,555grt. 137.37×17.46×9.2 4,161n. 12k.

E.	Sgl. screw, tpl. exp., 632 nhp, 225 psi, 3 sgl. blrs. By Central Marine Engineering Works, West Hartlepool.
B.	William Gray & Company, West Hartlepool.
1923	March. Delivered.
1924	March. Damaged by an explosion and fire. Declared a total loss but was later rebuilt.
1929	Low-pressure turbines added, hydraulic coupling, 729 nhp.
1943	1 May. In convoy TS 37 on a voyage from Takoradi to Freetown she was torpedoed and sunk by U-515.

City of Osaka 1923 6,614grt. 131.98×17.49×9.2 4,223n. 12k.

E.	Sgl. screw, tpl. exp., 617 nhp, 225 psi, 3 sgl. blrs. By Central Marine Engineering Works, West Hartlepool.
B.	William Gray & Company, West Hartlepool.
1923	January. Delivered as *Colorado* to Ellerman's Wilson Line.
1924	Transferred to Ellerman Lines, Hall Line as managers.
1930	22 September. Wrecked near Buchaness, Aberdeenshire.

Rydal Hall (5) / *City of Khios* (2) 1925 5,574grt. 127.25×16.76×8.84 3,537n. 12k.

E.	Sgl. screw, tpl. exp., 474 nhp, 225 psi, 3 sgl. blrs. By builder.
B.	Barclay, Curle & Company, Glasgow.
1924	28 November. Launched.
1925	January. Delivered as *Rydal Hall*, renamed *City of Khios*.
1955	6 June. Sold to Securities Shipping Company, renamed *Empire Merchant*, operated by Pacific Export Lines, Hong Kong.
1956	Owned by Stanley Shipping Company, Hong Kong.
1962	Renamed *Rantau Panjang*.
1963	25 February. Arrived at Nanao to be broken up.

City of Wellington 1925 5,733grt. 130.3×16.76×9.05 3,642n. 12k.

E.	Sgl. screw, tpl. exp., 551 nhp, 225 psi, 3 sgl. blrs. By builder.
B.	Barclay, Curle & Company, Glasgow.
1925	26 August. Launched.
1925	November. Delivered.
1932	Low-pressure turbines added, hydraulic coupling, 647 nhp.

1942	21 August. Torpedoed and sunk by U-506 off Freetown, on a voyage from Lourenco Marques to the United Kingdom.

City of Lyons	1926 7,063grt. 138.84×17.71×9.69 4,461n. 12½k.
E.	Sgl. screw, 3 srg turb., 709 nhp, 240 psi, 3 sgl. blrs. By Wallsend Slipway & Engineering Company, Wallsend.
B.	Swan Hunter & Wigham Richardson, Newcastle.
1926	February. Delivered.
1960	Her final voyage was from Chalna to Dublin.
1960	5 December. Sold to P. & W. Maclellan for £13 per light displacement ton.
1960	10 December. Arrived to be demolished.

City of Roubaix	1928 7,108grt. 139.02×17.8×9.69 4,555n. 12½k.
E.	Sgl. screw, 3 srg turb., 1,029 nhp, 240 psi, 3 sgl. blrs. By Wallsend Slipway & Engineering Company, Wallsend.
B.	Swan Hunter & Wigham Richardson, Newcastle.
1928	February. Delivered.
1941	6 April. She was sunk at Piraeus. The Clan Line vessel *Clan Fraser*, which was loaded with explosives, received a direct hit when she was bombed by German aircraft. *City of Roubaix*, *Cyprian Prince* and *Patris* were also destroyed as a train full of ammunition on the quayside was also blown up.

City of Bath	1926 5,079grt. 124.36×15.91×8.59 3,154n.
E.	Sgl. screw, quad. exp., 532 nhp, 265 psi, 3 sgl. blrs. By Central Marine Engineering Works, West Hartlepool.
B.	William Gray & Company, West Hartlepool.
1926	June. Delivered.
1942	2 December. Torpedoed and sunk by U-508 off Trinidad.

City of Bath.

City of Worcester	1927 5,469grt. 121.1×16.28×8.59 3,430n.
E.	Sgl. screw, tpl. exp., 523 nhp, 225 psi, 3 sgl. blrs. By builder.
B.	Earle's Shipbuilding Company, Hull.
1927	October. Delivered.
1952	25 January. Fire in cargo hold.
1955	19 May. Sold to Navigazione Peloritana SpA, Messina., renamed *Scillin II*.
1959	Broken up at Genoa.

Sandon Hall (2) / *City of Dundee* (2)   1921   5,273grt.   129.02×15.88×8.9   3,309n.

E.	Sgl. screw, 3 drg turb., 609 nhp, 220 psi, 2 sgl. blrs. By builder.
B.	Palmers Shipbuilding Company, Newcastle.
1921	March. Delivered as *Sandon Hall.* The line's final 'Hall' vessel.
1926	Renamed *City of Dundee.*
1957	January. Arrived at Manchester and placed on the for sale market.
1957	20 August. Arrived at Port Glasgow to be broken up by Smith & Houston.

City of Yokohama 1922   7,341grt.   141.76×17.71×9.69   4,721n.

E.	Sgl. screw, 2 drg turb., 917 nhp, 220 psi, 2 sgl. blrs. By builder.
B.	William Gray & Company, West Hartlepool.
1922	March. Delivered.
1958	January. Sold to Transatlantic Navigation Corporation, Monrovia, renamed *Trinity Pioneer.*
1959	Renamed *Transpioneer* and broken up at Hong Kong.

City of Yokohama.

City of Bedford   1924   6,407grt.   131.06×16.79×9.48   4,107n.

E.	Sgl. screw, quad. exp., 728 nhp, 250 psi, 2,280 ihp, 2 sgl. blrs. By builder.
B.	William Gray & Company, West Hartlepool.
1924	October. Delivered.
1940	30 December. While in convoy 280 miles off Iceland she collided with the Elder Dempster vessel *Bodnant. City of Bedford* sank with a loss of 7.5 million rifle cartridges, which was the largest munitions loss of the war to that date. The Prime Minister, Winston Churchill, gave orders that all large munitions consignments should be spread over a number of vessels in the future.

City of Salisbury   1924   5,946grt.   126.49×16.46×9.23   3,794n.

E.	Sgl. screw, tpl. exp., 574 nhp, 220 psi, 2 sgl. blrs. By Central Marine Engineering Works, West Hartlepool.
B.	William Gray & Company, West Hartlepool.
1924	June. Delivered.
1938	23 April. Grounded in fog near Graves Lighthouse, Boston, and broken in two.

City of Durban / City of Gloucester   1921   5,850grt.   115.73×15.88×8.11   3,672n.
E.   Sgl. screw, 3 drg turb., 607 nhp, 225 psi, 3 sgl. blrs. By builder.
B.   Earle's Shipbuilding Company, Hull.
1921   March. Delivered as a war loss replacement.
1945   Lifeboats abreast of the funnel were added.
1952   April. Renamed *City of Gloucester*.
1957   7 August. Arrived at Briton Ferry to be broken up by Thomas W. Ward.

City of Durban.

City of Boston   1912   5,885grt.   137.43×17.43×8.23   3,681n.
E.   Sgl. screw, tpl. exp. 697 nhp, 223 psi, 4 sgl. blrs. By builder.
B.   J.C. Tecklenborg AG, Geestemunde.
1912   4 February. Launched as *Dusseldorf* for DD-G Australische.
1912   26 March. Delivered.
1914   August. Interned at Barcelona at the start of the First World War.
1919   August. Operated by the French Government.
1921   14 February. Operated by Ellerman Lines, renamed *City of Boston*.
1927   Renamed Grandon for Norddeutscher Lloyd on the South American service.
1934   Transferred to Hamburg America Line.
1937   Renamed *Patagonia*.
1942   15 December. Operated as a naval transport.
1944   14 May. Target of Russian bombs at Kirkenes, damaged.
1945   15 May. At Brunsbuttel Koog when the war ended.
1945   4 October. Scuttled in the Skaggerak, loaded with ammunition.

City of Dunedin   1917   7,857grt.   144.87×18.5×10.03   4,870n.   12k.
E.   Sgl. screw, tpl. exp., 817 nhp. By builder.
B.   Bremer Vulkan, Vegesack.
1917   Delivered as *Porta* for Norddeutscher Lloyd.
1919   Responsibility of the British Shipping Controller, Lamport & Holt as
                  managers. She was used to transport the crews of German warships.
                  Surrendered in the Forth to Antwerp. Later laid up at Cowes.
1921   April. Purchased by Ellerman Lines Limited, renamed *City of Dunedin*, Hall
                  Line.

1927	August. Grounded for an hour on Pluckington Bank in the Mersey.
1928	Sold to Norddeutscher Lloyd, renamed *Lippe*.
1940	13 April. Sunk in Narvik Fjord in the Second Battle of Narvik.

City of Auckland	1914 8,336grt. 152.46×18.96×10.06 5,288n. 12k.
E.	Sgl. screw, quad. exp., 845 nhp, 213 psi, 4 sgl. blrs. By builder.
B.	A. G. Weser, Bremen.
1914	Delivered to DD-G 'Hansa', Bremen, as *Weissenfels*.
1919	Responsibility of the British Shipping Controller, Andrew Weir Bank Line as managers.
1921	Purchased by Montgomerie & Workman Limited, H.H. MacAllester as managers for the Hall Line, renamed *City of Auckland*.
1936	Transferred to Ellerman Lines Limited, Hall Line as managers.
1940	February–June. Transported military supplies to France.
1941	7 July. Attacked by four torpedoes fired by U-109. Retaliated by firing her guns at the submarine and laid a smoke screen which hid the ship completely The vessel took a course towards the submarine, firing shots at her as U-109 retreated, and *City of Auckland* was able to continue her voyage.
1947	17 October. Sold to Christopher Steam Ship Company, renamed *Karteria*.
1950	July. Owned by INSA, Genoa, renamed *Steva*.
1950	October. Broken up at La Spezia.

City of Stockholm	1915 5,075grt. 125.52×16.88×8.02 3,155n.
E.	Sgl. screw, oil, 3 cyl. 2S.SA. By North British Diesel Engineering Works, Glasgow.
B.	Barclay, Curle & Company, Glasgow.
1925	August. Laid down as *Frederick Gilbert*, purchased on the stocks as *City of Stockholm*.
1927	Sold to Hopemount Shipping Company, Stamp Mann & Company, Newcastle. Sold to Venatus Shipping Company, Howard Tenens Limited, London, renamed *Prunus*. Converted to triple expansion, 504 nhp, by Swan Hunter & Wigham Richardson, Newcastle.
1932	December. Sold to Hopemount Shipping Company, renamed *Hopetor*, Stott, Mann & Company as managers.
1936	January. Ashore in Australia but was refloated.
1937	Sold to Barry Shipping Company, renamed *St Merriel*.
1939	Owners became South American Saint Line.
1943	2 January. Bombed and sunk at Bona.
1950	Salvaged.
1950	4 August. Broke in two and sank off Capo Noli, while in tow to Savona to be broken up.

City of Hereford	1927 5,101grt. 117.47×15.76×9.23 3,215n. 12k.
E.	Sgl. screw, tpl. exp., 523 nhp, 225 psi, 2 sgl. blrs. By builder.
B.	Barclay, Curle & Company, Glasgow.
1927	May. Delivered to Hall Line's New York–Philadelphia–Far East service.
1940	Transferred to Ellerman & Bucknall Line.

1945	Managed by Westcott & Laurence Line.
1955	Sold to Williamson & Company, Hong Kong, renamed *Inchona*.
1956	Renamed *Golden Alpha* for the World Wide Steam Ship Company, London, World Wide Shipping Company, Hong Kong as managers.
1959	Broken up at Osaka.
City of Lille	1928 6,588grt. 141.94×17.65×10.33 4,052n. 13k.
E.	Sgl. screw, oil, 4 cyl. opposed Doxford, 5,000 bhp. By builder.
B.	Barclay, Curle & Company, Glasgow.
1928	July. Delivered as the first motorship for the fleet.
1933	23 January. As she cleared the Strait of Gibraltar on a voyage from Shanghai, Malaya, India and North Africa to New York, she received a radio message from the *City of Delhi*, saying that she had shed her propeller in a position some 500 miles north of the *City of Lille*. The *City of Lille* was ordered to go to the rescue and she set off northwards in deteriorating weather with the crew preparing two 100-fathom 5-inch wires and one 4½-inch wire joined in a single line to be attached to 40 fathoms of her anchor cable.
1933	25 January. Just after midnight *City of Delhi* was sighted and a couple of hours later a rocket succeeded in putting a line across her foredeck. The line was attached and the tow commenced at 06.09.
1933	27 January. The wind was strong and increased during the day, and it was decided to seep oil through the hawse pipes in an attempt to flatten the waves. Following damage to ventilators, the gangway and No. 2 lifeboat, the tow parted as the weather continued to deteriorate.
1933	28 January. The gale began to moderate and *City of Lille* turned to port to search for *City of Delhi*. However, by midnight, twenty-six hours after losing the tow, there was thick fog.
1933	January. In bad visibility, *City of Delhi* was sighted at 00.15, 1 mile ahead, but the wind soon increased to gale force again. At 13.30 *City of Lille* approached *City of Delhi*, the first rocket fell short as did the second, but contact was made at 13.41. The line was connected and the tow resumed at 15.31. However, the wind was so bad that both ships ended up heading east-south-east, not the way they wanted to go.
1933	30 January. The wind dropped in the early hours and the fog began to clear. By breakfast-time both ships were rolling and pitching heavily and shipping water, which continued for the rest of the day.
1933	31 January. Just after noon the *Sambro* light vessel was abeam and an hour later the fairway buoy was sighted. The ships proceeded to Chebucto Head, where the tug *Foundation Franklin* made fast to the *City of Delhi*, and *City of Lille* slipped the tow line. *City of Lille* resumed her voyage to New York, where she arrived on 8 February.
1955	December. Lost an anchor in the Bristol Channel.
1956	September. On a voyage from Newport to Beira she suffered an engine breakdown when several crosshead cooling brackets sheared off, and she docked at Cape Town for repairs to be carried out.
1957	27 May. Sold to the International Union Lines, Monrovia, renamed *Union Capitol*.
1963	Broken up at Taiwan.

*City of
Sydney* (2).

City of Sydney (2)	1930 6,986grt. 138.44×17.8×9.66 4,326n. 13k.	
E.	Sgl. screw, tpl. exp., 4 cyl. 2 LP turbines drg by hydraulic coupling, 905 nhp, 265 psi, 4 sgl. blrs. By builder.	
B.	Workman, Clark & Company, Belfast.	
1930	May. Delivered.	
1956	19 February. Collided with and sank the Cory vessel *Corchester* in a snow storm off the Haisborough Light. Eight crew from the *Corchester* lost their lives. *City of Sydney*, with a North Sea pilot on board had been proceeding southwards towards the *Corchester*. Both ships were equipped with radar and picked each other up on their screens. As they drew nearer, and at the critical time when visual contact might have occurred, the snow returned. The officer of the watch realised the probability of impact only moments before it happened and could not recall the master in time. The bow of the *City of Sydney* took the *Corchester* in the way of the forward end of No. 1 hold and continued right through the collier, severing the forward portion of the ship. Unfortunately, the *Corchester* was the only existing Cory collier to have forecastle accommodation for the deckhands and so the six men off watch were lost, as this forward section immediately sank. The rest of the ship, with the inrush of the sea through the severed hold, took a sharp pitch and a heavy list to starboard. All hands were ordered to the boat deck by Captain Northcott, who directed the launching of the ships' boat from the listed side. The deck was ice-covered and the dead ship was rolling heavily in the swell. The boat was swung out and took to the sea. Another Cory collier, the *Cormull*, arrived on the scene and assisted in the rescue operations, until *Corchester* heeled over and sank.	
1958	31 March. Rescued 1,300 people from the *Skaubryn*, which was on fire. She set off, heading to Aden but the Italian liner *Roma* assisted by taking the survivors on board.	
1958	28 May. Sold to Tsavliris (Shipping) Limited, London, renamed *Nicholaos Tsavliris*.	
1960	Broken up.	
City of Barcelona	1930 5,787grt. 135.33×17.74×8.32 3,524n. 12½k.	
E.	Sgl. screw, tpl. exp., 4 cyl., 2× LP turbines with electric drive, 638 nhp, 265 psi, 2 sgl. blrs. By builder.	

B.	Barclay, Curle & Company, Glasgow.
1930	12 February. Launched.
1930	May. Delivered as the first 'heavy lift' ship in the fleet with a 30-ton derrick.
1958	20 May. Broken up in Antwerp.

City of Manchester (4) 1935   8,917grt.   151.94×19.6×9.11   5,572n.   13k.

E.	Twin screw, 2×3 turbines, 1,625 nhp, 275 psi, 5 sgl. blrs. By builder.
B.	Cammell Laird & Company Limited, Birkenhead.
1935	July. Delivered. She was designed as a general and refrigerated cargo liner with accommodation for eight passengers and was built entirely of riveted mild steel with a raked stern, sheered foredeck and forecastle head and cruiser stern. The passenger accommodation consisted of four double-berth staterooms with adjoining bathroom and lavatory in a deckhouse at the forward end of the boatdeck. The master was provided with a self-contained suite comprising dayroom, bedroom and bathroom below the navigating bridge. The chief officer was housed forward, on the port side of the shelter deck. The crew accommodation, at the after end of the upper deck, provided space for a galley, a hospital, cabins and dormitory for twenty-six seamen. As she was designed for the Australasian trade she was provided with eleven insulated cargo chambers by the Liverpool Refrigeration Company Limited. Provision was made for the simultaneous carriage of both chilled and frozen goods. The propelling machinery consisted of two sets of Parsons steam turbines driving twin screws through single reduction mechanical gearing. Each set consisted of high pressure, intermediate pressure and low pressure ahead turbines driving separate pinions. Steam was provided by six single-ended cylindrical boilers at a pressure of 275 lb per sq. in. Each boiler was fitted with smoke-box superheaters and the furnaces were arranged to burn either coal or fuel oil under a combined system of forced and induced draught.
1942	27 February. Sailed from Tjilatjap, Java.
1942	28 February. Torpedoed and sunk by the Japanese submarine I-153 off Java.

City of Manchester (4).

City of Agra (3).

City of Agra (3)	1936 6,361grt. 140.18×17.13×9.33 3,866n. 13½k.
E.	Sgl. screw, 3 sgl. reduction Parsons geared turbines, 450 nhp, 275 psi, 3 sgl. blrs. By builder.
B.	William Denny & Brothers, Dumbarton.
1936	2 October. Launched.
1936	18 December. Delivered and operated on most of Ellerman Lines' regular services, rarely giving any trouble or problems.
1965	10 May. Sold as the oldest unit in the fleet to Dutch interests, re-sold.
1965	17 May. Arrived at Bilbao to be broken up.

City of Cape Town	1937 8,046grt. 157.12×19.02×9.54 3,935n. 13½k.
E.	Twin screw, 2×3 srg turb., 1,867 nhp, 265 psi, 6 sgl. blrs. By builder.
B.	Cammell Laird & Company Limited, Birkenhead.
1937	October. Delivered to Hall Line.
1939–45	Operated on commercial service during the Second World War.
1942	March. Transported a full cargo of munitions to India.
1962	Purchased by Harbour Line Limited, Bermuda, renamed *Mangrove Harbour*.
1951	May. She went ashore in the River Lawrence in thick fog. She was refloated later that day and after an inspection it was discovered that she had damaged her propeller. Towed to Halifax where a replacement was fitted.
1965	10 May. Sold to be broken up at Bilbao.

City of Bombay (4)	1937 7,140grt. 141.52×18.04×9.51 4,270n. 13½k.
E.	Sgl. screw, 3 srg turb., 750 nhp. By Parsons Marine Steam Turbines, Newcastle.
B.	Barclay, Curle & Company, Glasgow.
1937	23 July. Launched.
1937	Delivered. Designed with six cargo hatches to serve six holds and associated 'tween decks. Twenty-two Stewart and Lloyd's tubular steel derricks were fitted, powered by steam winches. A special derrick, stiffened to take a load of 45 tons, was arranged on the foremast. The masts and funnel were designed to be telescopic to enable her to navigate the Manchester Ship Canal. The crew were accommodated on the lower bridge and bridge deck with the master having a suite of rooms overlooking the foredeck. The officers' and

engineers' cabins were fitted with bed, setee, wardrobe and a combined writing desk and drawers. All cabins were provided with basins and running water. The Lascar crewmen were quartered in dormitory accommodation, spread around the poop on the upper deck. She was propelled by a single set of Parsons impulse-reaction steam turbines driving a single screw through single reduction gearing. Steam was supplied by four single-ended boilers. Each boiler had four furnaces and had a heating surface of 2,850 sq.ft. and was designed for either oil or coal burning. Normally the ship was oil-fired with coal being considered an alternative emergency fuel.

1942   3 December. Torpedoed and sunk by U-159, off St Paul's Rocks in the South Atlantic, with the loss of twenty lives.

City of Newport   1943   7,270grt.   134.63×17.37×10.61   4,452n.
E.   Sgl. screw, tpl. exp., 240 psi, 2 blrs, 2,500 ihp at 76 rpm. By General Machinery Corporation, Hamilton.
B.   Bethlehem Fairfield Shipbuilding Company, Baltimore.
1943   Launched as *William R. Cox*, completed as *Samtweed*, chartered to the Ministry of War Transport, Hall Line as managers.
1947   October. Purchased by Ellerman Lines, Hall Line, renamed *City of Newport*.
1961   23 May. Sold to Veritas Shipping Corporation, Greece, renamed *Istros II*.
1967   April. Broken up at Trieste.

City of Chester (2)   1944   8,380grt.   150.27×19.6×9.11   4,954n.
E.   Twin screw, quad. exp., 2×4 cyl., 9,000 bhp. By builder.
B.   Barclay, Curle & Company, Glasgow.
1943   30 December. Launched.
1944   March. Delivered to Hall Line.
1962   3 June. Arrived Wallsend for a special survey carried out by Swan Hunter & Wigham Richardson. This included the complete replacement of the port and starboard boat decks, and large-scale renewal of the poop and forcastle decks. A number of shell plates were also renewed. The cargo gear, including the electrically operated winches and control boxes, were overhauled. Survey of the main machinery, hull and boilers was also carried out.
1971   8 June. Sold to Embajada Cia. Nav. SA, Panama, renamed *Chester*. Broken up in Whampoa, China.

City of Madras (5)   1945   8,520grt.   143.74×19.6×9.11   4,270n.
E.   Twin screw, quad. exp., 2×4 cyl., 9,000 bhp. By Wallsend Slipway & Engineering Company, Wallsend.
B.   Swan Hunter & Wigham Richardson, Newcastle.
1945   February. Delivered.
1961   29 September. Sold to the Far Eastern Navigation Corporation, renamed *Wei Lee*.
1963   Broken up in Taiwan.

City of Khartoum (2)   1946   9,955grt.   145.00×19.57×12.19   6,128n.   14½k.
E.   Sgl. screw, oil, 6 cyl. Doxford 2S.SA, 6,600 bhp. By builder.
P.   12.
B.   Barclay, Curle & Company, Glasgow.

1945   24 August. Launched.
1946   January. Delivered, Hall Line as managers.
1968   15 February. Sold to the Ben Line, renamed *Benalligin*.
1972   27 September. Arrived at Kaohsiung to be broken up by the Nan Feng Steel
            Enterprise Company.

City of Lucknow (6)   1946   9,961grt.   145.00×19.57×12.19   5,954n.   14½k.
E.   Sgl. screw, oil, 3 drg Parsons turb., 880 nhp, 430 psi, 2× Babcock & Wilcox blrs. By
            builder.
P.   12.
B.   William Denny & Brothers, Dumbarton.
1945   21 November. Launched.
1946   14 May. Delivered, Hall Line as managers.
1963   12 December. Sold to the Alexandra Navigation Corporation, Liberia, renamed *Lisboa*.
1970   Owned by Outerocean Navigation Corporation, Taiwan.
1971   3 March. Left Esperance Bay to be broken up in Taiwan.

City of Lucknow (6).

City of Swansea (2)   1946   9,959grt.   145.00×19.57×12.19   7,053n.   14½k.
E.   Sgl. screw, oil, 6 cyl. Doxford 2S.SA, 6,600 bhp. By builder.
P.   12.
B.   Barclay, Curle & Company, Glasgow.
1945   21 December. Launched.
1946   April. Delivered, Hall Line as managers.
1968   29 March. Sold to the Ben Line, renamed *Benkitlan*.
1972   3 September. Arrived at Kaohsiung to be broken up by the Chin Tai Steel
            Enterprise Company.

City of Poona (2)   1946   9,962grt.   145.00×19.57×12.19   7,051n.   14½k.
E.   Sgl. screw, oil, 6 cyl. Doxford 2S.SA, 6,600 bhp. By builder.
P.   12.
B.   Swan Hunter & Wigham Richardson, Newcastle.
1946   July. Delivered, Hall Line as managers.
1968   26 April. Sold to the Ben Line, renamed *Benarkle*.
1974   16 June. Arrived at Kaohsiung to be broken up by Li Chong Steel & Iron Works.

City of New York   1947   8,420grt.   152.4×19.6×9.75   4,201n.   14k.
E.   Twin screw, 2×3 turb., HP, IP and LP srg, 430 psi, 3 blrs. By builder.
B.   Vickers Armstrong, Newcastle.
1947   January. Delivered to Hall Line.
1967   23 May. Sold to Mardevoto Cia. Nav. SA, Greece, renamed *Kavo Matapas*.
1969   31 July. Left Keelung to be broken up at Kaohsiung.

City of Hull 1947   8,458grt.   152.4×19.6×9.75   4,250n.   14k.
E.   Twin screw, 2×3 turbine, HP, IP and LP srg, 430 psi, 3 blrs. By builder.
B.   Vickers Armstrong, Newcastle.
1947   October. Delivered to Hall Line.
1950   Transferred to Ellerman & Bucknall Line.
1967   19 April. Sold to Embajada Cia. Nav., Panama, renamed *Essex* for the delivery
                voyage to the ship breakers at Aioi, Japan.

City of
Johannesburg (2).

City of Johannesburg (2)   1947   8,207grt.   151.64×19.57×9.84   4,831n.
E.   Twin screw, 2×4 cyl. 2S.SA, 4,000 bhp. By builder.
B.   Barclay, Curle & Company, Glasgow.
1947   23 May. Launched.
1947   November. Delivered to Hall Line. The *City of Johannesburg* was the fourth of the
                'City of New York' class but bore little resemblance to her sister ships in profile
                or proportion, and whereas the *City of New York*, *City of London*, *City of Hull* and
                City of Pretoria were steamships, the *City of Johannesburg* was a motorship. The
                next ten ships ordered after the *City of Johannesburg* were all fitted with steam
                turbine machinery. The hull, which was riveted throughout, was arranged on a
                three-island principle with a continuous main deck and an orlop deck in No.
                1 hold, and subdivided by seven watertight bulkheads. This provided five holds
                each with main 'tweendeck spaces and upper 'tweendecks in the way of Nos 1, 3
                and 4 hatches. No. 3 hold was fitted out as a deep tank for the carriage of edible
                oils, water ballast and dry cargo. However, with the exception of domestic fridge
                provision none of the 'tweendeck spaces were refrigerated. She was provided
                with fourteen Clarke Chapman electric winches and an outfit of twenty derricks
                varying in capacity from 7 to 10 tons. Passenger and public rooms were arranged

on the bridge deck at the forward end of the midship deckhouse with three double staterooms overlooking the forward welldeck and three single cabins on each side of the trunked No. 3 hatchway. A luxuriously appointed lounge and dining room were located to port and starboard, abaft of the stateroom accommodation. Access to the boatdeck, above, and the cocktail lounge was gained by either of the two main staircases which led from the public rooms. The master's and deck officers' accommodation was located on the bridge deck and engineers' cabins were also in the after part of the bridge deck, together with the ship's hospital and surgery. Accommodation for the Indian crew occupied the poop 'tweendeck spaces with an arrangement of compartments. Separate galleys, wash places and a hospital were located in the poop deckhouse. The propelling machinery was supplied by the builders and consisted of two sets of Doxford four cylinder, opposed-piston oil engines. which developed 10,350 hp at 119 rpm.

1953	24 December. In collision with and sank *Alf Everard* in the Thames Estuary. The coaster was inward bound in the Thames with a cargo of china clay from Charlestown when the collision occurred in the vicinity of No. 1 Sea Reach buoy. Her crew were rescued by a collier and transferred to the Southend lifeboat.
1970	26 January. Sold to Fairy Cia. Naviera SA, Greece, renamed *Filothei*.
1972	Owned by Rodini Cia. Nav. SA, Greece, renamed *Lykavitos*.
1973	7 February. Arrived at Kaohsiung to be broken up.

City of Gloucester (2) / *City of Brooklyn* 1949   7,557grt.   147.92×18.84×9.33   4,411n.   14k.

E.	Sgl. screw, 3 srg turb., 300 psi, 2 blrs. By Wallsend Slipway & Engineering Company, Wallsend.
B.	Swan Hunter & Wigham Richardson, Newcastle.
1949	May. Delivered to Hall Line, laid down as *City of Gloucester*.
1963	April. Collided with Bristol Steam Navigation Company's *Cato* at Avonmouth. It was reported that:

What was to have been a normal docking evolution became a disaster when the engines of the City of Brooklyn failed to go astern at the critical moment. Captain Tremlett, was ashore at the time, but the first mate, Mr. Foley was preparing to shave in his cabin when he heard anchors being dropped and the clatter of cables running. Glancing through his door he saw the bows of the City of Brooklyn slice through the starboard side of the Cato abreast of the after end of No. 2 hatch. Within 20 minutes all that was visible were the masts, the monkey island and funnel. The crew scrambled ashore in a hurry, half-dressed but unhurt. She was later salved by T.R. Brown & Sons and towed to the graving dock at Avonmouth where she was inspected and declared a total loss. A temporary patch was placed over the gash in her side to make her seaworthy enough for the trip down channel to the scrapyard at Newport.

1967	10 August. Sold to Astro Dinamicos Cia. Nav. SA, Panama, renamed *Lefkadios*.
1970	27 September. On a voyage from Bordeaux to Shanghai she was abandoned on fire, 600 miles south of Colombo.
1970	28 September. Sank.

City of Coventry   1949   7,568grt.   147.92×18.84×9.33   4,400n.   14k.

E.	Sgl. screw, 3 srg turb., 300 psi, 2 blrs. By Wallsend Slipway & Engineering Company, Wallsend.
B.	Swan Hunter & Wigham Richardson, Newcastle.
1949	May. Delivered to Hall Line.
1967	13 October. Sold to Austin Navigation Corporation, Liberia, renamed *Ingrid*.
1969	Owned by the Outerocean Navigation Corporation, Keelung, renamed *Annie*.
1970	27 April. Left Yokohama to be broken up at Kaohsiung.

City of Liverpool.

City of Liverpool   1949   7,612grt.   147.92×18.84×9.33   4,435n.   14k.

E.	Sgl. screw, Parsons srg impulse turb., 7,200 bhp, 115 rpm, 650 psi, 2× Babcock & Wilcox blrs. By builder.
B.	Cammell Laird & Company Limited, Birkenhead.
1948	4 November. Launched by the Mayoress of Liverpool, Mrs W. T. Lancashire.
1949	3 May. On trials the same day as *City of Birmingham* (3).
1949	4 May. Delivered to Hall Line. Designed with accommodation for twelve passengers, amidships on the shelter and boat decks in four single and four double rooms. Each room included a private bathroom and toilet en suite, with hot and cold freshwater services. The public rooms included a dining room with seating capacity for twenty-four people, a lounge, a library and a cocktail bar. There was an extensive sports deck and hand laundry for passengers' use. Also provided was a high standard of accommodation for the navigating and engineer officers and the crew.
1949	6 May. Maiden voyage Liverpool–Canada–USA–Far East.
1967	July. Sold to Astro Tridente Cia. Nav. SA, Panama, renamed *Kavo Grossos*.
1973	16 January. Left Singapore for Shanghai to be broken up.

City of Cardiff (3) / *City of Philadelphia*   1949   7,591grt.   147.92×18.84×9.33   4,464n.   14k.

E.	Sgl. screw, 3 srg turb., 300 psi, 2 blrs. By Parsons Marine Steam Turbine Company, Wallsend.
B.	Furness Shipbuilding Company, Haverton Hill.

1949	December. Delivered to Hall Line as *City of Philadelphia*, laid down as *City of Cardiff*.
1967	1 September. Sold to Marbrava Cia. Nav. SA, Piraeus, renamed *Kaptaspyro*.
1970	Owned by Spyros Shipping Company, Famagusta, renamed *Spyro*.
1971	4 March. Left Singapore Roads to be broken up at Whampoa.

City of Bath (3) / *City of Chicago* (3) 1950 7,622grt. 147.92×18.84×9.33 4,427n. 14k.

E.	Sgl. screw, 3 srg turb., 300 psi, 2 blrs. By builders at Barrow.
B.	Vickers Armstrong, Newcastle.
1950	June. Delivered to Hall Line, laid down as *City of Bath*. She was designed as a single-screw vessel, propelled by a set of three steam turbines connected to the screw shaft through single reduction gearing. She was built with accommodation for twelve passengers and was employed principally on the Hall Line's services to Indian and South and East African ports.
1967	7 July. Sold for £150,000 to Marapico Cia. Nav. SA, Pireaus, renamed *Kaptamarco*.
1970	Owned by Marcos Shipping Company, Famagusta, renamed *Marco*.
1971	29 November. Arrived at Shanghai to be broken up.

City of Guildford (2) / *City of Ottawa* / *City of Leeds* (5) 1950 7,622grt. 147.92×18.84×9.33 4,427n. 14k.

E.	Sgl. screw, 3 srg turb., 300 psi, 2 blrs. By builders at Barrow.
B.	Vickers Armstrong, Newcastle.
1950	August. Delivered as *City of Ottawa* to Hall Line, laid down as *City of Guildford*.
1971	Renamed *City of Leeds*.
1976	Sold to Gulf (Shipowners) Limited, London, renamed *Gulf Venture*.
1977	12 August. Arrived at Karachi on last voyage.
1977	November. Broken up at Gadani Beach.

City of Pittsburg (2) / *City of Birkenhead* 1950 7,942grt. 147.77×18.84×9.14 4,282n. 15½k.

E.	Sgl. screw, 3 srg turb., 300 psi, 2 blrs. By builder.
B.	Cammell Laird & Company, Birkenhead.
1949	22 November. Launched.
1950	March. Delivered to Hall Line as *City of Birkenhead*, laid down as *City of Pittsburg*. Final class of steamers built for the company.
1954	Transferred to Ellerman & Bucknall management.
1971	16 December. Sold to China Marine Investment Company, Hong Kong, renamed *Liberty Trader*.
1971	21 December. Left Hong Kong for Kaohsiung.
1972	5 August. Demolition commenced at Kaohsiung by Yi Ho Steel & Iron Works.

City of Bedford (2) 1950 7,341grt. 147.77×18.84×9.14 4,203n. 15½k.

E.	Sgl. screw, 3 srg turb., 300 psi, 2 blrs. By Cammell Laird & Company Limited, Birkenhead,
B.	Alexander Stephen & Sons, Glasgow.
1950	14 June. Launched.
1950	November. Delivered to Hall Line.
1972	5 June. Sold to Aguikar y Peris SL, Valencia and broken up.

City of Bedford (2).

City of Singapore (2)   1951   7,738grt.   147.77×18.84×9.14   4,204n.   15½k.

E.	Sgl. screw, 3 srg turb., 300 psi, 2 blrs. By builders.
B.	Alexander Stephen & Sons, Glasgow.
1950	26 October. Launched.
1951	March. Delivered to Hall Line.
1973	1 January. Transferred to Ellerman City Liners.
1973	10 November. On a voyage from the Tees to Lobitos she grounded off South Africa.
1973	26 November. Refloated with little damage.
1975	Sold to the Gulf Shipping Lines Limited, renamed *United Mariner*.
1976	Renamed *Gulf Mariner*.
1977	1 May. Arrived at Gadani Beach to be broken up.

City of Newcastle (2)   1956   7,727grt.   154.59×20.05×8.62   4,047n.   15k.

E.	Sgl. screw, oil, 6 cyl. 2S.SA Doxford, 8,000 bhp. By builder.
B.	Alexander Stephen & Sons, Glasgow.
1955	1 November. Launched.
1956	April. Delivered to Hall Line.
1956	9 April. Maiden voyage Liverpool–Beira.
1959	October. The Lord Mayor of Newcastle unveiled a coat of arms in the dining room of the ship when she visited Newcastle Corporation Quay for the first time.
1968	25 May. Chartered to the Ben Line, renamed *Benratha*.
1970	29 December. Renamed *City of Newcastle*, Ellerman & Bucknall as managers.
1973	1 January. Managed by Ellerman City Liners.
1978	Sold to Gulf East Ship Management Limited, Singapore, renamed *Eastern Envoy*.
1978	Purchased by Venture Bay Shipping Company, Singapore. Liberian flag.
1980	23 October. Arrived at Chittagong to be broken up.

City of Winnipeg (2) / *City of Delhi* (5)   1956   7,716grt.   154.59×20.05×8.62 4,020n.   15k.

E.	Sgl. screw, oil, 6 cyl. 2S.SA Doxford, 8,000 bhp. By Wallsend Slipway & Engineering Company, Wallsend.

B.	Caledon Shipbuilding & Engineering Company, Dundee.
1955	29 September. Launched without ceremony.
1956	March. Delivered to Hall Line.
1968	18 January. On charter to the Ben Line, renamed *Benedin*.
1970	23 November. Renamed *City of Delhi*, Ellerman & Bucknall as managers.
1973	1 January. Managed by Ellerman City Liners.
1976	Sold to Beaumaris Shipping Incorporated, Monrovia, Gulfeast Ship Management Limited as managers, renamed *Fexel Glory*.
1980	14 September. Arrived at Chittagong to be broken up.

City of Winnipeg (2) loading cargo in the West Float, Birkenhead.

City of Wellington (2).

City of Wellington (2)   1956   7,702grt.   155.00×20.05×8.62   4,041n.   15k.

E.	Sgl. screw, oil, 6 cyl. 2S.SA Doxford, 8,000 bhp. By Wallsend Slipway & Engineering Company, Wallsend.
B.	Cammell Laird & Company, Birkenhead.
1956	October. Delivered to Hall Line.
1973	1 January. Managed by Ellerman City Liners.
1978	June. Sold to Mulroy Bay Shipping Company, Liberia, renamed *Eastern Enterprise*, Singapore flag.
1979	13 February. Arrived at Kaohsiung to be broken up by the Tung Ho Steel Enterprise Corporation.

City of Guildford (3)   1957   4,945grt.   132.28×18.04×7.53   2,517n.   14½k.

E.	Sgl. screw, oil, 8 cyl. Sulzer 2S.SA, 5,600 bhp. By G. Clark and North East Marine (Sunderland) Limited.
B.	Swan Hunter & Wigham Richardson, Newcastle.
1957	January. Delivered to Hall Line.
1969	November. After arriving at Tilbury from Bombay she had a fire in No. 1 hold, which took three hours to extinguish.
1973	1 January. Managed by Ellerman City Liners.
1979	Sold to Eurydice Maritime Company Limited, Greece, renamed *Eurydice*.
1981	Owned by Chimadea Shipping Maritime Company (Mighty Management SA), Panama, renamed *Mighty Spirit*.
1984	Sold to Wonder Shipping & Maritime Company, Malta, renamed *Nirav*. Re-sold to Tricommerce Limited, Malta.
1984	17 September. Arrived at Chittagong to be broken up.

City of Guildford (3) on charter.

Lancaster at Stobcross Quay, Glasgow, on 27 June 1981.

City of Lancaster (2)   1958   4,949grt.   132.28×18.04×7.53   2,524n.   14½k.

E.	Sgl. screw, oil, 6 cyl. 2S.SA Doxford, 8,000 bhp. By Sulzer Brothers, Winterthur.
B.	Swan Hunter & Wigham Richardson, Newcastle.
1958	August. Delivered to Hall Line.
1973	1 January. Managed by Ellerman City Liners.
1979	Sold to Lancaster Shipping Company, Greece, renamed *Lancaster*.
1979	25 September. On a voyage from Calcutta to Glasgow she was in collision with the tanker *Thistle Venture* and arrived at Dublin later that day, where she was abandoned.
1980	16 March. Towed to Glasgow to discharge her cargo and she was put up for sale by the Clyde Port Authority.
1981	25 November. Sold to Andover Shipping Company, Greece and left the Clyde under tow for San Esteban de Pavia, Spain.
1981	4 December. Arrived at Aviles to be broken up.

City of Hereford (2) / *City of Glasgow* (5)   1958   4,954grt.   132.28×18.04×7.53   2,529n.   14½k.

E.	Sgl. screw, oil, 8 cyl. Sulzer 2S.SA, 5,600 bhp. By G. Clark and North East Marine (Sunderland) Limited.
B.	Robb Caledon Limited, Dundee.
1958	November. Delivered to Hall Line.
1971	Renamed *City of Glasgow*.
1973	1 January. Managed by Ellerman City Liners.
1978	Sold to Porter Shipping Company, Greece, renamed *Myrna*.
1980	23 April. Left Manila to be broken up at Kaohsiung.

City of Hereford (2).

City of Worcester (2)   1960   4,790grt.   132.28×18.04×7.56   2,517n.   14¾k.

E.	Sgl. screw, oil, 8 cyl. Sulzer 2S.SA, 5,600 bhp. By G. Clark and North East Marine (Sunderland) Limited.
B.	Robb Caledon Limited, Dundee.
1960	September. Delivered to Hall Line as the final vessel built for the line. She was designed as a single-screw closed-shelter deck vessel with poop, forecastle, cruiser stern and raked rounded stem. She had four cargo holds and of the four weather deck hatchways, three were fitted with MacGregor steel covers and the largest, 55 feet,

with wood slab covers. Four large deep tanks were situated in the wings at the fore end of the engine room for the carriage of liquid cargoes. She has two unstayed masts and two derrick posts with ten cargo derricks for 7- and 10-ton loads, the foremast being strengthened to allow the fitting of a 70-ton heavy derrick. The cargo winches, warping winch and windlass were all electrically driven, and the four cargo winches on the mainmast house top had remote controls at vantage points for the working of cargoes. All accommodation in the midship deckhouse was air conditioned, and the accommodation in the poop was mechanically heated and ventilated. She was also equipped with radar, direction finder, gyro compass and wireless telegraphy and the smoke detection system was centralised in the wheelhouse.

1973	1 January. Managed by Ellerman City Liners.
1979	Sold to the Vermont Steamship Company, Diamantides Maritime Company, Greece, renamed *Maria Diamanto*.
1982	Owned by Seadust Navigation Company, Cyprus, renamed *Cape Greco*.
1982	26 November. On a voyage from Turkey to Djibouti she suffered an engine failure.
1982	19 December. Arrived at Djibouti in tow, discharged her cargo.
1983	Sold to Ashraf Brothers.
1983	1 August. Arrived with cargo at Chittagong in tow.
1983	20 August. Beached and broken up at Chittagong.

Ellerman & Bucknall

Cambria	1825 124grt. Schooner, 1 deck.
B.	Sunderland.
1825	Delivered to the Cardiff & London Shipping Company. Sold to E. Bartlett, Exeter and Captain G. Treatt of Exeter.
1851	Purchased by Henry Corfield Bucknall.
1854	Sold.
1863–64	Out of register.

British Ensign	1857 196grt. Brig rig.
B.	Dumbarton.
1857	First vessel built for Henry Bucknall, operated on services to South America.
1861	Sold to King & Company. Bristol–Mediterranean service.
1876	Sold to William Kemp, Whitstable.
1880	Wrecked.

Alecto	1866 199grt. Brig, 1 deck
B.	Jenkins, Prince Edward Island.
1866	August. Delivered to Henry Bucknall for the Mediterranean services.
1878	Sold.

Lusitania	1867 219grt. Barque, 1 deck.
B.	W. Salisbury, London.
1867	August. Delivered for the Lisbon services.
1876	Sold.

Lisbon   1852   221grt.   Brig, 1 deck.
B.   Rostock, Germany.
1852   Delivered as *Alexander Brandt* to A. Brandt, Rostock.
1875   Sold to J. Mitchell, Glasgow.
1868   Purchased for the Lisbon services, renamed *Lisbon*.

Ocean Spray   1863   274grt.   Iron, 3-masted barquentine, 1 deck.
B.   Laroche, Quebec.
1863   October. Delivered to R. Beauvais.
1869   Purchased by Henry Bucknall.
1873   Sold and sunk.

Ruby   1868   266grt.   38.22×8.2×3.93   Barque rig, 2 decks.
B.   W. Salisbury, London.
1868   Delivered.
1869   Purchased by Henry Bucknall.
1889   Sold to East Downshire Sailing Ship Company, Belfast. The last sailing ship owned by Bucknall.
1900   Sold to John T. Williams, Fowey.
1914   Purchased by A. Anderson, Whitstable.
1915   13 November. On a voyage from London to Newcastle she was wrecked 6 miles north of Hartlepool.

Vanguard   1872   905grt.   67.88×9.14×4.9   Iron, 1 deck.
E.   Sgl. screw, 2 cyl. comp. inv., 75 nhp, 65 psi. By D. & W. Dudgeon, London.
B.   Cole Brothers, Newcastle.
1872   February. Delivered to Henry Bucknall & Sons for the Newcastle–Spain service.
1882   26 February. On a voyage from Lisbon to London she was declared missing with a cargo of cork and minerals. All twenty-three people on board were lost.

Tagus   1872   1,250grt.   69.8x9.26x5.06   Iron, 1 deck and spar deck.
E.   Sgl. screw, 2 cyl. comp. inv., 95 nhp, 75 psi. By D. & W. Dudgeon, London.
B.   Cole Brothers, Newcastle.
1872   September. Delivered to Henry Bucknall & Sons.
1890   Transferred to Bucknall Nephews.
1896   Sold to A. Gardella y Cia, Buenos Aires.
1900   Sold to S.N. Savas, Buenos Aires.
1901   6 January. While she was being loaded with coffee and tea for Buenos Aires she was destroyed by fire at Antonia.

Sydenham   1873   1,279grt.   70.59×9.08×5.01   Iron, 2 decks.
E.   Sgl. screw, 2 cyl. comp. inv., 75 nhp, 65 psi. By Ouseburn Engine Works Company, Newcastle.
B.   Cole Brothers, Newcastle.
1873   July. Delivered.
1886   8 August. On a voyage from Cartegena to Hartlepool with iron ore she sank off Portugal following a collision with the steamer *Lovaine*. One person died and the survivors were picked up by the *Lovaine* and taken to Lisbon.

San Domingo 1874   1,087grt.   70.01×9.48×4.88   Iron, 1 deck.

E.   Sgl. screw, 2 cyl. comp. inv., 142 nhp, 75 psi, 2 sgl. blrs. By Blair & Company,
            Stockton.

B.   M. Pearse & Company, Stockton on Tees.

1874   May. Delivered to Henry Bucknall & Sons.

1889   Sold to Hine Brothers, Maryport, Cumberland.

1899   Purchased by Angf Aktiebolaget Smaland, Oskarshamn, Sweden, renamed *Blenda*,
            T. Linnell as managers.

1920   21 November. On a voyage from Viborg to Hull she collided with a mine and sank
            off Hango.

John Dixon   1872   1,522grt.   76.23×9.81×5.91   Iron, 1 deck, schooner rig.

E.   Sgl. screw, 2 cyl. comp., 130 nhp. By C.D. Holmes & Company, Hull.

B.   Schlesinger Davies & Company, Newcastle.

1872   August. Delivered to E.W. King, Newcastle.

1876   Purchased by Henry Bucknall & Sons.

1889   Sold to North of England Shipping Company (G. Nelson & Sons), Liverpool.

1894   Owned by Hagerup, Doughty & Company, Grimsby.

1895   Sold to Act Dampskib Bengal, Drammen, Norway, renamed *Bengal*, Kr. Aug.
            Retvedt as managers.

1905   New boilers fitted.

1910   13 October. On a voyage from Kirkenes to Blyth she foundered off Finmark, north
            Norway in a hurricane. All seventeen crew were lost.

Joseph Dodds 1871   1,058grt.   66.84×9.17×5.33   Iron, 1 deck.

E.   Sgl. screw, 2 cyl. comp. inv., 99 nhp. By Blair & Company, Stockton.

B.   Richardson, Duck & Company, Newcastle.

1871   Delivered to W.T. Henley, Cardiff, Joseph Dodds as a partner.

1876   Purchased by Henry Bucknall & Sons.

1883   7 July. Struck a rock 40 miles north-west of Dog Rock Lighthouse, Tunisia. Captain
            was lost.

Egypt   1878   1,556grt.   76.2×10.18×5.91   Iron, 1 deck.

E.   Sgl. screw, 2 cyl. comp. inv., 140 nhp, 65 psi. By Tyne Engine Works, Newcastle.

B.   Wigham Richardson & Company, Newcastle.

1878   November. Delivered to Henry Bucknall & Sons.

1887   23 February. Departed New York with a cargo of wheat for Lisbon.

1887   3 March. On a voyage from New York to Lisbon in heavy seas the engine room
            flooded and she sank in position 58.44° N 64.8° W. All crew were saved by the
            Hannah Blanchard.

Madrid   1879   1,961grt.   85.34×10.73×7.5   1,270n.   9k.   Iron, 2 decks.

E.   Sgl. screw, 2 cyl. comp. inv., 200 nhp, 75 psi. By Wallsend Slipway & Engineering
            Company, Wallsend.

B.   Wigham Richardson & Company, Newcastle.

1879   5 June. Launched.

1879   26 July. Delivered to Henry Bucknall & Sons.

| 1887 | 16 June. On a voyage from Norfolk, Virginia, to Dublin, with a cargo of phosphates she was lost. Twenty-two members of her crew lost their lives. |

Manitoba   1887   2,127grt.   83.82×11.34×5.85   1,386n.   10k.

E.   Sgl. screw, 3 cyl. tpl. exp., 203 nhp. 160 psi, 2 sgl. blrs. By Blair & Company, Stockton. First steel vessel.

P.   12.

B.   Edward Withy & Company, West Hartlepool.

1887	March. Delivered to Henry Bucknall & Sons as the company's first steel hull and fitted with the first triple expansion engine in the fleet. All accommodation aft. Allocated to the Indian service and tramping duties.
1890	Owned by Bucknall Nephews.
1899	Sold to Orbe y Gobeo, Bilbao, renamed *Valle*. Owners later became Cia Cantabrica de Nav.
1900	28 January. She went missing off Bilbao on a voyage to Rotterdam with a cargo of iron ore. Twelve survivors were rescued by the *Servando*, but thirteen were lost.

Merida   1888   2,365grt.   88.39×11.61×5.8   1,383n.   10k.

E.   Sgl. screw, 3 cyl. tpl. exp., 212 nhp. 160 psi, 2 sgl. blrs. By Blair & Company, Stockton.

P.   12.

B.   Edward Withy & Company, West Hartlepool.

1888	10 February. Launched.
1888	March. Delivered to Henry Bucknall & Sons.
1890	Transferred to Bucknall Nephews.
1900	March. Sold to Orbe y Gobeo, renamed *Valle*. Owners then became Cia Cantabrica de Nav.
1917	17 January. Torpedoed and sunk by UC-18 in the Bay of Biscay.

Delcomyn   1880   1,827grt.   85.34×10.76×6.89   1,221n.   9k.

E.   Sgl. screw, 2 cyl. comp. inv., 260 nhp, 90 psi. By builder.

B.   Wigham Richardson & Company, Newcastle.

1880	6 October. Launched.
1880	27 November. Delivered to William Lund's Blue Anchor Line for the London–South Africa–Australia service.
1889	Purchased by Henry Bucknall & Sons.
1890	Transferred to Bucknall Nephews.
1897	Sold to J.B. Lussich, Buenos Aires, renamed *Felipe Lussich*.
1904	Sold to F. Francione, Buenos Aires, renamed *Corcega*. Later sold to Cia Argentina de Nav. (Nicholas Mihanovich) Limited, Buenos Aires, renamed *Patagonia*.
1914	Owned by A. Gardella.
1916	Broken up.

Elba   1889   2,293grt.   89.98×11.64×6.16   1,498n.   10k.

E.   Sgl. screw, tpl. exp., 300 nhp, 160 psi. By T. Richardson, Middlesbrough.

B.   Raylton Dixon & Company, Middlesbrough.

| 1889 | June. Launched for Henry Bucknall & Sons, completed for Bucknall Nephews. |
| 1893 | 4 July. On a voyage from Bombay to Hull she collided, in fog, with the *William Balls*, 30 miles north of the Humber. Both vessels sank but all were saved. |

Etona	1890	2,513grt. 90.52×12.19×5.79 1,613n. 10k.
E.		Sgl. screw, tpl. exp., 245 nhp, 160 psi, 2 sgl. blrs. By Blair & Company, Stockton.
B.		Richardson, Duck & Company, Stockton.
	1890	Laid down for Henry Bucknall & Sons, completed for Bucknall Nephews.
	1890	2 August. Delivered.
	1908	Sold to Nisbet, Calder & Company, Clydesdale Navigation Company.
	1913	Owned by George Nisbet & Company.
	1914	Sold to Moji Kisen KK, renamed *Buzen Maru*.
	1919	Owned by Kuribayashi Shosen KK.
	1934	Broken up in Japan.

Afrikander	1892	2,755grt. 100.27×12.37×5.3 1,793n. 10k.
E.		Sgl. screw, tpl. exp., 500 nhp, 160 psi, 2 sgl. blrs. By T. Richardson & Sons, Hartlepool.
B.		Raylton Dixon & Company, Middlesbrough.
	1891	28 December. Launched for the British & Colonial Steam Navigation Company, Bucknall Brothers as managers.
	1892	14 April. Maiden voyage London–South Africa. First of nine ships with a shallow draft designed to cross the bar at Durban and East London.
	1906	Sold to Adolphe Deppe, Antwerp, renamed *Uruguay* for the South America route.
	1907	Renamed *Bulgare* for the Black Sea services.
	1910	8 January. She went missing on a voyage from Kustindje to Antwerp. A lifeboat was found off Penmarch in March 1910.

Kaffir / Persian (2)	1891	2,374grt. 100.27×12.37×5.3 1,724n. 10k.
E.		Sgl. screw, tpl. exp., 500 nhp, 160 psi, 2 sgl. blrs. By T. Richardson & Sons, Hartlepool.
B.		Raylton Dixon & Company, Middlesbrough.
	1891	29 December. Launched for the British & Colonial Steam Navigation Company, Bucknall Brothers as managers.
	1906	Transferred to Ellerman & Papayanni, renamed *Persian*, Fred Swift as managers.
	1916	4 July. In collision with the Royal Mail Steam Packet vessel *Monmouthshire* off Cape Malea, Greece, and sank.

Zulu	1892	2,746grt. 94.43×12.37×5.3 1,724n. 10k.
E.		Sgl. screw, tpl. exp., 500 nhp, 160 psi, 2 sgl. blrs. By T. Richardson & Sons, Hartlepool.
B.		Raylton Dixon & Company, Middlesbrough.
	1892	29 February. Launched for the British & Colonial Steam Navigation Company, Bucknall Brothers as managers.
	1906	Sold to the Royal Mail Steam Packet Company, renamed *Marima*.
	1911	Owned by G. Coulouras, Andros, renamed *Marika*.
	1916	Sold to Hannevig Brothers, Christiansand, Oslo.
	1916	4 April. Foundered in South Atlantic.

Transvaal	1892	2,746grt. 94.37×12.37×5.3 1,781n. 10k.
E.		Sgl. screw, tpl. exp., 500 nhp, 160 psi, 2 sgl. blrs. By T. Richardson & Sons, Hartlepool.

B.	Raylton Dixon & Company, Middlesbrough.
1892	14 March. Launched for the British & Colonial Steam Navigation Company, Bucknall Brothers as managers.
1906	Sold to the Royal Mail Steam Packet Company, renamed *Manau*.
1906	March. Flooded and submerged while in dry dock, water pumped out.
1906	22 May. On a voyage from Bahia to Southampton she was wrecked 7 miles north of Bahia, Brazil. She later broke in two.

Basuto	1892 2,742grt. 94.49×12.37×5.3 1,784n. 10k.
E.	Sgl. screw, tpl. exp., 500 nhp, 160 psi, 2 sgl. blrs. By G. Clark & Company, Sunderland.
B.	James Laing & Company, Sunderland.
1892	Delivered to the British & Colonial Steam Navigation Company, Bucknall Brothers as managers
1901	11 December. She was last reported passing Anglesey on a voyage from Manchester to Bussorah, in the Persian Gulf.
1902	February. Posted missing. Fifty-seven crew were lost.

Bloemfontein / Arabian (2)	1892 2,745grt. 94.49×12.37×5.3 1,718n. 10k.
E.	Sgl. screw, tpl. exp., 500 nhp, 160 psi, 2 sgl. blrs. By G. Clark & Company, Sunderland.
B.	James Laing & Company, Sunderland.
1892	29 March. Launched for the British & Colonial Steam Navigation Company, Bucknall Brothers as managers
1906	Transferred to Ellerman & Papayanni, renamed *Arabian*, Fred Swift as managers.
1914	Operated on the London–East Africa service.
1915	2 October. Captured by U-33 off Cerigo Island, Greece and sunk by gunfire. Crew were saved.

Pondo	1892 2,741grt. 94.49×12.37×5.3 1,723n. 10k.
E.	Sgl. screw, tpl. exp., 500 nhp, 160 psi, 2 sgl. blrs. By G. Clark & Company, Sunderland.
B.	James Laing & Company, Sunderland.
1892	October. Delivered to the British & Colonial Steam Navigation Company, Bucknall Brothers as managers.
1912	Sold to G. Katsuda, Kobe, Japan, renamed *Taisho Maru*.
1914	Purchased by Uchida Kaisha KK, Nishonomiya.
1924	1 October. On a voyage from China to Yokohama she was wrecked on Kanabuse Rock, Shimonoseki Strait.

Mashona / Parana	1892 2,735grt. 94.49×12.37×5.3 1,781n. 10k.
E.	Sgl. screw, tpl. exp., 500 nhp, 160 psi, 2 sgl. blrs. By Central Marine Engineering Works, West Hartlepool.
B.	William Gray & Company, West Hartlepool.
1892	16 February. Launched for the British & Colonial Steam Navigation Company, Bucknall Brothers as managers.
1899	Transferred to Bucknall Nephews, renamed *Parana*.

1900	28 October. On a voyage from New York to Buenos Aires she was wrecked on Lobos Island, Uruguay. Broken in two.

Manica / Coronda   1892   2,733grt.   94.58×12.37×5.3   1,779n.   10k.

E.	Sgl. screw, tpl. exp., 500 nhp, 160 psi, 2 sgl. blrs. By Central Marine Engineering Works, West Hartlepool.
B.	William Gray & Company, West Hartlepool.
1892	May. Delivered to the British & Colonial Steam Navigation Company, Bucknall Brothers as managers.
1900	Transferred to Bucknall Nephews, renamed *Coronda*.
1908	September. Sold to Christian Salvesen.
1908	7 November. Left Tonsberg to establish a whaling station at New Island, Falkland Islands.
1909	October. Arrived at Leith Island, South Georgia to set up a whaling station.
1917	13 March. Torpedoed and sunk by U-18, 180 miles north-west of Tory Island, Northern Island.

Johannesburg   1895   4,495grt.   109.73×14.32×8.44   2,862n.   14k.

E.	Sgl. screw, tpl. exp., 578 nhp, 180 psi, 3 sgl. blrs. By Hawthorn Leslie & Company, Newcastle.
B.	Armstrong, Mitchell & Company, Newcastle.
1895	January. Delivered to the British & Colonial Steam Navigation Company, Bucknall Brothers as managers. Inaugurated the South African passenger service.
1900	Owned by Bucknall Steamship Lines.
1913	Sold to Andrew Weir & Company for their India–Africa passenger service, renamed *Surat*.
1926	April. Broken up at Shanghai by Sui Dah.

Fort Salisbury   1895   4,456grt.   109.73×14.32×8.44   2,824n.   14k.

E.	Sgl. screw, tpl. exp., 578 nhp, 180 psi, 3 sgl. blrs. By Hawthorn Leslie & Company, Newcastle.
B.	Armstrong, Mitchell & Company, Newcastle.
1895	March. Delivered to the British & Colonial Steam Navigation Company, Bucknall Brothers as managers, for the South African passenger service.
1900	Owned by Bucknall Steamship Lines.
1913	Sold to the Booth Steamship Company, Liverpool, renamed *Vincent* and then re-sold to Andrew Weir & Company, renamed *Gujarat*.
1919	Sold to Hajee M.H. Nemazee, Hong Kong.
1921	Renamed *Gorjistan*. Operating on pilgrim duties.
1923	Transferred to the Oriental Navigation Company.
1926	Transferred to Hajee M. H. Nemazee, Hong Kong.
1928	Purchased by Borg & Company.
1928	5 October. Arrived at Kobe to be broken up.

Bulawayo   1895   4,456grt.   109.73×14.32×8.44   2,824n.   14k.

E.	Sgl. screw, tpl. exp., 578 nhp, 180 psi, 3 sgl. blrs. By Hawthorn Leslie & Company, Newcastle.

B.	Armstrong, Mitchell & Company, Newcastle.
1895	May. Delivered to the British & Colonial Steam Navigation Company, Bucknall Brothers as managers, for the South African passenger service.
1900	Owned by Bucknall Steamship Lines.
1913	Sold to Andrew Weir & Company, renamed *Kathiawar*.
1921	5 September. Left Alexandria for Rotterdam to be laid up.
1926	Broken up in Belgium.

Bucrania	1896 4,069grt. 111.25×14.36×8.23 2,593n. 10k.
E.	Sgl. screw, tpl. exp., 368 nhp, 170 psi, 2 sgl. blrs. By North East Marine Engineering Company, Newcastle.
B.	Tyne Iron Shipbuilding Company, Newcastle.
1896	March. Delivered as *Fitzpatrick* to Charles Burrell & Sons, Glasgow.
1898	October. Sold to Elder Dempster & Company, renamed *Monmouth*.
1899	Purchased by Bucentaur Steam Ship Company, London, Bucknall Brothers as managers, renamed *Bucrania*.
1900	Owned by Bucknall Steamship Lines.
1911	Owned by B.G. Ashdown, then sold to Kishimoto Kisen Kk, renamed *Shinsei Maru*.
1915	Sold to M. Naruse, Kobe, renamed *Seiko Maru*.
1916	15 March. Sailed from Seattle.
1916	23 March. Left Port Townsend for Yokohama and disappeared.

Buceros	1894 4,038gt. 111.25×14.36×8.23 2,593n. 10k.
E.	Sgl. screw, tpl. exp., 368 nhp, 170 psi, 2 sgl. blrs. By Central Marine Engineering Works, West Hartlepool.
B.	William Gray & Company, West Hartlepool.
1894	Delivered as *Strathness* to Charles Burrell & Sons, Glasgow.
1899	Purchased by Bucknall Steam Ship Lines, London, renamed *Buceros*.
1911	Sold to J. Bryde, Sandefjord, renamed *Oestkysten* and later *Johan Bryde*.
1913	Renamed *Svend Foyn 1* for J.P. Bogen for use as an Antarctic whaling factory ship.
1923	Purchased by Johann Rasmussen, owned by Hvalfanger A/S Sydhavet, Sandefjord operating as an Antarctic supply and whale-oil carriage ship. She made annual voyages to South Shetland, Grahamland and the Palmer Peninsula, being laid up in Sandefjord in the summer.
1931	Laid up at Sandefjord.
1934	Broken up.

Bucentaur	1893 3,593grt. 109.73×13.47×8.2 2,223n. 10k.
E.	Sgl. screw, tpl. exp., 297 nhp, 160 psi, 2 sgl. blrs. By builder.
B.	London & Glasgow Shipbuilding Company, Glasgow.
1893	August. Delivered as *Oolong* to the China Mutual Steam Navigation Company, Liverpool for the Far East service.
1898	Sold to Bucentaur Steam Ship Company, Bucknall Brothers as managers, renamed *Bucentaur*.
1911	Sold to Meiji Kaiunk.K, Tarumi, Japan, renamed *Saikai Maru*.
1915	Owned by M. Naruse, Kobe.
1918	Sold to G. Katsuda, then Katsuda Kisen KK, Kobe.

| 1931 | Purchased by Nippon Kosan KK, Kobe, renamed *Shoechi Maru*. |
| 1935 | February. Broken up at Kobe. |

Beira	1894 4,120grt. 105.16×14.33×8.14 3,025n 10k.
E.	Sgl. screw, tpl. exp., 379 nhp, 160 psi, 3 sgl. blrs. By builder.
B.	Alexander Stephens & Sons, Linthouse.
1894	August. Delivered as *Turkistan* to Frank C. Strick & Company.
1897	Delivered to the British & Colonial Steam Navigation Company, Bucknall Brothers as managers, renamed *Beira*.
1900	Owned by Bucknall Steamship Lines.
1910	Sold to Kishimoto Kisen KK, renamed *Shinkai Maru*.
1915	Owned by Mitsui Bussan Kaisha, Kobe, renamed *Yubari Maru*.
1915	Sold to Hokkaido Tanko Kisen KK, Kobe.
1930	Purchased by Sugaya KK, renamed *Miharu Maru*.
1935	Broken up in Japan.

Mashona (2)	1894 4,142grt. 112.38×14.48×8.2 2,665n. 10k.
E.	Sgl. screw, tpl. exp., 399 nhp, 170 psi, 3 sgl. blrs. By Blackwood & Gordon, Port Glasgow.
B.	Russell & Company, Greenock.
1894	Delivered as *Strathairley* to Charles Burrell & Sons, Glasgow.
1899	Sold to the British & Colonial Steam Navigation Company, Bucknall Brothers as managers, renamed *Mashona*.
1900	Owned by Bucknall Steamship Lines.
1915	18 July. On a voyage from London to Beira she was wrecked, 30 miles west of Zavora Point, Lourenco Marques.

Bechuana	1894 4,148grt. 112.38×14.48×8.2 2,659n. 10k.
E.	Sgl. screw, tpl. exp., 399 nhp, 170 psi, 3 sgl. blrs. By Blackwood & Gordon, Port Glasgow.
B.	Russell & Company, Greenock.
1894	Delivered as *Strathtay* to Charles Burrell & Sons, Glasgow.
1899	Sold to the British & Colonial Steam Navigation Company, Bucknall Brothers as managers, renamed *Bechuana*.
1900	Owned by Bucknall Steamship Lines.
1915	Operated as a naval collier.
1919	Sold to Benito del Valle, then Cia Naviera Valle, renamed *Eusebia de Valle*.
1932	2 March. On a voyage from Follonica to Hamburg with a cargo of pyrites she foundered 60 miles south-west of Ushant.

Manica (2)	1900 4,117grt. 109.99×14.33×8.53 2,626n. 10k.
E.	Sgl. screw, tpl. exp., 530 nhp, 180 psi. 3 sgl. blrs. By T. Richardson & Sons, Hartlepool.
B.	James Laing & Sons, Sunderland.
1900	December. Delivered to Bucknall Steamship Lines, Bucknall Brothers as managers.
1914	August. Sold to Admiralty.
1915	Converted to a balloon observation ship for the Dardenelles campaign.

1915	April. Allocated to the 2nd Squadron at the Dardenelles.
1916	October. Converted to a bulk oil carrier for the Royal Navy, fitted with tanks and renamed *Huntball*.
1922	Sold to Anglo-Saxon Petroleum Company, renamed *Phorus*.
1930	12 August. Arrived at Hong Kong and laid up.
1931	3 July. Arrived at Osaka to be broken up.

Barotse	1901 4,119grt. 109.99×14.33×8.53 2,723n. 10k.
E.	Sgl. screw, tpl. exp., 530 nhp, 180 psi. 3 sgl. blrs. By T. Richardson & Sons, Hartlepool.
B.	James Laing & Sons, Sunderland.
1901	March. Delivered to Bucknall Steamship Lines, Bucknall Brothers as managers.
1922	Sold to Goshi Kaisha KK, renamed *Kyokutu Maru No 2*.
1925	Owned by Sanyo Sha Goshi Kaisha, Darien, renamed *Sanyo Maru*.
1932	30 November. Aground at Niigata and later salvaged.
1934	Broken up.

Baralong / Manica (3)	1901 4,192grt. 109.99×14.33×8.53 2,723n. 10k.
E.	Sgl. screw, tpl. exp., 530 nhp, 180 psi. 3 sgl. blrs. By T. Richardson & Sons, Hartlepool.
B.	James Laing & Sons, Sunderland.
1901	May. Delivered to Bucknall Steamship Lines, Bucknall Brothers as managers.
1902	8 September. Left builders towing a 30,000 dwt floating dock for Durban at a speed of 5 knots. In bad weather off Mossel Bay the towing line snapped and the dock went ashore and was lost.
1905	22 August. Collided with the Japanese ferry *Kinjo Maru* off Shimishima and 160 lives were lost. The inquiry established that the ferry was operating without the correct lights.
1914	September. Requisitioned as a naval supply vessel.
1915	Converted into a 'Q' ship and armed with concealed guns which could be used against enemy submarines, renamed HMS *Wyandra*.
1915	19 August. Sank the German submarine U-27 by gunfire as she was in the process of attempting to sink the Leyland steamer *Nicosian*. The crew of the *Nicosian* were picked up by HMS *Wyandra* and they informed the captain that there were German sailors on board their vessel. The boarding party that was sent onto *Nicosian* discovered enemy sailors who were all killed by gunfire. When the details of the incident reached Berlin, the German authorities demanded that the men be charged with murder.
1915 24	September. Sank the German submarine U-41.
1915	Transferred to Mediterranean duties. Following the outcry against the incident involving U-27 it was decided to change *Nicosian*'s name to *Nevision*, and the name *Baralong* was deleted from the register of shipping. The ship was given the name *Manica* when the original *Manica* (2) was renamed *Huntball*. Consequently, HMS *Wyandra* was decommissioned in 1917 as the balloon ship *Manica*.
1923	Sold to Goshi Kaisha KK, Dairen, renamed *Kyokuto Maru*.
1925	Owned by Shinsei Kisen Goshi KK, Dairen, renamed *Shinsei Maru No 1*.
1934	Broken up in Japan.

Bantu	1901 4,230grt. 109.72×14.33×8.53 2,655n. 10k.
E.	Sgl. screw, tpl. exp., 530 nhp, 180 psi. 3 sgl. blrs. By Wallsend Slipway & Engineering Company, Wallsend.
B.	Armstrong, Whitworth & Company, Newcastle.
1901	October. Delivered to Bucknall Steamship Lines, Bucknall Brothers as managers.
1911	Sold to Isthmian Steam Ship Company, renamed *Orpheus*. Later transferred to the American flag as owned by the United States Steel Corporation of New York.
1930	Purchased by M. Kulukundis, Piraeus, and later P. Hadjilias.
1931	Broken up at Blyth by Hughes, Bolckow.
Lotus	1863 621grt. 63.34×7.38×4.78 363n. 8k.
E.	Sgl. screw, 2 cyl. comp. By builder.
B.	Earle's Shipbuilding & Engineering Company, Hull.
1863	March. Delivered as *Cecile* to the Moss Steam Ship Company, Liverpool.
1873	New compound engines installed by T. Brassey, Liverpool.
1890	Sold to Walsh Brothers, Liverpool.
1891	Re-boilered.
1897	Sold to F. Alexander, Antwerp.
1900	Purchased by Bucknall Steam Ship Lines and operated in the Persian Gulf, based at Busoorah.
1914	January. Transferred to Ellerman & Bucknall.
1921	Broken up.
Balgay	1897 303grt. 39.68×6.95×2.96 131n. 8k.
E.	Sgl. screw, 2 cyl. comp., 60 nhp, 1 sgl. blr. By Cooper & Greig, Dundee.
B.	Dundee Shipbuilding Company, Dundee.
1897	October. Delivered to W. Kinnear & Company, Dundee.
1901	Purchased by Bucknall to tranship cargo at South African ports during the Boer War.
1904	2 May. Transported J.B. Turnbull and employees to Madagascar with the first gold dredging plant sent to the island.
1905	Sold to Hadjee Ahmed Nassam, Bombay.
1907	Purchased by the Bombay Steam Navigation Company.
1924	Sold to Nawanagar State Tramways Department.
1931	Broken up in India.
Balgowan	1897 286grt. 39.68×6.95×2.96 131n. 8k.
E.	Sgl. screw, 2 cyl. comp., 60 nhp, 1 sgl. blr. By A. Hall & Company, Dundee.
B.	Dundee Shipbuilding Company, Dundee.
1897	March. Delivered to W. Kinnear & Company, Dundee.
1901	Purchased by Bucknall to tranship cargo at South African ports during the Boer War.
1904	9 August. Sailing in ballast on a voyage from Swakopmund to Cape Town, she was wrecked in fog on Eastern Cliff, Spence Bay, 90 miles north of Luderitzbucht. Bucknall's *Ready* rescued the crew of nine.

Ready 1896 251grt. 36.45×7.65×2.5 137n. 8k.
E. Sgl. screw, 2 cyl. comp., 65 nhp. By J. Stewart & Sons, Middlesbrough.
B. R. Craggs & Sons, Middlesbrough.
1896 Delivered as *Ready* to Hawthorn Brothers, Middlesbrough.
1901 Purchased by Bucknall to tranship cargo at South African ports during the Boer War.
1907 Sold to George T. Wills, London, registered in Port Adelaide and sold to Charles F. Rischbeith.
1916 Purchased by Howard Smith's Australian Steamships Proprietary, Sydney.
1931 Owned by Penguin Limited, H.P. Stacey & J. Williams, and operated as a salvage vessel.
1938 Sold to E. Moller, Shanghai, renamed *Ready Moller*.
1941 8 December. Became the Japanese vessel *Amoy Maru II*.
1946 Reverted to E. Moller ownership as *Ready Moller*.
1949 Purchased by Anglo-Chinese Shipping Company, Shanghai, Moller as managers.
1951 Broken up at Shanghai.

Euphrates 1901 2,809grt. 91.44×13.32×5.12 1,794n. 10k.
E. Sgl. screw, tpl. exp., 280 nhp, 160 psi, 3 sgl. blrs. By North East Marine Engineering Company, Newcastle.
B. Armstrong, Whitworth & Company, Newcastle.
1901 24 October. Launched.
1902 25 January. Delivered to Bucknall Steam Ship Lines for the Persian Gulf services.
1906 Sold to Adolf Deppe's Cie Nationale Belge de Transportes Maritimes, Antwerp.
1917 22 January. Torpedoed and sank by U-57, 240 miles south-west of Fastnet.

Tigris 1901 2,805grt. 91.44×13.32×5.12 1,792n. 10k.
E. Sgl. screw, tpl. exp., 280 nhp, 160 psi, 3 sgl. blrs. By North East Marine Engineering Company, Newcastle.
B. Armstrong, Whitworth & Company, Newcastle.
1901 11 December. Launched.
1902 February. Delivered to Bucknall Steam Ship Lines for the Persian Gulf services.
1906 Sold to Adolf Deppe's Cie Nationale Belge de Transportes Maritimes, Antwerp.
1930 18 September. Left Antwerp for Alexandria, disappeared off the Isle of Wight, wreckage washed ashore at Dunkirk.

Swazi 1901 4,941grt. 115.82×15.24×8.87 3,174n. 10k.
E. Sgl. screw, tpl. exp., 443 nhp, 180 psi, 3 sgl. blrs. By Wallsend Slipway & Engineering Company, Wallsend.
B. Armstrong, Whitworth & Company, Newcastle.
1901 August. Delivered to Bucknall Steam Ship Lines.
1926 Sold to Z.M. Scheldestroom, Ghent, renamed *Scheldestroom*.
1933 November. Broken up in Italy.

Arabistan 1893 3,194grt. 99.06×12.8×5.76 1,928n. 10k.
E. Sgl. screw, tpl. exp., 306 nhp, 160 psi, 3 sgl. blrs. By builder.
B. Alexander Stephen & Sons, Linthouse.

1893	Delivered to F.C. Strick & Company as *Arabistan*.
1902	January. Purchased by Bucknall Nephews, Bucknall Brothers as managers.
1910	Sold to F. Chiama & Danova, Genoa, renamed *Giano*.
1911	24 December. Wrecked on the coast of Cyrenaica. All of the crew were saved.

Griqua	1902	3,344grt.	100.58×13.78×5.27	2,099n. 12k.

E.	Sgl. screw, tpl. exp., 387 nhp, 180 psi, 3 sgl. blrs. By North East Marine Engineering Company, Newcastle.
B.	Armstrong, Whitworth & Company, Newcastle.
1902	December. Delivered to Bucknall Steam Ship Lines for the Newcastle–Hamburg–Antwerp–South Africa service.
1914	1 January. Transferred to Ellerman & Bucknall.
1916	20 December. Attacked by a submarine in the Mediterranean.
1917	7 May. Attacked by submarine, escaped.
1927	Sold to Adria SA, di Nav. Marittima of Fiume, renamed *Aleardi*.
1934	June. Broken up in Italy.

Amatonga	1903	3,331grt.	100.58×13.78×5.27	2,093n. 12k.

E.	Sgl. screw, tpl. exp., 387 nhp, 180 psi, 3 sgl. blrs. By North East Marine Engineering Company, Newcastle.
B.	Armstrong, Whitworth & Company, Newcastle.
1903	10 January. Launched.
1903	10 February. Delivered.
1914	Transferred to Ellerman & Bucknall.
1927	Sold to Adria SA, di Nav. Marittima of Fiume, renamed *Foscolo*.
1933	13 April. Arrived at Fiume, sold and broken up.

Casilda	1902	3,928grt.	111.49×14.36×7.56	2,463n. 11k.

E.	Sgl. screw, tpl. exp., 362 nhp, 180 psi, 3 sgl. blrs. By G. Clark & Company Limited, Sunderland.
B.	Sir James Laing & Company, Sunderland.
1902	Delivered to Bucknall Nephews, Bucknall Brothers as managers.
1908	Sold to Soc. Les Affreteurs Reunis, Rouen, renamed *Ceres*.
1913	27 October. Sold to Deutsche Levante Linie, renamed *Lipsos*.
1914	1 August. Seized at Antwerp three days before Britain declared war.
1914	9 October. Ship still at Antwerp when Germany took the port.
1919	28 June. Responsibility of the British Shipping Controller, allocated to the Lyle Shipping Company, Glasgow.
1920	Owned by the Shakespeare Shipping Company, Glover Brothers as managers, renamed *Ovid*.
1933	Broken up by Alberto Trivero at Genoa.

Maritzburg	1904	6,847grt.	128.00×15.73×8.44	4,175n. 12½k.

E.	Twin screw, 2×tpl. exp., 851 nhp, 180 psi, 5 sgl. blrs. By Wallsend Slipway & Engineering Company, Wallsend.
B.	Armstrong, Whitworth & Company, Newcastle.
1904	16 May. Launched for Bucknall Steam Ship Lines. Because of a severe slump

following the Boer War she was put up for sale while under construction and was sold to Erasmo Piaggio for Soc. di Nav. Lloyd Italiano, Genoa as Mendoza.

1905	10 October. Maiden voyage from Genoa to Buenos Aires.
1912	Transferred to the Genoa to New York service.
1914	Renamed *Caserta*.
1918	1 June. The company took over Lloyd Italiano and she was painted in Navigazione Generale Italiana colours.
1923	Transferred to La Veloce, renamed *Venezuela* for the South American service, Valparaiso via the Panama Canal.
1924	21 September. Transferred back to Navigazione Generale Italiana.
1929	Broken up.

Matoppo	1904 3,942grt. 109.73×14.39×8.14 2,526n. 10k.
E.	Sgl. screw, tpl. exp., 403 nhp, 3 sgl. blrs. By Wallsend Slipway & Engineering Company, Wallsend.
B.	Armstrong, Whitworth & Company, Newcastle.
1903	5 November. Launched as *Lady Strathcona* for William Peterson Limited, Newcastle.
1904	Delivered.
1905	May. Purchased by Bucknall Steam Ship Lines, renamed *Matoppo*. Lost two of her three propeller blades on her maiden voyage and the spare blade was fitted by raising her bow. The second screw was fitted at Walvis Bay and on her way to Cape Town she lost another blade. Two new screws were fitted at Cape Town.
1905	October. Sold to the Union Steam Ship Company of New Zealand, renamed *Wairuna*.
1917	2 June. On a voyage from Auckland to San Francisco she was captured by the German raider *Wolf* off Kermadoc Island, New Zealand. She was taken to Sunday Island where 1,500 tons of coal was transferred.
1917	17 June. Towed out to sea and sunk by gunfire, 2 miles off the island.

Matoppo (2)	1905 5,280grt. 122.07×15.85×8.59 4,320n. 10k.
E.	Sgl. screw, tpl. exp., 487nhp, 200 psi, 3 sgl. blrs. By D. Rowan & Company Limited, Glasgow.
B.	William Hamilton & Company, Port Glasgow.
1905	November. Purchased on the stocks by Bucknall Steam Ship Lines.
1908	August. Transferred to the East Indies and Pacific services.
1914	1 January. Transferred to Ellerman & Bucknall.
1916	A man named Schiller was imprisoned after a plot was discovered to blow her up in the United States. He received a life sentence.
1930	December. Broken up by Thomas W. Ward at Preston.

Koranna	1905 3,585grt. 106.68×15.85×7.13 2,267n. 10k.
E.	Sgl. screw, tpl. exp., 337 nhp, 180 psi, 3 sgl. blrs. By North East Marine Engineering Company, Newcastle.
B.	Armstrong, Whitworth & Company, Newcastle.
1905	February. Delivered to Bucknall Steam Ship Lines.
1914	Transferred to Ellerman & Bucknall.
1916	April. Operated as an Indian Army Transport.
1929	Sold to Z. A. Valmos, Andros, renamed *Apikia*.

1936	Purchased by Ding Yao Dung, Chefoo, renamed *Chang Kwang*.
1937	Renamed *Shoko* for Japanese services.
1938	Owned by Akai Shoten KK, Osaka, renamed *Niitoku Maru*.
1944	14 February. Sunk by USS *Snook* in the Pacific in position 33.48° N 128.49°E.

Bloemfontein (2)   1906   4,654grt.   122.25×15.24×5.52   2,958n.   10k.

E.	Sgl. screw, tpl. exp., 478 nhp, 180 psi, 2 sgl. blrs. By Dunsmuir & Jackson Limited, Glasgow.
B.	A. McMillan & Son, Dumbarton.
1905	18 September. Launched.
1906	October. Delivered as the largest vessel in the fleet.
1914	1 January. Transferred to Ellerman & Bucknall.
1932	July. Sold to be broken up.
1932	31 July. Sailed from the Tyne for Trieste to be demolished.

Kasama   1907   4,635grt.   122.25×15.24×5.52   2,945n.   10k.

E.	Sgl. screw, tpl. exp., 478 nhp, 180 psi, 2 sgl. blrs. By Dunsmuir & Jackson Limited, Glasgow.
B.	A. McMillan & Son, Dumbarton.
1907	June. Delivered.
1914	1 January. Transferred to Ellerman & Bucknall.
1932	October. Sold for £2,700 to G. Ricardi, Genoa, to be broken up.

Kazembe   1907   4,658grt.   122.01×15.24×5.52   2,938n.   10k.

E.	Sgl. screw, tpl. exp., 478 nhp, 180 psi, 2 sgl. blrs. By builder.
B.	Alexander Stephen & Sons, Linthouse.
1907	May. Delivered.
1914	1 January. Transferred to Ellerman & Bucknall.
1915–18	Requisitioned by the Admiralty.
1932	July. Sold to Smith & Houston and broken up at Port Glasgow.

Kalomo / City of Halifax   1907   5.019grt.   121.32×15.94×6.13   3,209n.   10k.

E.	Sgl. screw, tpl. exp., 401 nhp, 180 psi, 3 sgl. blrs. By Rankin & Gilmore Limited, Greenock.
B.	Robert Duncan & Company, Port Glasgow.
1907	February. Delivered to Bucknall Steam Ship Lines.
1914	1 January. Transferred to Ellerman & Bucknall.
1926	Renamed *City of Halifax*.
1931	November. Sold to Thomas W. Ward and broken up at Inverkeithing.

Karonga   1907   4,665grt.   121.92×15.88×8.23   2,932n.   10k.

E.	Sgl. screw, tpl. exp., 477 nhp, 180 psi, 3 sgl. blrs. By North East Marine Engineering Company, Newcastle.
B.	Armstrong, Whitworth & Company, Newcastle.
1907	June. Delivered to Bucknall Steam Ship Lines.
1914	1 January. Transferred to Ellerman & Bucknall.
1917	29 April. Torpedoed and sunk by U–63 in the Strait of Messina. A Lascar fireman was trapped by the legs and as the ship began to sink Chief Steward Furneaux amputated

the leg and carried the man to the lifeboats. The seaman survived and Furneaux was awarded the Albert Medal. Eighteen of the crew lost their lives and her captain was taken prisoner.

Katuna / City of Swansea 1907 4,641grt. 121.92×15.88×8.23 2,927n. 10k.

E.	Sgl. screw, tpl. exp., 477 nhp, 180 psi, 3 sgl. blrs. Wallsend Slipway & Engineering Company, Wallsend.
B.	Armstrong, Whitworth & Company, Newcastle.
1907	May. Delivered.
1914	1 January. Transferred to Ellerman & Bucknall.
1929	Renamed *City of Swansea*.
1937	September. Sold to Barry Shipping Company, Cardiff, renamed *St Glen*.
1939	Owners renamed South American Saint Line.
1940	6 September. Bombed and sunk by German aircraft off the east coast of Scotland in position 57.25° N 01.38° W.

Kabinga 1907 4,657grt. 121.92×15.88×8.23 2,925n. 10k.

E.	Sgl. screw, tpl. exp., 477 nhp, 180 psi, 3 sgl. blrs. By North East Marine Engineering Company, Newcastle.
B.	Armstrong, Whitworth & Company, Newcastle.
1907	July. Delivered to Bucknall Steam Ship Lines.
1914	1 January. Transferred to Ellerman & Bucknall.
1914	11 September. Left Sandheads, River Hooghly, for Britain. The German light cruiser *Emden* and her collier *Markomannia* arrived in the Indian Ocean from Tsingtau.
1914	12 September. *Emden* captured *Kabinga* and because the captain's wife and daughter were on board the sinking of the ship was delayed until daylight.
1914	13 September. *Killin* was captured and sunk and her crew were transferred to *Kabinga*. This procedure was continued as other ships were captured and sunk. *Kabinga* was later released and sent to Calcutta.
1938	20 October. Sold to the African & Continental Steam Ship Company, renamed *Lulea*.
1939	August. Owned by Cia. Ligure di Nav., Genoa, renamed *San Leonardo*.
1940	10 June. Interned in the United States when Italy entered the Second World War.
1941	December. The United States Maritime Commission took over responsibility for the vessel, which was was renamed *Reigh Court*.
1943	5 June. Sunk following a collision off the east coast of America in position 44° N 63° W.

Kasenga 1907 4,652grt. 121.92×15.88×8.23 2,923n. 10k.

E.	Sgl. screw, tpl. exp., 477 nhp, 180 psi, 3 sgl. blrs. Wallsend Slipway & Engineering Company, Wallsend.
B.	Armstrong, Whitworth & Company, Newcastle.
1907	August. Delivered to Bucknall Steam Ship Lines.
1914	1 January. Transferred to Ellerman & Bucknall.
1915	Operated as a supply ship by the French Government to their colonies isolated during the war.

1917   1 April. Torpedoed and sunk by a German submarine 2 miles from the Hormigas, Cape Palos, near Cartagena, Spain.

Karema   1894   5,263grt.   124.97×15.1×9.78   3,362n.   10k.
E.   Sgl. screw, tpl. exp., 445 nhp, 180 psi, 3 sgl. blrs. By builder.
B.   Palmers Shipbuilding Company, Newcastle.
1894   Delivered as *Ranza* for the Caledonia Steamship Company, Liverpool.
1909   Sold to Bucknall Steam Ship Lines, renamed *Karema*.
1914   1 January. Transferred to Ellerman & Bucknall.
1917   25 November. Torpedoed and sunk by U–39, 33 miles south-east-by-east from Cape de Gata, Almeria, Spain.

Kansas / City of Winnipeg   1910   6,074grt.   131.58×16.73×9.42   3,931n.   11½k.
E.   Sgl. screw, tpl. exp., 403 nhp, 180 psi, 3 sgl. blrs. By builder.
B.   Workman, Clark & Company, Belfast.
1910   Delivered to Bucknall Steam Ship Lines for the United States service.
1914   1 January. Transferred to Ellerman & Bucknall.
1926   Renamed *City of Winnipeg*.
1932   March. When a leak was discovered she put into Plymouth. This was repaired without having to send her to dry dock.
1934   28 December. Sold to be broken up, renamed *Winny* and left Houston with cargo for Kobe.
1935   Broken up in Japan.

Kioto   1910   6,182grt.   131.67×16.5×9.42   4,020n.   11½k.
E.   Sgl. screw, tpl. exp., 403 nhp, 180 psi, 3 sgl. blrs. By Wallsend Slipway & Engineering Company, Wallsend.
B.   Swan Hunter & Wigham Richardson, Newcastle.
1910   Delivered.
1914   1 January. Transferred to Ellerman & Bucknall.
1917   11 July. Torpedoed and sunk by U–87, 20 miles west of Fastnet.

Kentucky / City of Mobile   1912   6,588grt.   131.67×16.5×9.42   4,020n.   11½k.
E.   Sgl. screw, 4 cyl. quad. exp., 403 nhp, 180 psi, 3 sgl. blrs. By builder.
B.   Swan Hunter & Wigham Richardson, Newcastle.
1912   29 October. Launched.
1912   10 December. Delivered. Maiden voyage Cardiff–New York.
1914   1 January. Transferred to Ellerman & Bucknall.
1926   Renamed *City of Mobile*.
1932–33   Laid up in the Gareloch.
1940   16 September. Bombed and sunk in an air attack in the Irish Channel.

Kafue   1913   6,064grt.   129.14×16.61×9.42   3,931n.   11½k.
E.   Sgl. screw, tpl. exp., 589 nhp, 180 psi, 3 sgl. blrs. By builder.
B.   Palmers Shipbuilding Company, Newcastle.
1913   April. Delivered.
1914   1 January. Transferred to Ellerman & Bucknall.

| 1915 | On charter to the Italian Government as a collier. |
| 1918 | 30 April. Torpedoed and sunk by U-86, 11 miles south-west of the Mull of Galloway. |

Karroo / City of Khartoum   1913   6,127grt.   129.14×16.61×9.42   3,941n.   11½k.

E.	Sgl. screw, tpl. exp., 601 nhp, 180 psi, 3 sgl. blrs. By builder.
B.	Palmers Shipbuilding Company, Newcastle.
1913	6 May. Delivered to Bucknall Steam Ship Lines, final ship with a counter stern.
1914	1 January. Transferred to Ellerman & Bucknall Line.
1914	4 August. She was berthed at Brisbane when the First World War was declared. Requisitioned as an American Government transport to convoy troops to Port Suez.
1914	9 November. She heard a message on her radio, which was sent from the cable station at Cocos Keeling Island, that there was a strange warship at the entrance of Suez. The vessel was the German cruiser *Emden*. *Karroo* radioed HMAS *Melbourne* and HMAS *Sydney*, who then followed and sank *Emden* later that day.
1917	22 April. On a voyage from Halifax to Devonport she was attacked by a submarine and two torpedoes were fired at her. She managed to escape without any injury or damage.
1917	21 May. Attacked by U-6 in the English Channel. She also survived this incident without any damage.
1918	6 July. Attacked in the English Channel by a German submarine. Escaped.
1927	Renamed *City of Khartoum*.
1936	September. Sold to Stephens, Sutton Limited, and scrapped in Italy by Luigi Pittaluga.

Saldanha   1912   4,594grt.   117.62×14.87×9.08   2,950n.   10k.

E.	Sgl. screw, tpl. exp., 339 nhp, 180 psi. By Wallsend Slipway & Engineering Company, Wallsend.
B.	Swan Hunter & Wigham Richardson, Newcastle.
1912	Delivered to Bucknall Steam Ship Lines.
1914	1 January. Transferred to Ellerman & Bucknall.
1918	19 March. Torpedoed and sunk by UB-52, 95 miles north of Algiers. Six of her crew lost their lives.

Kathlamba / City of Carlisle   1913   6,382grt.   132.28×16.67×9.51   4,104n.   12k.

E.	Sgl. screw, tpl. exp., 586 nhp, 220 psi, 3 sgl. blrs. By Central Marine Engineering Works, West Hartlepool.
B.	William Gray & Company, West Hartlepool.
1913	2 August. Delivered to Bucknall Steam Ship Lines.
1914	1 January. Transferred to Ellerman & Bucknall.
1917	18 June. Attacked and hit by a torpedo in the English Channel. Survived and made it to port.
1920	Collided with British India's *Nerbudda* in the Thames when both ships were at anchor. *Nerbudda*'s propeller damaged the hull of *Kathlamba*.
1927	Renamed *City of Carlisle*.
1932–34	Laid up in the Gareloch.
1934	June. Arrived at Dalmuir to be broken.

Kandahar / City of Perth (4)   1913   6,415grt.   132.47×16.67×9.51   4,104n.   12k.

E.	Sgl. screw, tpl. exp., 586 nhp, 220 psi, 3 sgl. blrs. By Wallsend Slipway & Engineering Company, Wallsend.
B.	Swan Hunter & Wigham Richardson, Newcastle.
1913	September. Delivered to Bucknall Steam Ship Lines as the final ship for the company.
1914	1 January. Transferred to Ellerman & Bucknall.
1926	Renamed *City of Perth*.
1943	26 March. Torpedoed and sunk by U-431 off Oran.

Keelung   1914   6,672grt.   136.92×17.31×9.39   12k.

E.	Sgl. screw, tpl. exp., 641 nhp, 220 psi, 3 sgl. blrs. By builder.
B.	Earle's Shipbuilding & Engineering Company, Hull.
1914	First ship to enter service for Ellerman Lines Limited with Ellerman & Bucknall Steamship Lines as managers.
1918	27 June. Torpedoed and sunk by U-53, 110 miles west-by-south of Ushant.

Keelung (2) / *City of Keelung*   1919   5,186grt.   125.58×15.91×8.69   3,199n.   12k.

E.	Sgl. screw, tpl. exp., 368 nhp, 220 psi, 3 sgl. blrs. By builder.
B.	Earle's Shipbuilding & Engineering Company, Hull.
1919	October. Built as *War Walrus* as a standard Type B hull. Taken over by Ellerman & Bucknall and completed to their specifications.
1936	Renamed *City of Keelung*.
1947	June. Sold to China Hellenic Lines, renamed *Hellenic Trader*.
1951	Owned by Nissan Kisen KK, renamed *Nichian Maru*.
1960	March. Broken up at Shimizu, Japan.

Rialto   1911   2,948grt.   103.33×14.66×6.37   1,773n.   10k.

E.	Sgl. screw, tpl. exp., 309 nhp, 190 psi, 2 sgl. blrs. By builder.
B.	A.G. 'Neptun', Rostock.
1911	11 March. Launched.
1911	10 May. Delivered to Deutsche Levante Linie as *Olympos*.
1914	1 August. Berthed in Germany at the start of the First World War.
1919	Responsibility of the British Shipping Controller, Thomas Law & Company, London as managers.
1921	Purchased by Ellerman & Bucknall, renamed *Rialto*.
1928	Sold to Les Cargoes Algeriens SA, Algiers, renamed *Madali*.
1940	June. Escaped from Rouen to Bordeaux.
1940	8 August. Captured by the Germans.
1941	Renamed *H 7* for the invasion of the United Kingdom, later decommissioned and chartered to Johs Fritzen & Sohns to operate as a supply ship to the Channel Islands.
1943	27 September. Attacked by British and Dutch patrol vessels. Torpedoed and sunk off Etaples.

Kosmo   1913   5,170grt.   127.18×16.5×8.05   3,106n.   10k.

E.	Sgl. screw, tpl. exp., 577 nhp, 180 psi, 3 sgl. blrs. By builder.
B.	William Doxford & Sons, Sunderland.

1913	Built for the Hamburg America Line as *Nordmark*.
1919	23 March. Responsibility of the British Shipping Controller.
1920	Purchased by Ellerman & Bucknall, renamed *Kosmo*.
1928	Sold to Norddeutscher Lloyd, Bremen, renamed *Nurnburg*.
1932	Renamed *Wellen* for Russian interests, registered at Vladivostok.
1959	Broken up.

Kasenga (2) 1899 7,160grt. 139.00×17.71×6.86 4,634n. 10k.

E.	Sgl. screw, 4 cyl. quad. exp., 588 nhp, 210 psi, 3 sgl. blrs. By builder.
B.	Wigham, Richardson & Company, Newcastle.
1899	December. Delivered to DD-G 'Hansa', Bremen as *Drachenfels*.
1919	Responsibility of the British Shipping Controller, British India Steam Navigation Company as managers.
1920	Purchased by Ellerman & Bucknall, renamed *Kasenga*.
1929	Sold to INSA (Industrie Navali SA), Genoa, renamed *Adelia*.
1933	Broken up in Italy.

Lorenzo / City of Christchurch 1915 6,009grt. 149.65×18.93×7.71 11k.

E.	Sgl. screw, 4 cyl. quad. exp., 725 nhp, 180 psi, 4 sgl. blrs. By builder.
B.	Tecklenborg, Geestemunde.
1915	July. Delivered to DD-G 'Hansa', Bremen as *Aschenburg*.
1919	Responsibility of the British Shipping Controller, Rankin, Gilmour & Company, Liverpool, British & Foreign Steam Ship Company's Saint Line as managers.
1920	Purchased by Ellerman & Bucknall, renamed *Lorenzo*.
1929	Renamed *City of Christchurch*.
1943	21 March. Sunk off Lisbon by German bombers.

City of Batavia 1907 5,597grt. 133.29×16.18×8.87 3,457n. 10k.

E.	Sgl. screw, tpl. exp., 556 nhp, 180 psi, 3 sgl. blrs. By Wallsend Slipway & Engineering Company, Wallsend.
P.	12.
B.	Swan Hunter & Wigham Richardson, Newcastle.
1907	July. Delivered to Roland Line AG, Bremen, as *Ganelon*.
1920	Purchased by Ellerman & Bucknall, renamed *City of Batavia*.
1938	November. Sold to Soc. Anon. Industria Armamento, Genoa, renamed *Voluntas*.
1940	June. When Italy entered the Second World War she was interned at Buenos Aires and was taken over by the Argentine Government. She was renamed *Teuco*, managed by Flota Mercante del Estado.
1946	Reverted back to Soc. Anon. Industria Armamento, Genoa, renamed *Voluntas*.
1949	Renamed *Volonta*, owned by Trasmarina S.p.A., Genoa.
1955	12 April. Wrecked at Ushant.

City of Harvard 1907 7,091grt. 130.64×16.61×8.5 4,410n. 12k.

E.	Sgl. screw, 4 cyl. quad. exp., 606 nhp, 180 psi, 3 sgl. blrs. By builder.
P.	83 (first), 46 (second).
B.	Bremer Vulkan AG, Bremen.

1907	4 December. Launched as *Giessen* for Norddeutscher Lloyd, Bremen, for the African and Far East services.
1913	May. Operated on the Bremen–New York service.
1919	March. Responsibility of the British Shipping Controller.
1920	Purchased by Ellerman & Bucknall, renamed *City of Harvard*.
1921	April. Operated on the New York–Port Said–Bombay–Karachi–Abadan service for the American & India Line. Later placed on the New York–India–Rangoon route.
1933	Laid up in the Gareloch.
1933	Broken up in Italy.

City of Alexandria   1905   4,697grt.   110.37×14.23×7.98   2,866n.   11k.

E.	Sgl. screw, tpl. exp., 415 nhp, 205 psi, 3 sgl. blrs. By builder.
B.	J.C. Tecklenborg, Geestemunde.
1905	20 May. Launched as *Dalmatia* for Hamburg America Line.
1905	1 September. Maiden voyage Hamburg–Rio Grande.
1907	21 June. Sold to Hamburg Süd-Americanische, renamed *Rio Pardo*.
1914	August. Taken over by the Kreigsmarine, renamed *Sperrbrecher II*, later *Sperrbrecher 4*.
1919	25 March. Responsibility of the British Shipping Controller, Orient Line as managers.
1920	Managed by Ellerman & Papayanni Line.
1921	29 January. Purchased by Ellerman & Bucknall, renamed *City of Alexandria* for the South African passenger service.
1933	July. Sold to Petersen & Albeck, Hamburg.
1936	Broken up.

City of Palermo   1905   4,699grt.   110.43×14.23×7.98   2,866n.   11k.

E.	Sgl. screw, tpl. exp., 415 nhp, 205 psi, 3 sgl. blrs. By builder.
B.	J.C. Tecklenborg, Geestemunde.
1905	20 February. Launched as *Rio Negro* for Hamburg Süd-Americanische.
1905	29 April. Maiden voyage Hamburg–Rio Grande.
1914	4 August. Operated as a supply ship at Para, Brazil for the German cruiser *Karlsruhe*.
1914	4 November. *Karlsruhe* was destroyed by an internal explosion, with 263 of her crew losing their lives. *Rio Negro* returned to Keil.
1917	Renamed *Sperrbrecher 1*.
1918	November. Reverted to the ownership of Hamburg Süd-Americanische.
1919	29 March. Responsibility of the British Shipping Controller, Orient Line as managers.
1920	October. Ellerman & Papayanni as managers. Transported refugees to Istanbul and Piraeus from Yalta and Black Sea ports.
1921	29 January. Purchased by Ellerman & Bucknall, renamed *City of Palermo*.
1933	Sold to Italiana Generale Navagazione and broken up.

Karonga (2) / *City of Derby*   1921   6,616grt.   131.98×17.5×9.20   4,190n.   12k.

E.	Sgl. screw, 2 drg steam turb., 767 nhp, 225 psi, 3 sgl. blrs. By Central Marine Engineering Works, Newcastle.
B.	William Gray & Company, Sunderland.
1921	November. Delivered as *Karoonga*.
1927	Renamed *City of Derby*.
1934	January. Operated on the line's last Manchester–New York sailing.
1940	24 December. In convoy attacked by the German heavy cruiser *Admiral Hipper*.
1957	February. Sold to the Fairtrade Steamship Company, Monrovia, renamed *Fairtrade*.
1959	February. Broken up.

City of Kimberley   1925   6,169grt.   133.04×17.16×9.20   4,190n.   12k.

E.	Sgl. screw, tpl. exp with LP turb. to electric drive, 767 nhp, 225 psi, 3 sgl. blrs. By Central Marine Engineering Works, Newcastle.
B.	William Gray & Company, Sunderland.
1925	April. Delivered.
1960	Sold for £60,000 to the Argonaut Shipping & Trading Company, renamed *Fairhurst* to replace *Fartrade*.
1964	Sold to the People's Republic of China.
1964	5 September. On tow from Hong Kong to Shanghai she broke adrift and was driven ashore.

Knaresborough / *City of Windsor*   1923   7,247grt.   136.4×17.62×9.78   4,616n.   12k.

E.	Sgl. screw, tpl. exp. with LP turbine drg hydraulic coupling to shaft. By Central Marine Engineering Works, Newcastle.
B.	William Gray & Company, Sunderland.
1923	Delivered for the United States–Canadian services to Africa and India.
1928	July. Renamed *City of Windsor*.
1939	3 September. Discharged at Glasgow and proceeded to Southampton to load munitions for France.
1940	June. Sailed to Cherbourg and evacuated soldiers under air attack. She carried over 1,000 men and then took 1,070 Vichy French sailors to Casablanca. Then she carried British civilians and refugees from Gibraltar, and later operated from Alexandria.
1941	Took part in the Greek campaign and evacuation in June that year. On one voyage to Alexandria with troops she was attacked by three bombers, three torpedo planes and a submarine. Later based at Basra in the Persian Gulf.
1943	Operated in the Mediterranean and carrying munitions from South Africa.
1943	9 September. Present at the Salerno landing.
1944	Overhauled at Liverpool and returned to Ellerman Lines.
1945	In service with Ellerman & Bucknall service.
1953	14 July. Arrived at Briton Ferry to be broken up.

City of Pretoria   1899   6,237grt.   129.75×16.48×9.08   4,025n.   12k.

E.	Sgl. screw, tpl. exp., 628 nhp, 180 psi, 5 sgl. blrs. By builder.
P.	4 (first), 209 (emigrants).
B.	William Denny & Brothers, Dumbarton.

1898	15 December. Launched.
1899	26 February. Delivered to Shaw, Savill & Albion as *Waiwera*, operated as a Boer War transport.
1917	Attacked and avoided a torpedo off the Lizard, Cornwall.
1926	30 September. Purchased by Ellerman & Bucknall, renamed *City of Pretoria*.
1928	5 March. Sold to Thomas W. Ward and broken up at Barrow.

City of Canberra   1927   7,485grt.   138.13×17.62×9.72   4,681n.   12k.

E.	Sgl. screw, 4 cyl. quad. exp., LP turb. electric drive, 984 nhp, 265 psi, 4 sgl. blrs. By Central Marine Engineering Works, West Hartlepool.
B.	William Gray & Company, West Hartlepool.
1927	December. Delivered.
1957	31 July. As the sale to Yugoslavian ship-breakers did not materialise, she was sold to Thomas W. Ward at Inverkeithing to be broken up.

City of Pretoria (2)   1937   8,046grt.   157.27×19.02×9.54   3,977n.

E.	Twin screw, 2×3 srg turb., 1,867 nhp, 265 psi, 6 sgl. blrs. By builder.
B.	Cammell Laird & Company Limited, Birkenhead.
1937	December. Delivered.
1942	26 November. Sailed from the Clyde for Gibraltar in convoy KMF4 with thirty other ships carrying reinforcements for Operation Torch, the North African landings.
1943	27 February. Left New York on a voyage to Liverpool with munitions and general cargo.
1943	3 March. Torpedoed twice by U-172 off Cape Race, Newfoundland. The ship exploded and all on board were lost.

City of Lincoln (2)   1938   8,039grt.   157.27×19.02×9.54   3,963n.

E.	Twin screw, 2×3 srg turb., 1,867 nhp, 265 psi, 6 sgl. blrs. By builder.
1938	December. Delivered.
1939–45	Requisitioned by the Admiralty.
1947	9 November. On a voyage from Baltimore to Beira she was wrecked at Quoin Point, Cape L'Agulhas, South Africa. She was moved to the Eastern Mole at the Duncan Dock, Table Bay, where she was broken up after being declared beyond repair. An earlier *City of Lincoln* also came to her end less than a mile away on the Woodstock Beach in February 1902 when she was inward bound with sheep and cattle from the River Plate (she was built in 1866 as the *Manhattan* for the Guion Line).
1950	8 May. The hull was towed out to sea and sunk by the South African Air Force.

City of Cardiff (2)   1942   6,987grt.   135.94×17.13×10.42   4,193n.   12½k.

E.	Sgl. screw, tpl. exp., 520 nhp, 220 psi, 2 sgl. blrs. By Fullerton, Hodgart & Barclay, Paisley.
B.	William Lithgow, Port Glasgow.
1942	April. Built as *Empire Spartan* for the Ministry of War Transport. Clark & Service, Glasgow, then Ellerman & Bucknall as managers.

1946	Owned by the Ministry of Transport.
1947	Managed by Ellerman & Bucknall.
1951	June. Purchased by Ellerman & Bucknall, renamed *City of Cardiff*.
1959	27 November. Sold to Kam Kee Navigation Company, Hong Kong, renamed *Shun Wing*.
1971	Purchased by Chan Moo Chu, Kam Kee as managers. Later managed by Jebshun Shipping.
1972	29 September. Arrived at Kaohsiung to be broken up.

City of Chelmsford 1943 7,271grt. 129.14×17.37×10.61 4,457n. 11k.

E.	Sgl. screw, tpl. exp., 2,500 bhp at 76 rpm, 240 psi, 2 blrs. By General Machinery Corporation, Hamilton, Ohio.
B.	Bethlehem Fairfield, Baltimore.
1943	Launched as *Lionel Copley*.
1943	August. Delivered to the Ministry of War Transport as *Sambrake* on charter, Ellerman & Bucknall as managers.
1946	Chartered by the Ministry of Transport.
1947	July. Renamed *City of Chelmsford*.
1958	First ship to berth at Princess Margaret Quay, Dar es Salaam.
1959	24 June. Sold to Cia. Naviera Vaptistis, Panama, renamed *San George*.
1960	Converted to diesel by Mirrlees, Bickerton, Newport, Monmouthshire.
1968	Owned by Suerte Shipping Company, Cyprus, renamed *Suerte*.
1971	6 October. Arrived at Split to be broken up by Brodopas.

City of Doncaster 1943 7,257grt. 129.14×17.37×10.61 4,452n. 11k.

E.	Sgl. screw, tpl. exp., 2,500 bhp at 76 rpm, 240 psi, 2 blrs. By General Machinery Corporation, Hamilton, Ohio.
B.	Bethlehem Fairfield, Baltimore.
1943	Launched as *Emma Lazarus*.
1943	September. Completed as *Samara* and delivered to the Ministry of War Transport as *Samshire* on charter, Ellerman & Bucknall as managers.
1946	Chartered by the Ministry of Transport.
1947	September. Purchased by Ellerman & Bucknall, renamed *City of Doncaster*.
1961	13 January. Sold to Trader Line Limited, London, renamed *Pembroke Trader*.
1966	Owned by Doreen Steam Ship Corporation, Liberia, renamed *Galletta*.
1970	10 April. On a voyage from Chittagong to Chalna with a cargo of rice she went aground 60 miles from Chalna.
1970	12 May. Part of the cargo was removed and several unsuccessful attempts were made to refloat the vessel. She was then abandoned.
1970	21 May. Salvaged and towed to Chalna and then to Singapore.
1970	1 July. Sold to Fuji, Marden & Company and arrived at Hong Kong to be broken up.

City of Portsmouth 1943 7,216grt. 129.14×17.37×10.61 4,440n. 11k.

E.	Sgl. screw, tpl. exp., 2,500 bhp at 76 rpm, 240 psi, 2 blrs. By General Machinery Corporation, Hamilton, Ohio.
B.	Bethlehem Fairfield, Baltimore.
1943	Launched as *Henry Van Dyke*.

1943	August. Delivered as *Samhain*, Ministry of War Transport.
1946	Chartered by the Ministry of Transport.
1947	October. Purchased by Ellerman & Bucknall, renamed *City of Portsmouth*.
1959	14 September. Sold to Demetrios P. Margaronis, Piraeus, renamed *Efcharis*.
1970	13 December. Laid up at Piraeus.
1971	July. Broken up at Kynosoura, Greece.

City of Colchester 1944 7,238grt. 129.14×17.37×10.61 4,408n. 11k.

E.	Sgl. screw, tpl. exp., 2,500 bhp at 76 rpm, 240 psi, 2 blrs. By Ellicott Machinery Corporation, Baltimore.
B.	Bethlehem Fairfield, Baltimore.
1944	March. Delivered as *Samlea*, Ministry of War Transport, Ellerman & Bucknall as managers.
1946	Chartered by the Ministry of Transport.
1947	August. Purchased by Ellerman & Bucknall, renamed *City of Colchester*.
1959	25 March. Sold to Alberta Steam Ship Limited, Monrovia, renamed *Sunset*.
1966	Owned by M. & A. Shipping Company, Liberia, renamed *Maria Eleni*.
1967	Sold to Island Maritime Associates SA, Monrovia, renamed *Blue Wave*.
1967	23 December. Left Osaka to be broken up at Matsuyama.

City of Leeds (1) 1947 7,250grt. 129.14×17.37×10.61 4,473n. 11k.

E.	Sgl. screw, tpl. exp., 2,500 bhp at 76 rpm, 240 psi, 2 blrs. By General Machinery Corporation, Hamilton, Ohio.
B.	Bethlehem Fairfield, Baltimore.
1944	May. Delivered as *Samcrest*, Ministry of War Transport, Ellerman & Bucknall as managers.
1946	Chartered by the Ministry of Transport.
1947	May. Purchased by Ellerman & Bucknall, renamed *City of Leeds* (1).
1960	3 June. Sold to the Grosvenor Shipping Company, London, renamed *Grosvenor Explorer*.
1965	March. Broken up at Hong Kong.

City of Carlisle (2) 1946 9,913grt. 151.57×19.63×12.19 5,900n. 14½k.

E.	Sgl. screw, 3 drg turb., 2 blrs. By builder.
B.	Cammell Laird & Company Limited, Birkenhead.
1946	February. Delivered to Ellerman & Bucknall.
1963	Final voyage Yokohama–London.
1963	27 August. Sold for £110,000 to Waywiser Navigation Corporation, Keelung, renamed *Jeannie*.
1970	Broken up at Kaohsiung.

City of London (4) 1947 8,434grt. 152.4×19.6×10.03 4,220n. 15k.

E.	Twin screw, 2×3 turb., 3 blrs. By Wallsend Slipway & Engineering Company, Wallsend.
P.	12.
B.	Swan Hunter & Wigham Richardson, Newcastle.
1947	May. Delivered to Ellerman & Bucknall.
1953	15 June. Participated at the Coronation Spithead Review.

1967	11 January. Sold to Somia Cia. Mar, Greece, owned by Union Commercial Steam Ship Company, renamed *Sandra N*.
1968	30 December. Arrived at Kaohsiung to be broken up.

City of London (4) at the Spithead Review on 15 June 1953.

City of Pretoria (3) in the East Float, Birkenhead.

City of Pretoria (3) 1947 8,450grt. 152.4×19.6×10.03 4,152n. 15k.

E.	Twin screw, 2×3 turb., 3 blrs. By builder.
P.	12.
B.	Cammell Laird & Company Limited.
1947	November. Delivered to Ellerman & Bucknall.
1967	2 February. Sold to Embajada Cia. Navigation, Panama, renamed *Proxeneion*.
1967	Following her last commercial voyage to the Far East she was broken up at Osaka, Japan.

City of Bath (2) 1947 7,030grt. 147.4×19.05×8.41 3,699n. 15½k.

E.	Sgl. screw, oil, 6 cyl. 2S.SA, 6,800 bhp at 116 rpm. By Barclay Curle & Company Limited.
P.	12.
B.	Blythswood Shipbuilding Company, Glasgow.
1947	June. Delivered as *Langleescot* for the Medomsley Steam Shipping Company, British subsidiary of the Van Ommeren Group.

1952	July. Purchased by Ellerman Lines Limited, Ellerman & Bucknall as managers, renamed *City of Bath*.
1969	Sold to Constantinos Shipping Company, Famagusta, renamed *Lena*.
1972	22 March. Arrived at Castellon in tow from St John, New Brunswick, and broken up by I.M.Varela Davalillo.

City of Ripon (2) / *City of Brisbane* (3) 1951 10,595grt. 142.61×21.73×9.57 6,087n. 17½k.

E.	Sgl. screw, 3 drg turb., 14,300 shp, 490 psi, 4 blrs. By builder.
B.	Cammell Laird & Company Limited.
1951	Laid down as *City of Ripon*.
1951	November. Delivered to Ellerman & Bucknall as *City of Brisbane*.
1970	27 October. Sold to the Ben Line, renamed *Bencairn*.
1975	21 March. Arrived at Kaohisung and broken up by Sing Cheng Yung Iron & Steel Company.

City of Winchester (3) 1949 10,594grt. 173.16×21.73×9.57 6,087n. 17½k.

E.	Sgl. screw, 3 drg turbines, 14,300 shp, 490 psi, 4 blrs. By builder.
B.	William Denny & Brothers, Dumbarton.
1952	27 March. Launched.
1952	16 October. Delivered to Ellerman & Bucknall.
1970	18 September. Sold to the Ben Line, renamed *Benvannoch*.
1975	2 July. Arrived at Kaohsiung and broken up by the Li Chong Steel Company.

City of Port Elizabeth 1952 13,363grt. 164.9×21.7×10.97 7,573n. 16½k.

E.	Twin screw, oil, 2×6 cyl. Doxford 2S.SA, 12,650 bhp at 115 rpm. By Hawthorn, Leslie & Company, Newcastle. P.107 first.
B.	Vickers Armstrong Limited, Newcastle.
1952	12 March. Launched.
1952	10 December. Delivered to Ellerman & Bucknall. Designed with three complete decks with a long bridge deck, poop and forecastle with promenade and boat deck superimposed. The rounded cruiser stern, raking plate stem combined with a well-balanced superstructure and single funnel with a raked top. She was built with seven watertight bulkheads carried to the upper deck, with further local subdivision in way of cross-bunkers, cargo oil and fresh water tanks. Forward of the cross-bunkers, the double-bottom tanks were reserved for fresh water, and under the bunkers for oil fuel or water ballast. Diesel oil was carried in wing tanks under the machinery space. Five cargo holds were provided, with upper and lower 'tweendecks to each, except that No. 5 upper 'tweendeck space was occupied by crew accommodation. Deep tanks were provided at the after end of No. 4 hold to carry latex, cargo oils, dry cargo or water ballast. Cargo handling gear included fourteen tubular steel derricks. Accommodation was provided for 107 passengers in double-bed sitting rooms, fourteen double and eight single rooms, all with private bathrooms and nineteen double and four single rooms. A lounge, smoke room, writing room and veranda café were located on the promenade deck. Ladies and gentlemen's hairdressing saloons and a permanent swimming pool were also provided. Propelling machinery consisted of twin opposed-piston oil engines of Doxford design and capable of developing a total of 12,650 bhp at 115 rpm.

City of Port Elizabeth.

1953	January. Maiden voyage London–Las Palmas–Cape Town–Port Elizabeth–East London–Durban–Lourenco Marques–Beira.
1961–62	Completed special survey by Swan Hunter & Wigham Richardson involving extensive steel renewals to shell plating and frames, machinery repairs and redecoration of passenger and crew accommodation.
1967	Passenger accommodation was renovated.
1969	City of London Livery Club charter for a cruise, and the master, Captain Norman Allan Perry of West Kirby, Wirral, was made a freeman of the City of London at a ceremony at Guildhall. As a coincidence, Captain Parry was then appointed to command the new *City of London*, which was under construction by Upper Clyde Shipbuilders. He took his new ship on its maiden voyage in 1970.
1971	July. Laid up and placed on the for-sale market. It was reported that 'we shall be witnessing the passing of the last of the ultra-luxury passenger cargo vessels, certainly under the British flag.'
1971	10 September. Sold to Michail A. Karageorgis Lines Corporation, renamed *Mediterranean Island*, owned by Occidental Ultramar SA, Piraeus, for service between Patras and Ancona.
1975	Conversion commenced but later suspended as it was decided to convert her for cruising. The original intention was to convert the sister ships as car and passenger ferries. Renamed *Mediterranean Sun* and laid up.
1980	12 March. Left Piraeus in tow of tug *Amsterdam* for Kaohsiung.
1980	3 June. Demolition by Long Jong Industry Company commenced.

City of Exeter (2)   1952   13,363grt.   164.9×21.7×10.97   7,573n.   16½k.

E.	Twin screw, oil, 2×6 cyl. Doxford 2S.SA, 12,650 bhp at 115 rpm. By Vickers Armstrong & Company Limited, Barrow.
P.	107 (first).
B.	Vickers Armstrong Limited, Newcastle.
1952	7 July. Launched.
1953	29 April. Delivered to Ellerman & Bucknall.
1961–62	Completed special survey by Swan Hunter & Wigham Richardson involving extensive steel renewals to shell plating and frames, machinery repairs and redecoration of passenger and crew accommodation.
1971	September. Sold to Michail A. Karageorgis Lines Corporation, renamed *Mediterranean Sea*, owned by Benigno Navigation SA, Piraeus. Rebuilt for a car

and passenger service between Patras and Ancona. Two decks were stripped out and new ones built, to provide one principal car deck and two lower car decks, having a capacity of 400 vehicles including large trucks and lorries, with additional accommodation for 850 passengers above the car decks.

1972	December. Entered service on the Patras–Brindisi–Ancona route.
1974	Registered at Famagusta.
1975	Owned by Mikar Limited, Limassol.
1996	Owned by Deep Ocean Shipping, Panama, renamed *Tutku*.
1996	Renamed *Alice*.
1998	9 July. Beached at Aliaga and broken up.

City of York (4)   1953   13,363grt.   164.9×21.7×10.97   7,573n.   16½k.

E.	Twin screw, oil, 2X6 cyl. Doxford 2S.SA, 12,650 bhp at 115 rpm. By Hawthorn, Leslie & Company, Newcastle.
P.	107 (first).
B.	Vickers Armstrong Limited, Newcastle.
1953	30 March. Launched.
1953	26 October. Delivered to Ellerman & Bucknall.
1953	November. Maiden voyage London–Las Palmas–Cape Town–Port Elizabeth–East London–Durban–Lourenco Marques–Beira.
1961–62	Completed special survey by Swan Hunter & Wigham Richardson involving extensive steel renewals to shell plating and frames, machinery repairs and redecoration of passenger and crew accommodation.
1971	4 June. Left Cape Town on her final passenger sailing.
1971	10 September. Sold to Michail A. Karageorgis Lines Corporation, renamed *Mediterranean Sky*. Rebuilt for a car and passenger service between Patras and Ancona.
1974	June. Entered service on the Ancona–Rhodes route.
1996	August. Arrested at Patras.
1999	Towed to Eleusis.
2002	26 November. Beached at Eleusis.
2003	January. Capsized.

City of York (4).

City of Durban (2)   1954   13,363grt.   164.9×21.7×10.97   7,573n.   16½k.

E.   Twin screw, oil, 2×6 cyl. Doxford 2S.SA, 12,650 bhp at 115 rpm. By Hawthorn,
            Leslie & Company, Newcastle.

P.   107 (first).

B.   Vickers Armstrong Limited, Newcastle.

1953   28 May. Launched.

1954   May. Delivered for the London–Las Palmas–Cape Town–Port Elizabeth–East
            London–Durban–Lourenco Marques–Beira service.

1961–62   Completed special survey by Swan Hunter & Wigham Richardson involving
            extensive steel renewals to shell plating and frames, machinery repairs and
            redecoration of passenger and crew accommodation.

1971   24 September. Sold to Michail A. Karageorgis Lines Corporation, Mundial
            Armadora SA, Panama, renamed *Mediterranean Dolphin*. Laid up at Perama.

1974   30 March. Arrived at Kaohsiung to be broken up.

City of Durban (2).

City of Melbourne (2) / *City of Cape Town* (2)   1957   9,914grt.   166.18×21.7×8.81   5,312n.   18k.

E.   Sgl. screw, oil, 12 cyl. Sulzer 2S.SA, 14,700 bhp. By builder.

B.   Alexander Stephen & Sons, Linthouse.

1957   Delivered.

1959   21 April. Launched.

1959   Delivered to Ellerman Lines Limited and specially designed for the service
            between the United Kingdom, Canada and Australia. She was built to Lloyd's Class
            +100A1 with refrigeration, and had five main cargo holds with corresponding
            lower and upper 'tween decks. No. 2 lower and No. 3 upper and lower 'tween
            decks and No.4 hold were insulated for the carriage of frozen or fruit cargo. No.
            2 lower and No.3 upper 'tween decks were also arranged for chilled cargo. Deep
            tanks between No.2 and No. 3 holds and 'tween decks were arranged for the
            carriage of latex, mineral oil, vegetable oil or general cargo and were coated with
            vinyl lacquer. No. 1 hold and No. 5 lower 'tween deck and hold, and also deep
            cargo and ballast tanks, could be fitted out for the carriage of grain in bulk. She had

six 5-ton, four 7-ton, eight 10-ton and one 20-ton derricks, all served with Clarke Chapman electrically operated winches of the 'Autocon' type, excepting the two aftermost which were of the contractor type and used for warping in addition to cargo handling. The Asian crew accommodation was arranged on the shelter deck and second deck aft in four berth rooms. Two galleys were provided on the poop for the Asian seamen and engine-room crew. Cabins in the midship deckhouse on the shelter deck were provided for the purser, junior ship and engineer officers, cadets and petty officers and also a hospital and surgery. The dining room was situated at the aft end of the midship deckhouse on the shelter deck.

1968	Transferred from the Australian routes to the South African services, renamed *City of Cape Town*.
1973	1 January. Transferred to Ellerman City Liners.
1978	Sold to Atlantic Gold Shipping Pte., Singapore, renamed *Ota Gold*.
1979	19 May. Sold to Goldwils (Hong Kong) Limited, re-sold to ship-breakers at Taiwan.
1979	22 May. Arrived at Kaohsiung.

City of Cape Town (2).

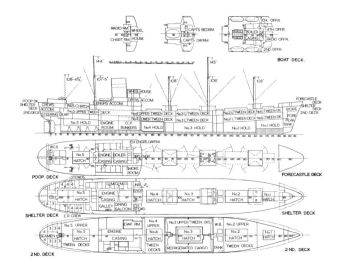

Deck plan of *City of Sydney* (3).

City of Auckland (2) 1958 8,181grt. 154.59×20.42×8.53 4,359n. 15k.
E.   Sgl. screw, oil, 6 cyl. 2S.SA, 8,000 bhp. By Vickers Armstrong Limited, Barrow.
B.   Vickers Armstrong Limited, Newcastle.
1958   February. Delivered to Ellerman & Bucknall.
1971   Laid up at Barry Docks.
1973   1 January. Transferred to Ellerman City Liners.
1978   Sold to Gulf Shipping Lines Limited, London, renamed *Gulf Falcon*.
1982   24 August. Laid up at Jebel Ali, UAE.
1983   27 July. Arrived at Bombay to be broken up.

City of Sydney (3) / *City of Montreal* 1960 10,155grt. 155.97×20.51×9.3 5,888n. 17½k.
E.   Sgl. screw, oil, 9 cyl. Sulzer 2S.SA, 11,535 bhp. By builder.
P.   12.
B.   Barclay Curle, Glasgow.
1960   24 May. Launched by Mrs D.F. Martin-Jenkins.
1960   October. Delivered to Ellerman & Bucknall as a closed shelter deck type with
              forecastle, cruiser stern and raked rounded stem. She had five cargo holds with
              complete upper and lower 'tween decks, No.3 upper and lower 'tween decks and
              No.4 hold having insulated capacity of 111,000 cu ft for the carriage of refrigerated
              cargoes. Double bottom tanks were arranged for the carriage of oil fuel or water
              ballast, the aftermost double bottom tank being arranged for feed water. Deep
              tanks between Nos 2 and 3 holds were arranged for the carriage of vegetable oil
              and latex. She was fitted with ten 5-ton derricks, eight 10-ton derricks and one
              20-ton derrick, two of the aft cargo winches were fitted with geared warping ends
              for mooring purposes. Fire detection and CO_2 fire-extinguishing installations,
              covering all the cargo and machinery spaces, were fitted.
1973   1 January. Transferred to Ellerman City Liners, renamed *City of Montreal* and
              transferred to the St Lawrence service.
1977   Sold to the Hooton Shipping Company Incorporated, Panama, owned by Yatco
              Enterprises Limited, renamed *Yat Fei*.
1979   25 May. Arrived at Kaohsiung.
1979   19 June. Demolition commenced by the Han Tai Iron & Steel Company.

City of St Albans (2) 1960 6,980grt. 132.19×18.04×8.2 3,911n. 14¾k.
E.   Sgl. screw, oil, 8 cyl. Sulzer 2S.SA, 5,600 bhp. By builder.
B.   William Denny & Brothers, Dumbarton.
1960   1 August. Launched by Mrs R. A. Lloyd, wife of director of Ellerman & Bucknall
              Steamship Company Limited.
1960   December. Delivered to Ellerman & Bucknall. Completed as a closed shelter
              deck vessel, arrangements were made for easy conversion to an open shelter deck
              type and also for the ship to be quickly converted, if necessary, for the carriage
              of grain in bulk. The cargo gear consisted of six 7-ton derricks and four 10-ton
              derricks, serving four large cargo hatchways. The derricks were operated by ten
              electric improved over-drive 'Autocon'-type winches of Clarke Chapman &
              Company make; topping winches were also provided for each derrick. An air-
              conditioning system with mechanical ventilation was installed for the midship
              accommodation, also a mechanical ventilation and heating system for the crew

accommodation aft. Special consideration was given and arrangments made to safeguard the vessel against the spread of fire with the equipment comprising of a combined CO_2 fire-extinquishing and smoke detecting system for all cargo spaces, engine room and auxiliary boiler room.

1971   November. On a voyage from Calcutta to Chalna during the Pakistan civil war she was attacked and hit forty-nine times by 40mm shells. There were no casualties and she returned to Calcutta to be repaired.

1973   January. Transferred to Ellerman City Liners, owned by Ellerman Lines Limited.

1977   June. Represented Ellerman Lines at the Queen's Silver Jubilee review on the Mersey.

1979   Sold to Venture Investment Trust Incorporated, Piraeus, renamed *Island of Marmora*. Collided with Everard's Conformity in St George's Channel on her first voyage. Towed to Swansea to be repaired.

1983   29 September. Left Dubai to be broken up.

1983   8 October. Demolition commenced at Jamnagar by Mastan Taherbhai.

Island of Marmora
(ex–City of St
Albans [2]).

City of Lichfield (2)   1961   4,795grt.   132.19×18.04×8.2   2,530n.   14¾k.

E.   Sgl. screw, oil, 8 cyl. Sulzer 2S.SA, 5,600 bhp. By builder.

B.   William Denny & Brothers, Dumbarton.

1960   22 November. Launched by Mrs E.L.Denny, OBE, wife of the chairman of the builders. The time taken from the keel laying to the launch was twenty-five working weeks.

1961   March. Delivered to Ellerman & Bucknall. Completed as a closed shelter deck vessel, arrangements were made for easy conversion to an open shelter deck type and also for the ship to be quickly converted, if necessary, for the carriage of grain in bulk. The cargo gear consisted of six 7-ton derricks and four 10-ton derricks, serving four large cargo hatchways. The derricks were operated by ten electric improved over-drive 'Autocon'-type winches of Clarke Chapman & Company make; topping winches were also provided for each derrick. An air-conditioning system with mechanical ventilation was installed for the midship accommodation, also a mechanical ventilation and heating system for the crew accommodation aft.

1973   January. Transferred to Ellerman City Liners.

1978	Sold to Serenity Maritime Company, Cyprus, renamed *Leeds*.
1980	Purchased by Ross Navigation Company, Cyprus, renamed *City of Leeds*.
1980	11 November. Damaged after stranding at Antalya in heavy weather.
1981	12 January. She was refloated and returned to port where she was abandoned.
1982	20 September. Sold by public auction to Onur Marine Limited.
1983	29 December. Left Antalya for Aliaga.
1984	30 January. Sold to be broken up at Aliaga.

City of Dundee (3)   1961   4,798grt.   132.28×18.04×8.2   2,530n.   14¾k.

E.	Sgl. screw, oil, 8 cyl. Sulzer 2S.SA, 5,600 bhp. By G. Clark & Company Limited, Sunderland.
B.	Robb Caledon, Dundee.
1961	May. Delivered to Ellerman & Bucknall. Designed as a closed shelter deck vessel with poop, forecastle, cruiser stern and raked rounded stem. She was built with four cargo holds, three fitted with MacGregor steel covers and the largest with wood slab covers. Four deep tanks were situated in the wings at the fore end of the engine room for the carriage of liquid cargoes. Shifting boards were also provided for when cargoes of bulk grain were carried. She was fitted with two unstayed masts and two derrick posts with ten cargo derricks for 7- and 10-ton loads, the foremast being strengthened to allow the fitting of a 70-ton heavy lift derrick.
1961	20 June. Maiden voyage to Bombay and Karachi.
1973	January. Transferred to Ellerman City Liners.
1978	Sold to the Dundee Maritime Company (Richmond Shipping Company Limited), Cyprus, renamed *Dundee*.
1980	Owned by Kilkis Navigation Company, Cyprus, owned by Lifedream Cia. Naviera, Limassol, renamed *City of Dundee*.
1984	17 January. Arrived at Gadani Beach and broken up by the Panama Shipbreaking Company.

Suerte (ex–*City of Gloucester* [3]).

City of Gloucester (3)   1963   4,803grt.   132.28×18.04×8.2   2,521n.   14¾k.

E.	Sgl. screw, oil, 8 cyl. Sulzer 2S.SA, 5,600 bhp. By builder.
B.	William Denny & Brothers, Dumbarton.
1962	18 September. Launched.
1963	March. Delivered to Ellerman & Bucknall.
1973	January. Transferred to Ellerman City Liners.
1979	Sold to Lionheart Maritime Incorporated, Piraeus, owned by Ilios Shipping SA, renamed *Suerte*.
1985	1 April. Arrived at Dalian, China to be broken up.

City of
Canberra (2).

City of Canberra (2)   1961   10,306grt.   155.69×20.51×9.14   5,318n.   18k.

E.	Sgl. screw, oil, 9 cyl. Sulzer 2S.SA, 11,700 bhp. By builder.
B.	Barclay Curle, Glasgow.
1961	25 August. Launched.
1961	December. Delivered to Ellerman & Bucknall. Designed as a closed shelter deck type with forecastle, cruiser stern and raked round stem on which was placed a bow crest bearing the coat of arms of the city of Canberra. She had five cargo holds with complete upper and lower 'tween decks, No. 2 upper and lower 'tween decks and hold. No. 3 upper and lower 'tween decks and No. 4 upper and lower 'tween decks and hold had insulated capacity of 240,000 cu. ft. for the carriage of refrigerated cargoes. Double bottom tanks were arranged for the carriage of oil fuel or water ballast, the aftermost double bottom tank being arranged for feed water. She was fitted with ten 5-ton derricks, eight 10-ton derricks and one 20-ton derrick. The captain and chief engineer each had a suite of rooms, comprising dayroom, bedroom and bathroom, the chief officer and 2nd engineer were provided with a private bathroom. The dining room was situated at the starboard side forward on the shelter deck and on the starboard side forward on the poop deck was the smoking room for the use of officers. A permanent swimming pool was built into the structure at the aft end of the boat deck.
1973	January. Transferred to Ellerman City Liners.
1978	Sold to Tasman Gold Shipping Pty Limited, Singapore, renamed *Tasgold*.
1978	31 March. Aground on a reef off Rossel Island, Louisiade Archipelago.
1978	5 May. Refloated.

1979	18 October. Sold to Wiltopps (Asia) Limited, Hong Kong.
1979	20 October. Left Hong Kong for Taiwan.
1979	21 October. Re-sold to ship-breakers at Kaohsiung.
1979	10 November. Arrived at Kaohsiung and broken up.

City of Eastbourne (2) / *City of Toronto*   1962   10,006grt.   154.84×20.36×9.02   5,500n.   18k.

E.	Sgl. screw, oil, 8 cyl. Sulzer 2S.SA, 10,300 bhp. By Vickers Armstrong Limited.
B.	Vickers Armstrong, Newcastle.
1962	March. Delivered to Ellerman & Bucknall.
1971	Renamed *City of Toronto* for the St Lawrence services.
1973	January. Transferred to Ellerman City Liners, Ellerman Lines Limited as owners.
1978	Sold to Y.C. Cheng's Pacific International Lines (Pte), Singapore, renamed *Kota Cantik*.
1984	16 October. Arrived at Kaohsiung to be broken up.

City of
Eastbourne (2).

City of Glasgow (6) / *City of Ottawa* (2)
1963   10,017grt.   154.84×20.36×9.02   5,576n.   18k.

E.	Sgl. screw, oil, 8 cyl. Sulzer 2S.SA, 10,300 bhp. By Vickers Armstrong Limited
B.	Vickers Armstrong Limited, Newcastle.
1962	Launched by Mr R. Gerner, resident engineer of the naval yard attached to the staff of the Engineer Superintendent, Ellerman Lines.
1963	April. Delivered to Ellerman & Bucknall. Constructed to Lloyds special survey for class 100A1 incorporating a curved and raked stem, cruiser stern, six cargo holds with cargo-oil deep tanks in the engine room and water ballast or general cargo in Nos 1 and 3 holds. Fuel oil was carried in the double bottom, and the cargo-oil deep tanks in the engine room could be used for oil fuel bunkers in an emergency. The second deck extended the full length of the ship. She was designed to be readily converted to carry grain in bulk when required.
1971	Renamed *City of Ottawa* for the Canadian services.
1973	January. Transferred to Ellerman City Liners.
1978	Sold to Y.C. Cheng's Pacific International Lines (Pte), Singapore, renamed *Kota Cahaya* for the Singapore–Persian Gulf service.
1985	31 July. Arrived at Nantong, China to be broken up.

City of Adelaide (3) / *City of Canterbury* (3)   1964   10,511grt.   155.66×20.54×9.3   5,934n.   18¼k.

E.   Sgl. screw, oil, 9 cyl. Sulzer 2S.SA, 14,200 bhp. By builder.

B.   Barclay Curle, Glasgow.

1964   January. Delivered to Ellerman & Bucknall. Completed as a closed shelter deck type with forecastle, cruiser stern and raked round stem. She had five cargo holds with complete lower and upper 'tween decks. Double bottom tanks were arranged for the carriage of oil fuel or water ballasts, the aftermost double bottom tank being arranged for feed water. She had ten 5-ton, eight 10-ton derricks and a 60-ton derrick. Amongst the many installations provided were fire detection and CO_2 fire-extinguishing covering all cargo spaces and machinery, sewage disposal plant, water treatment plant and thermal injection for the elimination of condensation around boundaries of the insulated cargo spaces. The captain and chief engineer each had a suite of rooms comprising dayroom, bedroom and bathroom, and the chief officer and second engineer were each provided with a private bathroom. The remainder of the deck officers' and engineer officers' accommodation was provided in the deckhouse on boat deck, poop deck and shelter deck. Crew accommodation was aft on the poop deck, shelter deck and second deck and a permanent swimming pool was built into the structure at the aft end of the boat deck. Air conditioning was provided for the European personnel and mechanical ventilation and heating for the remainder of the crew.

1972   Renamed *Cap Cleveland* for a charter to Hamburg Süd-Americanische.

1973   Returned to Ellerman Lines, renamed *City of Canterbury*.

1976   Sold to Cie. Maritime Belge SA, Antwerp, renamed *Rubens*.

1983   Purchased by Crisela Limited, Gibraltar, renamed *A.L. Pioneer*.

1983   28 August. Arrived at Chittagong to be broken up.

Cap Cleveland (ex–City of Adelaide [3]).

City of Bristol (3)   1945   7,096grt.   137.46×17.92×8.63   4,019n.   14k.

E.   Twin screw, oil, 2×3 cyl. 2S.SA, 5,200 bhp. By William Doxford & Sons Limited, Sunderland.

B.   Cammell Laird & Company Limited, Birkenhead.

1945   August. Delivered as *Sacramento* to Ellerman's Wilson Line.

1964   Transferred to Ellerman & Bucknall, renamed *City of Bristol*.

1969	Sold to Anna Shipping Company, Famagusta, renamed *Felicie*.
1970	Sold to the Republic of Cuba, renamed *30 de Noviembre* by Lineas Mambisa (Empresa Consolidada de Navigation), Mambisa, Havana.
1977	27 July. Arrived at Faslane to be broken up by Shipbreaking Industries Limited.

City of Bristol (3).

City of Liverpool (2).

City of Liverpool (2)   1970   7,093grt.   152.98×22.28×8.05   3,612n.   18¼k.

E.	Sgl. screw, oil, 7 cyl. Doxford J-type 2S.SA, 17,500 bhp. By Doxford & Sunderland Shipbuilding & Engineering Company, Sunderland. Engine controlled from bridge.
B.	Robb Caledon Shipbuilders, Dundee.
1970	24 March. Launched by Mrs D.F. Martin-Jenkins, wife of the chairman of Ellerman Lines Limited.
1970	September. Delivered to Ellerman & Bucknall to operate on the Hull–South Africa service
1970	8 December. Collided with the Norwegian vessel *Jark* off the mouth of the Humber. *Jark*, owned by the Norwegian line A.J. Bronner of Oslo was on a voyage from Immingham to Naples with coke and was extensively damaged on her stern port side. She was abandoned by part of her crew and later towed back to Immingham. *City of Liverpool* was not seriously damaged and continued her voyage to Rotterdam.

1973	January. Transferred to Ellerman City Liners, owners HLL Shipping Limited, London.
1981	November. Sold to Sun Horizon Navigation SA, Piraeus, owned by Diana Shipping Agencies, renamed *Marianthe*.
1985	25 November. On a voyage from Puerto Caballo to Baltimore she grounded off Turks Island.
1986	16 September. Arrived at Kaohsiung to be broken up.

City of London (5)   1970   7,415grt.   152.98×22.28×8.05   3,579n.   18¼k.

E.	Sgl. screw, oil, 7 cyl. Doxford J-type 2S.SA, 17,500 bhp. By Barclay, Curle & Company Limited. Engine controlled from bridge.
B.	Upper Clyde Shipbuilders, Scotstoun.
1970	23 June. Launched.
1970	November. Delivered to Ellerman & Bucknall.
1973	Transferred to Ellerman City Liners, owners HLL Shipping Limited, London.
1981	November. Sold to Paros Shipping Company, Piraeus, owned by P&P Shipping Company (Hellas) SA, renamed *Sea Lord*.
1987	2 December. Arrived at Kaohsiung to be broken up.

City of London (5).

City of Hull (2)   1971   7,093grt.   152.98×22.28×8.05   3,579n.   18¼k.

E.	Sgl. screw, oil, 7 cyl. Doxford J-type 2S.SA, 17,500 bhp. By Doxford & Sunderland Shipbuilding & Engineering Company, Sunderland. Engine controlled from bridge.
B.	Robb Caledon Shipbuilders, Dundee.
1970	27 November. Launched.
1971	April. Delivered to Ellerman & Bucknall, maiden voyage on the Strick–Ellerman service to the Persian Gulf.
1973	Transferred to Ellerman City Liners, owners HLL Shipping Limited, London. Operated on the joint P&O–Ellerman service to the Persian Gulf.
1980	May. Sold to Waveney Shipping Corporation, Liberia, renamed *St John*.
1982	Owned by Jorama Cia. Naviera SA, Pireaus, renamed *Seagull*.
1983	Stranded and repaired at Durban.
1985	February. Owned by Best Maritime SA, Piraeus, renamed *Sea Lady*.
1995	Became *Magdalena*.

| 1996 | 28 August. Arrived at Alang to be broken up. |
| 1996 | 15 September. Beached. |

City of Hull (2).

Ellerman's Wilson Vessels

Operated by Ellerman Lines sectors without change of ownership

Lepanto / City of Ripon   1915   6,394 grt.
B.	Russell & Company, Port Glasgow.
1934	Transferred to Hall Line as managers, renamed *City of Ripon*.
1942	11 November. Torpedoed and sunk by U-160, south-east of Trinidad. Fifty-seven of her crew were lost.

City of Ripon.

Urbino   1918   5,198 grt.
B.	Earle's Shipbuilding Company, Hull.
1934	Managed by Ellerman & Bucknall for the Glasgow–South Africa service.
1937	Damaged in a collision on a Glasgow–Cochin Voyage.
1940–44	Operated on the Cape Town–South African Ports–East Africa–Middle East service.
1948–49	Major engine overhaul at Earle's & Company, Hull, but continued with mechanical problems.
1954	March. Sold and broken up at Faslane.

Urbino.

Ships Managed for the Ministry of War Transport (MOWT)

Empire Comfort
Empire Comfort
Empire Shelter

Empire Clyde   1925   7,515grt.
B.   Ansaldo San Giorgio, La Spezia. As *Leonardo da Vinci* for Lloyd Triestino.
P.   100 (first), 200 (second), 1,500 (third).
1941   Captured at Somalia.
1943   Managed by City Line. Converted to a hospital ship.
1946   Hospital ship at Hong Kong.
1948   1 January. Requisitioned by the Admiralty as a hospital ship, renamed *Maine*.
1950–53   Hospital ship in the Korean War.
1954   26 April. Broken up at Hong Kong.

Empire Faith   1941   7,061grt.
B.   Barclay Curle & Company, Glasgow.
1941   June. Delivered as *Empire Faith*, managed by Westcott & Laurence, London.
1946   Sold to Johnston Warren Lines, renamed *Jessmore*.

Empire Gauntlet   1944   7,177grt.
B.   Consolidated Steel Corporation, Wilmington, California.
1944   Launched as *Cape Comorin*, Type C1-S-AY1, United States standard ship.
1944   January. Completed on charter to MOWT as *Empire Gauntlet* and converted to
                a landing ship, infantry, renamed HMS *Sefton*.
1944   June. At Utah and Omaha Normandy invasion beach landing. Renamed *Empire
                Gauntlet* as a supply ship, Ellerman City Lines as managers.
1945   Renamed *Cape Comorin*, US Department of Commerce, Los Angeles.

Empire Irving   1944   7,081grt.
B.   William Gray & Company, West Hartlepool.
1944   June. Delivered to MOWT, Hall Line as managers.
1946   Sold to Ropner Shipping Company, renamed *Bellerby*.

Empire Pendennis   1944   7,058grt.
B.   Short Brothers, Sunderland.
1944   June. Delivered as *Empire Pendennis* for MOWT, Ellerman Hall Line as managers.
1946   April. Sold to Cunard-White Star Line, renamed *Vasconia*.

Empire Viceroy   1943   7,803grt.
B.   Vickers Armstrong Limited, Barrow.
1943   August. Delivered, Hall Line as managers.
1947   Transferred to Counties Ship Management.

Empire Wallace   1946   7,800grt.
B.   Greenock Dockyard Company, Greenock.
1946   February. Delivered to MOWT, Hall Line as managers.
1947   Haddon Steam Ship Company, London as managers.

Taiposhan   1901   2,143grt.
B.   London & Glasgow Engineering & Iron Shipbuilding Company, Glasgow.
1901   October. Delivered as *Hang Sang* for the Indo-China Steam Navigation
                Company.
1940   Purchased by Pang Kwok Sui, managed for the MOWT by Ellerman &
                Papayanni, renamed *Taiposhan*.
1946   Owned by Tai On Steam Navigation Company, Hong Kong.

Andrea Gritti   1943   6,404grt.
B.   Cantieri Riuniti del Adriatico, Monfalcone.
1943   July. Delivered to Soc. Italiana di Armamento 'Sidarma', Venice.
1943   September. She came under Allied control with Hall Line as managers.
1945   Returned to Italian control.

Fort Constantine   1944   7,221grt.
B.   Burrard Dry Dock Company, South Yard, Vancouver.
1944   25 April. Delivered to MOWT, Ellerman & Bucknall as managers, as a stores-
                issuing ship (air stores) to operate with aircraft carriers.
1949   Transferred to the Admiralty, Royal Fleet Auxiliary.

Fort Dunvegan   1944   7,221grt.
B.   Burrard Dry Dock Company, South Yard, Vancouver.
1944   14 April. Delivered to MOWT, Ellerman & Bucknall as managers, as a stores-
                issuing ship (air stores), to operate with aircraft carriers.
1949   Transferred to the Admiralty, Royal Fleet Auxiliary.

Fort Edmonton   1944   7,221grt.
B.   Burrard Dry Dock Company, South Yard, Vancouver.
1944   13 September. Delivered to MOWT, Ellerman & Bucknall as managers, as a
                stores-issuing ship (air stores), to operate with aircraft carriers.
1947   Sold to Federal & Commercial Navigation Company, Montreal, renamed
                Federal Voyager.

Fort Kilmar   1944   7,221grt.

B.	Burrard Dry Dock Company, South Yard, Vancouver.
1944	25 May. Delivered to MOWT, Ellerman & Bucknall as managers, as a stores-issuing ship (air stores), to operate with aircraft carriers.
1947	Sold to Andros Shipping Company, Montreal, renamed *Ironside*.

Fort Providence   1944   7,221grt.

B.	Burrard Dry Dock Company, South Yard, Vancouver.
1944	8 July. Delivered to MOWT, Ellerman & Bucknall as managers, as a stores-issuing ship (air stores), to operate with aircraft carriers.
1948	Sold to Eastboard Navigation Company, Montreal, renamed *Eastwater*.

Fort St James   1942   7,130grt.

B.	Burrard Dry Dock Company, South Yard, Vancouver.
1942	29 January. Delivered as the first ship of the 'North Sands' type, managed by Ellerman & Bucknall and later Ellerman's Wilson.
1947	Sold to Lambert Brothers Limited, London, renamed *Temple Bar*.

Fort Tadoussac   1942   7,129grt.

B.	Davie Shipbuilding & Repairing Company, Lauzon, Quebec.
1942	18 April. Delivered to the Canadian Government and transferred to the MOWT, Ellerman & Bucknall as managers.
1947	United States Maritime Commission as owners.

Cape Douglas   1944   7,156grt.

B.	Pusey & Jones, Wilmington, Delaware.
1944	January. Delivered.
1946	March. Laid up.
1947	On charter to Ministry of Transport, Ellerman Lines as managers.
1948	Operated by the United States Maritime Commission.

Cap Padaran   1922   8,009grt.

B.	Ateliers et Chantiers de la Lore, St Nazaire.
P.	154 (first), 70 (second).
1941	Seized by British warship, south of Durban. Managed by City Line for MOWT.
1943	September. Operated as a troopship in the Mediterranean.
1943	9 December. Torpedoed and sunk by U-596 in the Adriatic.

Cap Tourane   1923   8,009grt.

B.	Ateliers et Chantiers de la Lore, St Nazaire.
P.	154 (first), 70 (second).
1940–45	Served with the Free French.
1946	Returned to Chargeurs Reunis.

D'Entrecasteaux 1922 7,642grt.

1941   1 July. Captured at sea by the British cruiser HMS *Dunedin*, MOWT, Ellerman City Line as managers

1942   7 November. Torpedoed and sunk by U-154 in the South Atlantic.

Ellerman 20 per cent Owned, Ben Line 80 per cent Owned

Benalder 1972 55,889grt. 289.6×32.3×13.0 23k.

B.   Howaldtswerke-Deutsche Werft, Kiel.

1993   *Maersk London*

1993   *London Maersk*

1999   *London*

2001   Broken up.

Benavon 1973 55,889grt. 289.6×32.3×13.0 23k.

B.   Howaldtswerke-Deutsche Werft, Kiel.

1993   *Maersk Paris*

1993   *Paris Maersk*

1998   *Paris*

2001   Broken up.

Vessels Chartered for the Ellesmere Port–Mediterranean Services

City of Lisbon 1978 3,598grt.

1985   In Ellerman City Liners service.

1986   Renamed *Manchester City* for Manchester Liners.

City of Manchester 1984 2,778grt.

1984   In Ellerman City Liners service.

1985   Charter completed, renamed *Hasselwerder*.

City of Oporto 1979 1,599grt.

1984   In Ellerman City Liners service.

1985   Charter completed, renamed *Royal Prince*.

City of Oporto (2) 1981 1,599grt.

1984   In Ellerman City Liners service.

1986   Charter completed, renamed *Nord*.

City of Salerno 1981 1,598grt.

1984   In Ellerman City Liners service.

1985   Charter completed, renamed *Nordstar*.

City of Salerno   1977   1,599grt.
1985   In Ellerman City Liners service.
1986   Charter completed, renamed *Peter Knuppel*.

City of Salerno   1983   1,599grt.
1986   In Ellerman City Liners service.
1987   Charter completed, renamed *Ocean*.

Ellerman City Liners

City of Liverpool   1982   18,575grt.
B.   Howaldtswerke Deutsche Werft, Kiel.
1982   Delivered to Christian F. Ahrenkial, Hamburg as City of Liverpool.
1985   Renamed *Campania*, owned by Navifonds, West Germany.

City of London   1980   16,482grt.
1981   5 December. *Mentor* was renamed *City of London* on a one-year charter to the
              Overseas Container Line and laid up in the River Fal in 1982 when the charter
              was completed. She returned to the Overseas Container Line on charter in
              1984, and became *Normannia* when sold to the Hake Shipping Company
              Limited in 1985.

Mentor as *City of London* in Ellerman Lines colours.

Ellerman Asia Limited (Andrew Weir Shipping Limited), London

City of London   1997   23,500grt.   188.1×30.0×10.0   21k.
B. Stocznia Gdynia SA, Gdynia, Poland.

City of Lisbon
City of Manchester

Other Charters

City of Athens   1945   8,965grt.   John L. Jacobs & Company

1945	Delivered as *Beechwood*, a tanker.
1955	Sold to Soc. de Nav. Magiveras, Panama and converted to a dry cargo vessel.
1955–57	Chartered to Ellerman Lines, renamed *City of Athens*. In Ellerman livery.
1957	Renamed *Marianne*.
1964	Became *Constellation*.
1970	Golden *Moon*.
1973	Broken up.

City of Athens.

City of Pretoria   1973   7,100grt.   Common Brothers / Hindustan Steam Shipping Company

1973	Delivered as *Ria Jean McMurty*, newsprint carrier.
1976	Chartered to Ellerman Lines, renamed *City of Pretoria*.
1977	Renamed *Simonburn* when charter was completed.
1979	Sold to Vast Shipping, Jersey, renamed *Gomba Challenge*.
1980	Owned by Challenge Shipping, renamed *Ocean Challenge*.
1985	Purchased by Portline Transportes Maritimos, Portugal, renamed *Fernao Gomes*.
1994	*Fusaro*.
1995	*Gido*.
1996	*Kianda*.
1997	*Cem Pumper*.
1999	*Sofia G.*
2002	*Cem Adriatic.*
2003	*Cem Rol.*
2004	*Adriatic Arrow.*
2010	28 May. Wrecked at 30.11° N 47.54° E.

City of Athens   1980   5,065grt.

B.	J.J. Sietas Schiffswerft, Hamburg.
B.	As *Estrader*.
1987	*City of Athens*.
1991	*Emstader*.

City of Rotterdam   1982   5,931grt.
B.   Singapore Eagle.
1985   *City of Rotterdam.*
1989   *Woermann Sankuru.*

Isnes   1976   2,978grt.
B.   Schulte & Bruns Schiffswerft, Emden, Germany.
B.   as *Dollard.*
1987   *Isnes.*
1994   *Gardsky.*